OUT OF THE BLUE

First published in 2005 by

WOODFIELD PUBLISHING
Bognor Regis, West Sussex, England
www.woodfieldpublishing.com

© George Edwards, 2005

ISBN 1-873203-91 8

Out of the
BLUE

Tales of a RAF Airman 1965 –2005

L4281028 GEORGE G EDWARDS BEM

Woodfield

THE AIRMAN'S PRAYER

The first thing we'll pray for we'll pray for some beer
Glorious glorious glorious beer!
If we only have one beer may we also have ten,
May we have a whole brewery? Said the airmen "Amen"

The next thing we'll pray for we'll pray for some girls,
Glorious glorious, glorious girls!
If we only have one girl, may we also have ten,
May we have a whole harem? Said the airmen, "Amen"

The next thing we'll pray for we'll pray for the King,
If he only has one son may he also have ten,
May he have a whole squadron? Said the airmen, "Amen"

The last thing we'll pray for we'll pray for the Erk
The poor wretched blighter who does all the work,
If he only serves one year, may he also serve ten,
May he blinking serve forever. Said the airmen. "Amen"?

from Harold Bennett's
Bawdy Ballads and Dirty Ditties of the Wartime RAF
(Woodfield Publishing)

Contents

List of illustrations

Introduction

Out of the Blue is the well-considered title for an Air Force autobiography. The working blue and best blue uniforms of the RAF airmen symbolise the everyday events and social and adventure highlights of RAF life, not forgetting, of course, the blue of the sky.

Written in an easy style the book charts the progress of George Edwards from 'erk' to experienced airman and SNCO and latterly an Air Cadet Squadron Commander. In all ranks and in his many different employment and social experiences his enthusiasm and commitment shines through.

I knew the author as a clean-cut, equable, sporting young man. I did not appreciate the depth of his life experiences then and could not imagine his subsequent career and altruistic attainments, culminating in the award of the British Empire Medal on completion his RAF service. This fascinating portrait of the man and his career will surely stir memories for servicemen/women everywhere and may well make civilians who thought about enlisting wish they had 'taken the shilling' – after reading George's revelations about sand, sea and sex I would expect armed forces recruiting offices to be inundated with enquiries!

In common with the author, I served as a fireman in the Royal Air Force, although a bit prior to and a bit after him (1953-90). We were both stationed at RAF Brize Norton (but never met) and were later stationed together at RAF Gutersloh. I now know he passed through Aden on his way to Masirah and later, when I was up to my neck in muck and bullets at RAF Khormakser (Aden) he was on his way to Mombasa for a period of "rest and recuperation" (booze and debauchery more like it!).

Reading this fascinating tale I recognised many places, people and postings. I too did a spell on recruiting duties, tours in Germany and the Gulf and the almost mandatory Falklands detachment. I also did my recruit training on the Wirral (RAF West Kirkby) not a million miles from the author's Liverpool home. George refers to the Grafton Rooms where he met the future Mrs Edwards. Together with the

Tower Ballroom in New Brighton the Grafton Rooms was a regular haunt for servicemen of the day. It was the start of the Teddy Boy era and because of their bad reputation for trouble the doorkeepers at the Grafton would measure the length of the lads' drape jackets to decide if they were a Teddy Boy and therefore unfit to enter –although you would have thought that the velvet drainpipe trousers and thick crepe-soled shoes (brothel creepers) were a dead give-away! The other essential ingredient was the hair, slicked back into a centre parting at the back called a 'DA' (Duck's Ass). RAF recruits were not allowed to wear civilian clothes, so our Best Blue and short back and sides always gained us entry.

I undertook my recruit training during the winter of 1953/54 and I remember it being very cold. As I headed back to camp one evening, to keep out the bitter Mersey wind I turned up my collar on my greatcoat uniform. No sooner done than I was accosted by two 'Snowdrops' (RAF Policemen) and promptly charged with being improperly dressed. Two days later I was 'arraigned' before my Flight Commander. He accepted my plea that I did not know that turning up my collar was wrong but he was duty bound to punish me in some way. I was quite a good cross-country runner in those days and to teach me a lesson he said I would not be allowed to run for RAF West Kirkby against RAF Bridgnorth on the coming Saturday.

As intimated this was a bitter winter and the punishment was timely in the extreme. Instead of turning out in running kit I was able to attend a football match at Anfield (complete with greatcoat) and I remember Liverpool were playing Blackpool, Stanley Matthew's and all. As a neutral I remained strictly unbiased and chanted throughout "Come on the Pool"

Unlike George I never played sport to an appreciable level but I thoroughly enjoyed watching service sport and supported my colleagues in sport were possible. When I was the senior NCO in charge of RAF West Drayton Fire section, I supervised a Welsh Corporal fireman who was of national standard in throwing the discus. I managed to change rosters and arrange cover for his duties whilst he participated in sport. I noticed one day that his hair was very long and told him to get it cut.

"But Sir my long hair helps me blend in to the civilian environment at the sports events."

"Get it cut," I said, but he countered in his rich Welsh accent.

"But Sir, if I get it cut my yers stick out!"

I told him I could live with sticky-out ears and off to the barbers he went. Talking about barbers, in my youth barbers used to be the only source of condoms or 'French letters' as they were known then. Newly-married and returning home on leave to Hull I had not got anything for the weekend. I had a long wait for a train in Birmingham and was delighted to find a large Boots the chemist open. As I waited nervously in the enormous queue my turn came to step forward and I blurted out "a packet of Durex please." The sales assistant, a rather prim woman, was not impressed and obviously full of disdain (or envy) for my prospective licentiousness and said rather grandly and loudly, "Boots the chemist has a Catholic ownership, which does not condone the sale of such items" and off I slunk.

In those awkward days there was another young man who said to a lady chemist, "A packet of three please Miss."

"Don't you 'Miss' me, young man," she replied icily.

"OK," said the young man, "a packet of four please."

Like the author and all those who are aspiring to be, or are, fire-fighters, there is a vision of 'going to blazes' every day, but that is not the case. Serious incidents, thankfully, are becoming increasingly rare in the RAF, but during the 1950s and 60s aircraft crashes were quite frequent. This was in partly due to the age of many of the aircrew, who were mainly ex-wartime and still a bit gung-ho. Modern technology, flight safety, health and safety and bureaucracy was in its infancy. There was also still an attitude of 'kick the tyres and light the fires' and aircrew tended to press on regardless even if their aircraft was unserviceable or the weather was unfit for flyling.

I can relate to the author's experiences of mind-numbing routine and listening to old firemen as they related horrible details of 'prangs' they had attended and of mangled and charred human remains they had removed from crashed aircraft. Perversely, it was some relief to be 'blooded' in this gruesome experience but the first prang I attended remains vivid in my memory fifty years after the event – a Vampire crash in a paddy-field in the Hong Kong hinterland. Lifting the remaining body parts out of what was left of the cockpit is something I shall never forget, but in those days, of course, we were not allowed to be 'traumatised'.

However, George's book is not about prangs, it's about the humour, comradeship and responsibility of the airman's way of life, which brings out the best in an individual.

George makes reference to RAF Gutersloh and one of his old crew chiefs, Tom Dolman. Tom was a very good friend of mine. One fine day Tom, Warrant Officer Jack Morrell, the Senior Air Traffic Controller (SATCO) and myself were on the top floor of the RAF Gutersloh fire section looking across towards the airfield. Tom was a Derbyshire man and an ex-farmer, I believe. He had a lived-in face and a forthright manner; human sensibilities were not part of his management style. A very likeable man and truly one of the most unforgettable characters you could ever meet. Tom noticed a fire vehicle on the far side of the airfield, which, as crew commander, he should have been aware of, but obviously was not.

"What's that poxy fire truck doing over there?" he exclaimed.

"What truck?" asked the SATCO.

"That poxy Mk7," replies Tom and continues. "Your eyesight must be bad Sir. If you can't see that, you must have played with yourself when you were a boy."

All present except, of course, Tom stood agog as he continued.

"Do you know sir I never played with myself till I was twenty-three. I used to get my brother to do it for me."

The book has caused me to look back and recall the many deeds and the many characters that have contributed to the development and history of the fireman trade in the RAF. Years ago RAF firemen were called upon to undertake a host of unrelated tasks. I remember for instance being called upon by the station Warrant Officer at RAF Wellesbourne-Mountford (circa 1958) to bring my ladder, place it against the station flagpole and measure its height from the ground. I pointed out that there was a mechanism to lower the flagpole and it could be lowered to the horizontal position and then measured. He looked at me as if I was out on day release from the local Funny Farm and rasped, "Corporal I want to know its *height* not its bleeding *length*!" It was rumoured that the same SWO was present at a Sergeants' Mess meeting where it was proposed that the mess purchase an expensive chandelier to enhance the Mess entrance. "It's all very well spending all this money," he declared, "but who knows how to play one?"

Nowadays, as so aptly recorded in George's story, the RAF Fire service has moved on. Its men (women as well these days) and machines are amongst the finest to be found in any fire-fighting organisation. I suspect that similar situations to those experienced by the author continue to this day in fire crew rooms around the world. As for me, I was back in the crew room again, picturing all the disparate characters who make up any fire crew, each with their own hopes and aspirations, abilities and failings, yet all able to switch from dormant inactivity to controlled action in an instant.

All this is aptly encapsulated in the author's description of working on the short landing strip that was RAF Stanley in the South Atlantic. Imagine operating in the dark with a face-numbing Antarctic wind chill, recovering jet aircraft with the engines running (speech impossible) from ice-clad runway arresting cables. Speed and accuracy are imperative if the aircraft is to be removed and the cable prepared for the imminent landing of another fast jet or transport aircraft; both at the limit of their endurance, with no diversionary airfield. Only this dangerous situation could give you any idea of the essential mutual support and teamwork that bonds a fire crew.

I always said I would write a book, but George has beaten me too it and well done to him for doing so. I am sure the book will bring pleasure to many, not just firemen, but also those who have an interest in military life or just enjoy a good read. Read on, and in parallel with the author, recall your own adventures.

Steve Davey
Warrant Officer, RAF Fire Service, 1953-90

Acknowledgements

I would like to thank the many people who have encouraged me to write this tale. My Probation colleagues Jean Woods and Anne Owens, who read a few chapters and went on to give me great encouragement to finish my story. To another Probation colleague Jean McCooey, who for many years provided invaluable voluntary administration support when I was a voluntary youth worker and caseworker for SSAFA. Jean also carried out the initial proof-read. To my colleagues from the RAF & Defence Fire Service Association, especially Steve Davey, Dennis McCann and Bob Feather. Thanks also to Dave Kenyon and his wife Jacky for kindly undertaking the final proof read. To my son-in-law Lawrence, who worked tirelessly with me copying my collection of photographs into acceptable format. Special thanks to my wife Anne and two children Peter and Christine who shared the best part of my RAF career with me and more recently have accepted my nightly disappearance to my computer as almost normal behaviour over the last year or so.

Finally the book is dedicated to my late dad, whose five years spent in the Royal Air Force during the Second World War were, he would often say, the best years of his life. Throughout my RAF career my dad never failed to turn up to see me and then my family set off on our various journeys and was always pleased to see us return home. I think he may have been a bit embarrassed by some of my exploits but he would, I'm sure, have been pleased to see me complete an autobiography. I mustn't forget my dear late mum who made so many of my RAF mates welcome at our home. I know she would have been proud of my humble achievements.

George Edwards
November 2005

RAF fire truck MFV.

RAF fire truck TACR2.

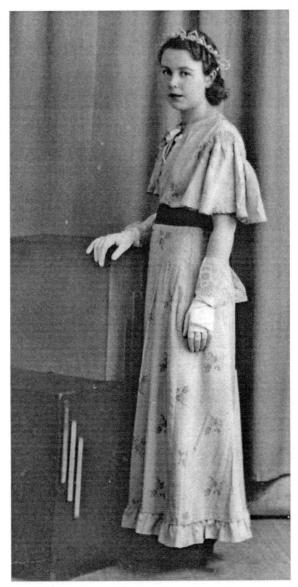

RAF Bride (my mum) Joyce Edwards.

1. Early Days ~ Marham & Honington

My story begins on 3rd September 1965 at Lime Street Station, Liverpool. On that day I set off for RAF Swinderby in Lincolnshire to commence my Royal Air Force career. I had passed the necessary entrance examinations and medical at the RAF Careers Office, Pall Mall, Liverpool and left my employment as a saw doctor at Holloway's timber importers in Grafton Street. My parents came to Lime Street, along with a few friends, to wave me off and that was it – my journey had begun...

1100170 G Edwards My Dad who served in the RAF 1939-45.

I knew to an extent what to expect – my father had spent five years in the RAF during World War Two, as did his two brothers and one of his sisters, so I had been well briefed. My dad's recollections of his RAF days were, however, somewhat blurred with the passing of time, and as one does, it is easy to forget the bad times and re-member only the good. My dad had been an RAF Regiment drill instructor stationed at those two infamous RAF recruit-training camps, Bridgnorth and Padgate. He also spent time at the Butlin's holiday camps at Filey and Ayr, which served as recruit training centres during the war. It was hardly surprising that my dad had such fond memories of his RAF service, none of which was spent over-seas – other than the time he spent at the RAF camp on the Isle of Man, which, if my sums are right, is the place where I was con-ceived. In memory of my dad, and as my own little pilgrimage, I have visited all the above locations. It can be an eerie feeling to visit a disused RAF camp that is now no more than a car-park or indus-trial estate, but being blessed with a vivid imagination it was easy for me to transport myself back to its heyday. I could hear my dad barking out his drill orders and imagine him on parade, resplendent in his RAF uniform, pleased as Punch.

My dad's service amounted to no more than five years, but those five years, he would often say, were the best time of his life. My dad had left school with a good education but was unable to obtain employment befitting his educational ability. It is hard for our generation to imagine what it must have been like leaving school in the 1930s. The world's economy was in a deep depression, unem-ployment was rife, employment opportunities were very few and most school-leavers had to take whatever came their way.

My dad was the eldest of five children whose father was a Liver-pool dockworker already experiencing the ravages of unemployment and irregular work. My dad went looking for work at the same time as his father was looking for work. As it was, my dad obtained work as a labourer at a large timber importers and, such was the measure of my dad, he remained a loyal employee for that same company for forty years with a five-year break for his RAF wartime service.

I left school (Gateacre Comprehensive) at the age of fifteen. I left school one day and started work the following day for the same employers as my dad. I had previously been interviewed and ac-cepted for an apprenticeship as a saw doctor, probably the most prestigious job in the timber trade. I was required to attend Liverpool College of building one full day a week and, whereas some of the other students would bunk off for the evening class, I had to remain, as the tutor was a friend of my dad. I soon became disillusioned with the job; it was repetitive, quite boring and I had more or less mastered it after a few months. I knew I had to wait five years before I would earn a reasonable wage – an apprentice's pay was abysmal and I was doing a man's work, including setting up and operating the big band saws and wood cutting machines. Most of the men I worked with had completed some form of military service and would regale me with tales of their life in uniform. These were fine men who worked hard in terrible conditions for a pittance of a wage. With no health and safety regulations in those days it was not uncommon to see men lose a finger as they worked in close proximity to a 12-inch band saw blade or huge crosscut saw. It wasn't long before I found myself on my way to Liverpool Infirmary. Operating a cross cut saw one day, something distracted me and I sliced off the top of my left thumb. Still to this day I have the scar where the surgeons stitched it back on.

Another unpleasant aspect of this work was the constant presence of sawdust – it was everywhere. Nowadays, if I ever sense that generally pleasant smell of recently cut timber it evokes pleasant memories of my dad coming home from work. However, being covered in sawdust on a daily basis was a very unpleasant business. I was soon to find out that I was allergic to some hardwoods, notably mahogany and teak. Just a short time spent sawing or machining these fine timbers and I would come out in rash, or worse, boils would appear on my face and neck. Such is the vanity of adolescence I would apply all sorts of lotions and locally-produced potions, but none of them seemed to do any good.

Many of the men I worked with had badly pockmarked skin, the result of many years spent working in sawmills. Even if there were shower facilities I doubt if they would have been used: after all, a nine-hour shift was a long enough day. I was generally disillusioned with the job, the working conditions and the lack of prospects. My dad, like many of his mates, had spent all their working life in the one job and at the same location. That prospect did not appeal to me and I had already made up my mind to seek alternative employment.

Prior to leaving school, I applied for RAF service as a Boy Entrant. I sat and passed all the tests but my mother was not keen for me to join at such an early age. I withdrew that application but, for the next three years, I harboured thoughts of joining the RAF when I was eighteen years of age. My eighteenth birthday duly arrived and, with my mother's agreement, I applied once more for the RAF. My dad and my work mates all thought it was the best thing I could do, although my dad would have preferred me to enlist in one of the engineering trades, but I wanted to be a RAF fireman and that is what I joined as.

I joined the RAF shortly after my eighteenth birthday. My RAF career was to last slightly longer than my dad's and whilst, I would say I enjoyed my RAF service, there were many ups and downs, happy times, sad times but it would be unfair to say they were the best times of my life. Let's just say they were very eventful times. They were also rewarding and satisfying times; I felt I was valued for the work I did and financially rewarded. Social and economic opportunities came my way that would never have come my way had I remained at home and it was in a determined and confident mood that I left Liverpool for RAF Swinderby.

Recruit training presented no problems for me – quite the opposite. I thoroughly enjoyed every aspect of recruit and trade training. I was quite happy with my "bed space" – the small area that encompasses your bed, bedside table and a wardrobe. Effectively it became your sanctuary; the fact that there were other recruits no more than an arm's length away made no difference – it was your space and you were alone with your thoughts. It was, in fact, an improvement on the rather cramped conditions I was used to at home and I could also have a shower on a daily basis. At home we had to make do with an old tin bath that was filled by pans of tepid water and then we were restricted to the number of times we could bathe in a week. Recruit training was difficult for some and probably still is but it is all about a mind set. Our billet consisted of a collection of generally cheerful, enthusiastic young men who, like me, had completed a lengthy selection process. We were all fit, healthy, motivated, free of criminal convictions and vices. How different the RAF that Aircraftman 352087 Ross (better known as Lawrence of Arabia) wrote about in his remarkable study of RAF life in his book, The Mint. The following is just an extract.

"Our hut is a fair microcosm of unemployed England; not of unemployable England, for the strict RAF standards refuse the last levels of the social structure. Yet a man's enlisting is his acknowledgement of defeat by life. Amongst a hundred serving men you will not find one whole and happy. Each has a lesion, a hurt open or concealed, in his late history. Some of us here had no money or no trade and were too proud to join the ranks of labours unskilled. Some faltered at their jobs and lost them. The heartbreak of seeking work had driven many into the feeble satisfaction of "getting in". Some have blacked their character and dodge shame or the Police Court. Others have tangled with women or ejected by women and are revenging the ill – usage of society upon their smarting selves. Yet aloud we all claim achievement, moneyed relatives, a colourful past. We include lads and their shady equivalent the hard case. Also the soft and the silly the vain the old soldier who is lost without the nails of service; the fallen officer sharply contemptuous of our raw company, yet trying to be well fellow and not proud. The dressy artisans, the Glasgow blacksmith, the axed Devenport apprentice and The Great Western Railway machinist who rejected all kindness and swilled beer solitarily. There were chauffeurs, van men, dapper handed clerks, photographers, mechanics, broken men and bright lads from school. We are tossed through the day haphazardly from hand to hand like the golden balls of a juggler; and with some apprehension of the balls lest we be dropped suddenly and bruised. Bruised not broken and that makes part of the sorrow. We can be half killed, but not killed; punished but not capitally. There is no thrill of a real danger to graze and avoid only the certainty of minor accident and no way of escape- from a self-built prison. However tired the day has left me, I cannot sleep a whole night away: not once since my enlistment. The dark hours march by me and I lie half indifferent to them, not particularly wanting to sleep, but still less wanting to think consecutively, to attend to the hut sounds: for our hut persists in being a main intruder upon what should be mental piece. After midnight, my head jars at every vibration across the still air: fellows dream vocally of girls, muttering their pet names aloud: or shortly moan "Don't, don't" (the day long complainant grumble of the service man is his night habit too: mutely he begs always for pity, having no self defence).

They sigh and fart, amid the piano janglings of their wire beds and reveille shatters the end of the night like a last exasperation, just when I have sunk into the custom of lying still. In the morning our sergeants are waiting always wanting to spread blind terror have transformed us civilians into very frightened troops in a few days. We recruits are counselled always the road of least resistance to dodge everything earned or unearned – except our pay. At the end of every exhortation we remind one another that we are Airmen in the Royal Air Force."

Life at RAF Swinderby bore no resemblance to that experienced by Aircraftman Ross at the RAF Uxbridge Depot in the 1920s, although I can identify with some of the characters so vividly recorded by him. We had our own tinkers, tailors, soldiers and sailors, broken-hearted, hard-cases, soft-cases but training was short and relatively sweet. One thing for sure, Thomas Ross, although not by choice, was probably the most famous RAF Airman of all time. He, like his predecessors and like those who came later, endured recruit training and went on to play their part in the development of the Royal Air Force. It is important we remember that the RAF's history is not restricted solely to the Officer core. Trenchard, Mallory, Harris, Bader et al are immortalised in RAF history but the Ross's and thousands of others, including my own extended family (over a hundred years collective RAF service for this Liverpool family), played their part in the development of the Royal Air Force.

Our drill instructors had a job to do; some shouted louder than others and some were nastier than others but, in my experience, they had no favourites and there are very few recruits who go through training without a bollocking or two, I was no exception. You have to accept that a bollocking was a bollocking and it was no good writing home and telling my parents I had been shouted at. I thought it best to grin and bear it. Recruits need to realise that basic training does not last forever; there is a beginning, a middle and an ending and one can't get to the end without first completing the two other salient parts. There is also a purpose and that's the same if you're a raw Russian Air Force recruit or a more pampered Royal Air Force recruit – you have to learn to live and work together. There are no differences for the privileged or underprivileged, we all looked the same in denims or sports kit. We all ate the same food, shared the same accommodation and basically began to think the same way. We all learnt to hate, if that's the right word, our drill instructors, yet we thought the world of them when we left and even bought them presents – what a difference a few weeks made! I particularly enjoyed recruit training because I was free of the constraints and boredom of my previous employment. In my job as a saw doctor I was confined to a small dingy room, unable to leave until the work's hooter sounded for the two ten minute breaks in the day, the thirty minute lunch break and the end of the work day.

Now I was out in the fresh air almost all day undertaking healthy activities. I was blessed with the ability to master foot drill and arms drill quite quickly – must be in the genes – and I was already practised in ironing and bulling my shoes, something I used to do with my dad. Above all, I loved sport. I never knew till I joined the RAF that I could run. At school I was never in any sports teams, mainly I think because my parents could not afford to buy me sports kit or football boots and it was something that never particularly bothered me. I had only been at Swinderby a few days and we were sent off on the first of our many cross-country runs. We all wore mandatory RAF PT kit, complete with RAF blue plimsolls. Off we went and I couldn't believe it, I was the first to finish. When I arrived back I very politely asked the Corporal what he wanted me to do then. Not so politely, he said, "Are you from Liverpool?" and I answered in the affirmative, at which he told me to go round again. I also played compulsory football, which I loved, the only drawback being we were still wearing our RAF plimsolls. I was selected for our recruit's flight football team, the first time in my life that I had ever been selected for any team. I felt like I was representing my country. Being part of a drill squad is another team event but unique in that there are no weaknesses or strengths, one mistake and we're all failures; hence the enormous sense of bonding that goes into making a good drill squad.

The vast majority of those completing recruit training look back on it with fondness and affection. It was without doubt a relatively stress free business. All decisions were made for you, recruits simply responded to orders, and there was little time for reflection. Days were very long – up at 5.30 a.m., bed at maybe 11.00 or 12.00 p.m., but those few hours sleep were the best I have ever had. Friendships were formed that have lasted forever in the memory and even those mean drill instructors are remembered with increasing affection. Recruit training completed and fond farewells to all our Flight, we set off to the many trade training schools scattered throughout the UK. I was the only one of our flight travelling to RAF Catterick, home to the RAF Regiment Depot and the RAF Fire School. Catterick was, if anything, more likes a Guards depot. There were no basic recruits struggling with the rudiments of drill, men marched everywhere looking as if they were on a Queen's Birthday parade.

We had to be very careful that we marched to the best of our ability or it would be a serious bollocking from the Regiment Depot Warrant Officer, the infamous Mr Gaunt. Alas the RAF Fire School also had its own infamous Warrant Officer the redoubtable, Mr Shearn. To get bollocked by either gentleman was something you never forgot. I was put in something of a dilemma at Catterick; I joined the RAF as a Fireman and that was all I wanted to be; however, when I arrived at Catterick I was summoned before a Squadron Leader. He had before him my file from Swinderby and I had apparently done very well in all sporting activities, drill and weapons training – just the qualities needed for an RAF Regiment Gunner. I could have been coerced into changing trades but an RAF Fireman was all I wanted to be and he must have realised that, so the interview concluded quite quickly.

Practice Crash (photo courtesy of Pete (Scouse) Carter).

Trade training was another wonderful experience. We didn't do a lot of drill but we spent the best part of our day outdoors learning all sorts of fire skills; ladder drills, hose drills, hydrant drills, etc. Dry fires, wet fires, solid fires, liquid fires, fuel fires, domestic fires and the big one, aircraft fires. In those days, anyone driving past RAF

Catterick (situated on the A1) would have seen huge plumes of smoke billowing from the burning area as old aircraft were set on fire to allow us trainees to practice our newfound skills. Once again, teamwork was the order of the day; any fire crew is only as good as the weakest link so we had to ensure we had no weak link. This was serious stuff – even on a training fire ground, accidents regularly happened both to trainees and staff. I was probably more in my element now than I was at Swinderby. I soon realised I had no fear of heights or no claustrophobic tendencies; unfortunately, some did. There was no way of finding this out until you were put in these situations: panic or fear meant failure and transfer to another trade. I'm pleased to say I passed trade training without too many problems and left Catterick ready to face the world.

RAF Catterick Fire School, 'burning area'.

I arrived at my first operational posting RAF Marham, a V Bomber station in Norfolk on a bleak winter's day in January 1966. I arrived quietly confident and half-expected some sort of welcome or acknowledgement. Burdened down with kitbags and recruits mentality, I saluted and informed all who passed that I was Leading Aircraft Man (LAC) Edwards arriving for duty until one kindly soul directed me to general office. At least someone there would know of my arrival and, more to the point, my existence. I was given a form with the names of the various sections I had to report to and notify of my arrival. I seem to remember reporting to the bedding store, the bicycle store and many other obscure stores before finally landing at the fire section. At least I could expect a welcome there – after all I was a fully trained Fireman. My arrival at the fire section was even more of a non-event. I was keen to meet my fellow firemen but those I met were not at all interested in meeting me. One of the first people to speak to me was a very strange looking man who spoke to me in an accent I could not understand. I had no idea who this man was until, a few hours later, someone mentioned they had seen me talking to the section Warrant Officer whose name was Ben Skie. I was called into an office and told by a Corporal, unlike any Corporal I'd meet during training, that I would be going onto A crew and they were on nights tonight.

He issued me with my fireman's kit; axe, quick release knife, ejection seat pins, helmet boots and the cumbersome crash kit. The Corporal then informed me that the kit I had received belonged to another sprog who was killed when he was sucked into a V Bomber's engine, coming out the other end as mincemeat. If he wanted to frighten me, he certainly did. He then sent me away with instructions to get a few hours sleep and report back at 16.00 hours. Sleep was out of the question, adrenaline kept me awake. I could only lie there and think of the emergencies likely to be encountered that night and that poor sprog reduced to mincemeat. Would I cope or would I be sent home in disgrace or, even worse, returned home as mincemeat.

I had no time to dwell on that; a giant of a man was shouting at me in a broad Irish brogue "Get into the back of the truck and move it!" Who was I to argue? If he was a giant, the rest of the men in the back were gargantuan. Yet, despite their enormity, they were strangely quiet and did not radiate any enthusiasm or share my sense of occasion. Climbing into the back of that four ton truck was the culmination of many months training, years of preparation and the fulfilment of a long held ambition. I was about to take my place as a fully trained Fireman, with an RAF crash crew on an operational RAF station. All sorts of thoughts flashed through my mind as I joined the eighteen-man crew, embarking on a fifteen-hour night shift, at the very sharp end of the cold war, or so I thought. This is what I'd always dreamt about as I travelled to work each morning in Liverpool. The excitement of it, those then unfamiliar sounds and smells of throbbing aircraft engines, taxiing aeroplanes, a veritable hullabaloo of noise, movement and intense activity.

That journey across the airfield to the crash bays was probably the most bewildering journey I have ever undertaken. Here I was, fully trained, highly motivated, and desperate to be acknowledged by the crew but they sat motionless, totally oblivious to my presence. The roar of a passing Victor bomber interrupted my thoughts, yet the others remained unperturbed. Another roar, this time that Irish brogue ordered every one out of the truck and a semblance of a line took shape. Whilst those disembarking shuffled and groaned, the off-going crew threw themselves into the truck amid shrieks and howls of abuse. I was almost transported back across the airfield; it was only the shouts of the Irishman that prevented me returning to base. I quickly worked out for myself that, in the makeshift line, I would be shortest on the right. As the Irishman gave out the crew positions, I waited eagerly for my name to be called. Each man in turn fell out and I knew that I would soon be recognised and given a position. That was not to be – I stood alone.

"Who are you?" asked the Irishman.

"LAC Edwards," I beamed.

"Not another sprog?" came the reply. "Straight from training are you lad?"

"Yes Sergeant."

"That's all we need! Get the tea on for the lads and then report to my office."

As I struggled with the urn, I wanted desperately to be with my friends from training, at least then we were all in it together. It seemed an eternity waiting for the men to come in from their vehicle and equipment checks. What would happen, I thought, if the alarm went? I won't even go with them. What if the phone goes? What if that Sergeant starts asking me questions? I really wished I had travelled back on the truck.

It wasn't long before the first fireman drifted into the crew room, a grubby dishevelled hulk of a man, the seat of his trousers almost touching the floor; a cigarette stuck to his lip, and an accent I could hardly understand.

"Three sugars for me," he said, before collapsing in a heap. He sat down, pulled out a paper from the front of his trousers and remained motionless. I must, I thought, have to take his tea over to him, and was on my way over when the Sergeant burst in and shouted,

"Stiff... get out there and finish off your vehicle checks!"

I was terrified at the sound of the sergeant's voice, but Stiff remained unperturbed, stuffed the paperback down his trousers and drifted back out into the vehicle bays, closely followed by the Sergeant. As I watched I could hardly fail to notice the difference in the two men. Stiff was almost ape-like, bent over, long arms, dragging his heels and his protective clothing added to his bizarre appearance. The Sergeant, meanwhile, was stocky, had a healthy glow about him and was bolt upright, totally the opposite to Stiff. I went back to my tea duty and waited eagerly for the men to come in. I could see the rest of the crew carrying out their checks. Men were on the roof of the fire trucks checking water and foam tanks, others were checking breathing apparatus, cutting gear, rescue equipment, engines were running, klaxons were being tested; it all looked very business-like and purposeful. As I surveyed the scene and looked at the huge fire vehicles and the men tending to them, I wondered if I would ever be in that position. My thoughts were interrupted by the Sergeant's raucous voice.

"Into my office lad." Up until now, every time a Sergeant had spoken to me I had automatically come to attention. I was about to do that when the Sergeant said, "Come on, follow me…"

As I entered his office I felt ill at ease like never before. During my recruit and trade training I had no time to think, everything happened so quickly and bollockings only lasted a few minutes. This was totally different. "Right lad, my name is Sergeant Burns, and it looks as though you have been detailed to my crew and I am your Crew Commander. Do you know what that means?"

"Yes Sergeant," I replied, not knowing really what it meant.

"Well, let's get one thing straight from the start; I don't want to see you sat in the tea room with Stiff again, understand?"

"But Sergeant…"

"Understand?"

"Yes Sergeant."

"Now go out and find Stiff. He is probably sat on the steps of crash five reading his paper. Seeing you two get on so well together, you are on his vehicle."

That was it. My introduction to a lengthy RAF Fire service career.

I trundled out into the bays looking for Stiff. Sergeant Burns was right, he was sat on the steps of the last vehicle in the line reading his paper and he had what looked like the same cigarette stuck to his lip.

"Come to bring me my tea?"

"No, I have been sent by Sergeant Burns. I am on your truck."

"Well go and get me a cup of tea and I will show you where to put your kit."

I went back up the bays to the tea-room, my intention being to bring Stiff his tea, when Sergeant Burns burst in.

"What are you doing?" I tried to explain but when I saw his face go red and the veins in his neck bulge I knew I had no chance. "Go and get Stiff, and the two of you, in my office now!" Back down the bays I went. Stiff was totally unperturbed and more concerned that I had not brought his tea than the fact that Sergeant Burns wanted to see us. Over the tannoy came a message:

"Stiff and the sprog to Sarge's office, and I would hurry up if I were you two, Sarge has thrown a wobbly."

Stiff got up and more or less dragged himself down to the office with me in tow. "Looking for me Sarge?"

"Stiff, you know this is your last chance, mess it up on my crew and you are out and I mean *out* of the Air Force and, as for you lad, if you don't buck up your ideas, you will be going with him."

I could have cried but I thought better of it and followed Stiff out.

Crash five was the last in the line of fire vehicles that made up the crash combine, and certainly the least important. It was used to replenish the major foam trucks, wash down fuel spillages and carry out any unimportant tasks. I can understand why Stiff was allocated to that truck, but why me? Stiff had still not passed comment to me as we climbed on the truck.

"Where do I put my kit?" I asked. Stiff was totally disinterested so I made my own arrangements. After what appeared to be a cursory check of the vehicle, I followed Stiff back into the Crew room. The place resounded to a clatter of noise, different dialects, accents and unfamiliar language. All this interspersed with the sound of aircraft overhead and continuous tannoy messages. As I walked into the crew room behind Stiff, the place fell silent and then uproar. I was greeted with screams of derision, the urn had boiled dry and I was held responsible. There was no point in apologising. I tried to say sorry but that only worsened the situation.

"Bloody sprogs! Don't they teach you anything at Catterick?"

Before I could attempt to made amends the tannoy went.

"Pan Wash pan 21." I wasn't aware then that this was a job for crash five but the rest of the crew made it plain it was Stiff's job; "Try not to get lost", "Make sure you don't hit any aircraft", "See

you in the morning" and other such comments. Stiff remained his unperturbed self and it was only when Sergeant Burns came in and shouted that Stiff decided to move.

When an aircraft is refuelled, it is not uncommon to overfill the aircraft and fuel to overspill. The split fuel is easily ignited and has to be washed away. This was my first operational task and, however mundane it may seem, I was at last leaving the crew room and about to embark on an operational airfield for the first time. Leaving the bright lights of the crash bays behind and moving into a dark, toned down airfield complex is a frightening experience at the best of times but, with an incongruous driver at the controls of a huge fire truck, my fears were further heightened. A maze of different coloured lights lay ahead – some static, some flashing and some moving. I was really quite mesmerised and it was only Stiff asking me directions that brought me to my senses.

"Do you know where we are?" said Stiff.

"Hardly," I thought "this is an alien world for me."

"Have a look at that map," he said.

"What map?" And there followed a frantic search on my part, for the map. I could almost hear Stiff thinking and, without further ado, he picked up the radiotelephone and, in his own inimitable style, he contacted air traffic control and asked for directions to Pan 21.

"Put your blue light on crash five – now we can see you – carry straight down the peri track, past the O.R.P, turn first left then right and Pan 21 is straight in front of you. Beware of taxiing aircraft."

"OK tower," replied Stiff and off we went. I thought 'this is not like the radio procedure I have been taught at Catterick'. However, I was just glad to arrive at Pan 21 without hitting any aircraft. On arrival Stiff operated a few controls and, amidst great crunching of gears and loud bangs, dismounted and went to the pump compartment. I ran out a length of hose and waited for what seemed like an eternity for water to appear at the branch. When it did come, it came at high speed and I had difficulty controlling the hose.

Once the task was completed we set off back to the crash bays with Stiff receiving directions from the tower. En route Stiff called in at several buildings, I didn't know then what he was up to but he was apparently a prolific scrounger and he would return from his visits laden down with odds and sods. As I sat alone in the vehicle, still totally bemused, Sergeant Burn's voice came over the radio.

"Crash combine manned and proceeding to 26 O.R.P."
"Roger, four jet inbound, engine malfunction, deploy crash one to the inter section," came the reply from air traffic control. Meanwhile, Stiff was doing what he is good at – scrounging – whilst I am left to sit, listen and wonder if one day I would be part of the team. It was some time before Stiff and I finally returned to the crash bays and on return I noticed the crew seemed much livelier than before.

Men were playing cards, throwing darts and some were in animated discussion. Stiff's arrival caused not the slightest interest, mine even less and it wasn't until Sergeant Burns came in and mentioned to Stiff that the duty air traffic controller had made a complaint about his radio procedure that we were acknowledged by the rest of the crew. Stiff was more concerned that there was no tea on the go! Throughout the night one pan wash followed another, whilst the rest of the crew went about their more urgent duties. I remember daylight dawning and feeling tired like never before, I didn't think I could stay awake, although Stiff seemed to drift in and out of sleep continuously. By the end of the shift I was painfully tired and eagerly awaited the arrival of the truck to take us back to base. The shift was virtually completed, yet I didn't know any other member of the crew but Stiff and Sergeant Burns. I knew there was a Tug and a Spud, a Geordie, a Jock and a Taff and I had been christened Junior. However, I just wanted my bed. I slept all the way back to base; those same sounds and smells that, only fifteen hours earlier had excited and thrilled me were now drowned out by my need to sleep. When I awoke in the truck I was all-alone had missed breakfast and ached all over. I made my way to the block, set my alarm clock for three p.m. and collapsed into a deep sleep. At least when I did wake I was slightly better prepared for the next duty.

Prior to going on shift I went to the Airman's mess for my evening meal. Marham was a huge base with a huge mess and not knowing another soul I sat down alone to eat my meal. Shortly after, another airman joined me, dressed in fireman's protective clothing. I recognised him as one of the card players from last night. "All right Junior?" or something like that he muttered in a pronounced Scottish accent. "My name is George or most people call me Scouse". "Och, all right Junior". I thought no more of that and Junior I remained during my time at Marham. Jock McCart was certainly at the other end of the airman's social and professional pecking order of things. I was well and truly a sprog compared to Jock, totally unversed in all aspects of Air Force life. Right from our first meeting, Jock captivated my imagination, his tales from abroad, conquests with the opposite sex, daring deeds on the crash line, his sporting prowess and his acceptance by other airmen quickly attracted me to him and he was, after all, a world apart from Stiff. I became apprenticed to Jock as he called it and he taught me so much, like how to deal from the bottom of a pack of cards and how to consume large quantities of beer. He also looked after me, took an interest in me and introduced me to the airman's way of life.

I went on shift that night mentally and physically prepared to cope with any situation. I'd found a role model and he had accepted me, however tenuously, and I would work on that. It didn't alter the fact that I was still on the same vehicle as Stiff and in the pecking order of the crew I remained bottom of the pile. Nevertheless, Sergeant Burns' voice didn't sound as raucous as the previous night, although the sight of him still struck fear in me, but I was determined to make a success of my new career after all, the prospect of returning home a failure was all the incentive I needed. Crash five remained my vehicle and Stiff continued to be the driver for those first few months of my RAF fire service career. Stiff had no intention of changing his ways and appeared content with his lot. There's no denying he was one of life's moaners, although no one took the slightest notice of him. I was, however, able to learn from Stiff's mistakes, I had to; yet despite all his shortcomings, Stiff remained an unflappable character, regardless of the situation or who he spoke to. Sad to say, there is no hiding place in the modern Royal Air force for characters like Stiff.

My knowledge of fire fighting, aircraft escape systems and airfield topography was all the time increasing. I knew Stiff would never find his way round the airfield in the dark so I had to learn fairly quickly. My imagination often drifted on to thoughts of arriving first at the scene of an incident and how would I react. I would listen intently to other crew members as they related tales of extricating aircrew from burning aircraft; all the time I was developing a quest for knowledge and more practical experience. I was also, like other young airmen, beginning to take a keen interest in the opposite sex. During recruit and trade training, women played little part in my thoughts or deeds. We were always to busy and some said bromide was put in our tea to dampen our ardour. However, I now found myself in the company of men, who seemed to occupy their thoughts with little else. It was, therefore, only natural for my thoughts to turn that way too. Even Stiff could recall tales of passionate lust during his time in the Far East whilst Jock McCart captivated my imagination with his tales from Gibraltar and of conquests much closer to home. It had been made clear to me by my crewmates that I really was a sprog, in all senses of the word. Yet I knew I could apply myself to my trade and with a bit of luck I too would be able to join in on an equal basis when the conversation turned to sexual exploits.

Thursday was, in those days before bank accounts pay day and if the shift roster worked out well, Thursday night was always a crew night out. Almost to a man, it was obligatory to meet at the Narborough Arms and spend the greater part of a week's pay on that one night, certainly a LAC's pay didn't go far. It was also a regular occurrence to visit the Sampson and Hercules dance hall in Norwich. My first visit to that venue was in the company of all the crew including Sergeant Burns. Out of uniform Sergeant Burns was a dapper dresser and he must have presented a favourable impression with any woman. He was also a snappy dancer, had an excellent repartee and a nice line in banter. Jock was certainly more devilish than Sergeant Burns; Jock's only intention with women was seduction and to elicit free drinks – the Sergeant was only there, it seemed, for the fun of it. My priority lay more in Jock's direction and I needed a conquest of some description if I was to become a fully-fledged Airman. The Samson and Hercules was not my favourite place, it attracted serious dancers and there was little opportunity for me to succeed in the company of my elders, who still looked upon me as junior. They had first choice – we sprogs were left the scraps and usually very ugly ones at that…

In addition to the crew night out, I had befriended another young fireman off B crew, Taffy Edwards. Taff was the same age, same rank and was experiencing the same difficulties on B crew as I was on my crew. Taff and I would meet in the NAAFI and over a few pints we would moan and groan about our plight. Marham really was in the wilds, El Adam with grass it was generally known as, not the ideal place for two young airmen. There were no women on the camp; none in the Narborough Arms and those who went the Sampson were out of our reach. We needed somewhere were we could at least meet women of our age and one of the NAAFI cowboys suggested we try the Saturday night dance at Swaffham. We managed to get a lift to Swaffham one Saturday and, sure enough, this proved to be our Mecca. This was 1966; the era of Beatle mania and all things Liverpool were in. The fact that I was a Liverpudlian and related to Ringo Starr (my paternal Nan was a Starkey) was just what the young women of Swaffham wanted to hear. Taff had a good line in patter also and our first visit to Swaffham proved highly successful. We duly picked up two women who agreed to take us back to base in their car.

I can remember to this day the absolute surprise when, as I was sat in the front seat next to my girl, I looked in the rear view mirror to see a smile on Taff's face that stretched from ear to ear. I couldn't see his girl and I was just about to ask were she had disappeared to when I realised where and why Taff had such a huge smile. My girl wasn't going to be out-done and she pulled the car into a lay-by and she showed me that she also knew how to bring a smile to a lonely Airman. Not only did Taff and I obtain fulfilment but also the women took us back to base and asked if they could use the toilets. The fire section toilets seemed as good as a place as any and, without further ado, the two women were taken to the fire section toilets. The sight of two attractive young women entering the fire section toilet obviously delighted the duty fire crew. The next day Taff and I were summoned to Warrant Officer Skie's office, a rare occurrence. We were marched in – also present were our two crew commanders. We were asked to account for our whereabouts last night, which we did. However, when asked had we brought loose women into the fire section, I said "No they weren't loose, they were with us."

The Warrant didn't agree and certainly didn't think it amusing. We were then given a rather stern lecture on morality and the need for young Airman to concentrate on more useful and purposeful activities than fornicating with the opposite sex. The euphoria of the night before soon disappeared and, once again, concerns for my future in the RAF were raised. We were duly marched out and pulled to one side by our respective crew commanders. I expected Sergeant Burns would take a very dim view of the proceedings but he reacted contrary to what I expected. "Never mind Junior", he said, "I'm sure the rest of the crew would have done the same" and left it at that. The next duty, I suddenly found myself the centre of attention. The crew were hurrying their vehicle checks and coming up to me asking me to relate details of the incident. The first tea break I was asked to explain exactly what happened, lurid details and all. I'd very quickly been elevated to celebrity status amongst the crew and, despite the elevation, I found it somewhat disconcerting.

Nevertheless, the whole incident seemed to meet with approval from all the crew and, in the cut and thrust of inter crew banter, Junior had played his part in maintaining 'A' Crew's position as the crew to be on. Coincidentally, Sergeant Burns decided it was time I came off crash 5 and moved to one of the major foams. Taking my kit off crash 5 and moving up the line was a poignant moment for me. I was obviously leaving Stiff behind, probably for good, and my elevation, however slight, was a move up the social pecking order of the crew. I had also grown to like Stiff; he was old enough to be my dad and he was at the end of a long RAF career and I respected him for that.

I also respected him for his honesty; in the sycophantic and highly competitive service life, one meets few genuinely honest and plain speaking individuals, and he was certainly that. Ironically, I met Stiff several years later. I was undertaking the fire service advanced course, a pre-requisite for promotion. Stiff was in charge of the burning area. A dirty, smelly, wet and indeed highly dangerous occupation, but essential if fireman were to receive quality training. Stiff was never one to seek praise but was quick to let you know if he didn't like you. He never fell out with me; that's probably because I always respected him. Stiff could well have moved on to that big fire section in the sky. I'm sure if St Peter wanted a reliable stoker, Stiff would be his man.

Whilst at Marham all the station firemen were required to under-take training in ornithology as bird strikes were becoming increasingly common occurrences. All sorts of schemes were set up to deter birds, certainly the larger of the species, from setting up home on RAF airfields. Marham obtained the services of a University of East Anglia Professor and he was tasked to train us in the identification of birds and the use of the newly designed bird scaring equipment known as SAPPHO. None of us had any idea what it stood for but we were well warned to treat the Professor with due decorum and civility. Fortunately the Professor was a pleasant individual, an archetypal boffin if ever there was such a person. He reminds me now of David Bellamy, full of enthusiasm for his subject. Unfortunately, none of us were the least bit interested. If anything, this new scheme was seen as hare-brained and interfered with our normal routine. We had to spend time in a classroom identifying the various types of birds and then selecting the appropriate bird distress tape. We would then play the tape on the loudspeakers fitted to the fire trucks. On reflection, it must have been an expensive operation with research and equipment costs, not to mention the professor's remuneration. It was, as far as we were concerned, destined to fail but we had to co-operate and be seen to be keen and attentive. We would be taken out on the airfield with the professor in tow and he would, with all his enthusiasm, ask us to identify an over flying bird and then play the appropriate tape. I don't think we made an impression on the local bird population – they probably knew we were RAF firemen and thought we were stupid anyway. Give the professor his due, he did persevere with us and never lost his composure. Surprising really, some of the old sweats would make the most outrageous comments. I remember the professor asking for a bird identification and an old sweat told him it was a B one RD (Bird). The professor searched frantically through his ornithological encyclopaedia but could not find a B one RD and then one of the crew responded to his question by stating he had just seen a "Shite hawk". Again the professor searched through his encyclopaedia but no Shite hawk could he find. On another occasion one of the crew asked how did they manage to record the bird distress calls. Poor old professor was stumped on that one but, as ever, one of the firemen had an answer! "That's easy," he said "just catch a bird stick a pencil up its arse and it will soon give out a distress call." I think the professor spent about a week with us and, despite his best efforts and his wonderful charm, he failed to convince us that SAPPHO was nothing more than a waste of money and our time.

My journey home to Liverpool in those days was done in uniform and I would hitchhike the two hundred or so miles. That could be a scary experience, especially the journey back to Marham and hitchhiking in the wilds of Norfolk, usually late at night and with a head full of scary stories that I had been told whilst on crew. I will always remember one winter's night hitch hiking just outside Kings Lynn. A car pulled up and a middle-aged woman asked where I was going and offered me a lift part way. Once in the car she said she could drop me off at Marham but she would need to call at her home first. I was quite happy with that and I suspected the woman took pity on this poor Airman. She took me to her home and left me in her living room and returned clad in night attire and it didn't take me long to respond to her overtures. Another older woman who was happy to teach this young airman a few tricks but, what a surprise, half way into this performance a man entered the room. Surprising what thoughts go through your mind in these situations and it wasn't the only time I found myself in a similar situation but on this occasion this was a planned scenario. I was stuck now and depended on the generosity of this woman to get me back to base so I had to carry on with my activities whilst her partner, obviously a voyeur, watched. I did get a lift back to base and the woman apologised for her behaviour, claiming she only did it to please her partner. She did offer to pick me up again and take me back to her home but I declined that offer

As the weeks and months went by I was gaining all sorts of experiences professionally and socially. I was gaining a reputation amongst the crew and also in that great sanctuary for Airmen, the Pigs Bar in the NAAFI. I could never understand why the bar in the NAAFI was referred to almost reverently as the Pigs Bar, it wasn't that bad. Likewise, one airman to another always referred to the RAF as the mob. "How long have you been in the mob?" and "I'll see you in the Pigs Bar at opening time" were two of the most common Airman phrases. By the time the tale of Taff's and my girlfriend's visit to the fire section toilets got back to the city fathers at the Pigs Bar, it had reached pornographic proportions. These two women had entertained all of the crew and the off duty crews. I was only glad the Warrant Officer never got to hear these exaggerated tales. Shortly after this escapade, RAF Marham closed down – nothing to do with our escapade. The runways at Marham had to be re-built and the aircraft, including all and sundry, were deployed to RAF Honington. The single airmen were billeted at Honington whilst the married men remained at Marham and travelled over each day by coach. RAF Honington was at the time also used as a record quarters, a base for families whose husbands were serving abroad or for those women who were estranged from their husbands and waiting for re housing. Honington was an ideal location for such a requirement; it was like Marham, a remote and secure base. However, the temptation for both parties, wives of husbands who were serving unaccompanied tours in the far-flung corners of the Empire and large numbers of young single airmen suddenly thrown together must, on reflection, have been enormous. I was still at this time apprenticed to Jock McCart and he was billeted with me at Honington.

This detachment resembled feeding time in the Atlantic when the great white whales gorge themselves on seals. Young airmen and not so young married women were gorging themselves in sexual activities. Jock McCart was the leader of the pack and I became his sidekick willing and able to perform whenever and wherever. I did get spoilt for choice and became quite selective, much to Jock's annoyance – he had no taste. All airmen had been well warned by the RAF Police that records quarters were definitely out of bounds. Nevertheless, the NAAFI dances were a common meeting place for both parties and whilst the vast majority of wives remained dutiful, there was obviously going to be some who would transgress. Those who did were fought over by desperate Airmen. Single Firemen seemed to be a particular attraction; maybe it was the string vest. I do remember checking fire extinguishers in the record quarters, an otherwise onerous and least liked of all fire service tasks suddenly became extremely popular. This was a legitimate and perfectly honourable reason to enter the record quarters patch, but I was glad to get out on many occasions.

One particular incident at Honington always comes to mind. I was on night shift, a domestic duty; the crew was reduced in numbers, flying had ceased for the day. I think it was a Corporal Stevenson in charge of the shift who received a phone call from a woman living in the record quarters; she had telephoned and asked if any Firemen wanted to call over to her quarter. The Corporal obviously thought it was a good idea for one of the crew to maintain the good name of the fire section and duly call over. He looked at me but there was no way I was going over. However, there was a newly posted-in Fireman on crew, just returned from a twelve-month tour in Gan. He volunteered to go and as I knew the area the Corporal asked me to take him over. One of the qualities of Firemen is the ability to work together and look after your mates. The whole ethos of training is geared round that, so I felt I had to take him. Corporal Stevenson said if we got a shout (a call out) they would come round and pick us up en route.

On our arrival at the particular quarter, a strange sight beheld us; most of the Pigs Bar regulars were sat round, in a queue, waiting for their turn to climb the stairs and meet the woman. Firemen are well-known queue jumpers and as we were on duty, we were able to go to the front of the queue. I went upstairs and I really had no intention of participating, I just wanted to introduce the newly posted in Fireman. The sight that greeted me was not the most pleasant; the woman lay on the bed ready for action, the remains of a fish and chip supper lay on the floor and she was sipping wine. I suppose for a woman with an insatiable appetite for sex this was the ultimate experience and she was certainly going to make hay while hubby was away in some foreign land that is forever England. I attempted to make my excuses and retreat back to the safety of the fire section but she climbed off the bed and attacked me where I stood. At a time when I was having enjoyable sexual relations with several young women, this escapade was generally an unpleasant experience. I was asked to call back anytime but she knew once I was out she wouldn't see me for dust. However, my mate waiting eagerly downstairs had just spent the last twelve months at RAF Gan on an Island in the Indian Ocean totally devoid of women; his needs were greater than mine.

As I left the quarter I could hear the earth move for them both; they were obviously ideally matched for that occasion. As I walked the few hundred yards back to the section with my tail literally between my legs, I suddenly realised I was being followed. I recognised the sound of the land rover slowly approaching from behind. Next thing I knew an RAF Policeman climbed out of the vehicle and I was stopped in my tracks.

"Where have you just come from?" asked the Policeman. My thoughts raced, "Oh shit, I'm really in it this time. I'm in an out of bounds area, absent from my place of duty and I could drop my mate and the duty fire crew right in it".

"Well... which quarter have you just come from?"

"I can't remember."

"Are you stupid? You must know were you have just been."

"I'm sorry I can't." I was really terrified and felt I was in real trouble this time but I just couldn't identify the quarter, I knew my mate would be hard at it by now and all the rest of the airmen waiting in the queue would also be in trouble.

"Well, do you know where you're going?" asked the Policeman.

"Back to the Fire Section," said I, knowing that I had already incriminated myself by acknowledging I was absent from my place of duty.

"Get in the Landrover," said the Policeman, and I was taken to the section. I was initially surprised at the reaction of the Policeman as he spoke to Corporal Stevenson. They both seemed nonplussed about the incident, whereas I was ready to carry the can for everybody and I was already thinking of how I would cope at Colchester military prison. Next thing, the Policeman was leaving the section and he seemed happy enough.

I stood all forlorn, waiting to be transported over to the guard-room, when Corporal Stevenson said, "What's up with you, Junior?"

"I'm sorry I got caught. I probably should have been more careful and looked about before I set off, but I was desperate to get away from that woman."

"Oh don't worry about that. The Policeman only wanted to know if you had been asked to *pay* for sex. When I told him where you'd been, he was all right." Apparently there were a number of women selling their wares and using one of the quarters as a brothel. I obtained greater satisfaction hearing that than my mate did back at the free sex married quarter.

Once I finally settled down after that nightmare I took myself off to the toilet and washed my willy all over, inside and out with RAF scouring powder. Not the most pleasant of detergents but we were always led to believe that RAF scouring powder kills all known germs! My mate did eventually return to complete his duty but he remained one of many who kept regular appointments with this insatiable woman. In all my time in the mob, I never refused to carry out an order but during that detachment at Honington, if I was asked to check the fire extinguishers in married quarters I would volunteer for any other task but that. It really took me a long time to get over the experience, both in the quarter and being caught on the way home.

That apart, Honington was a good learning experience. The Victors did not fly at weekends so this provided an opportunity to train and practice for the multitude and varied range of incidents that could befall any RAF fireman. The fire crews had to test their vehicles; producing foam as quickly as possible was one of the measurable yardsticks of a good fireman. Some firemen could have foam out of their truck monitors and sidelines in almost no time, whilst others could miss a gear or fail to engage a power take off lever or even stall the vehicle.

It really was a great skill producing foam from a crash tender because there were, depending on the type of vehicle, about ten separate operations to complete under enormous pressure, usually driving at high speed to an aircraft that could possibly explode at any time. There were set positions to take on arrival at an incident; crash one, the rescue truck always covered the cockpit area. The crew of crash one would run out their dry powder lines, enter the flame mass and make directly for the cockpit. Their sole task was to save the aircrew. A varied amount of rescue equipment was carried by the crew, including a pneumatic saw to cut in if necessary through the cockpit canopy, axe to shatter the canopy, ejection seat pins to secure the seat prior to extricating the aircrew.

At the crash as one crew entered the flame mass, the major foam trucks would arrive simultaneously and lay down a foam path covering the rescue crew, both during their rescue attempt and throughout their escape with the rescued aircrew. That was the plan, although every type of aircraft had to be approached differently. Some aircraft were armed and their armaments had to be made safe. Some aircraft had to have leg locks fitted, others had engine intakes that could suck in a fireman and spew him out the other end as mincemeat. Wheel chocks had to be put in place, ladders had to be placed correctly, engines closed down, batteries switched off, oxygen masks removed, seat harness released before finally removing the aircrew from his seat. An ejection seat is simply a rocket and that thought alone could send a tingling sensation through the most experienced fireman. There is no greater sensation than straddling an ejection seat and not knowing whether you have fitted the ejection seat pins correctly. Sad to say that more than one RAF Fireman has been torn in two by an ejecting, ejection seat.

Other lesser factors that also had to be taken into consideration included wind direction, stopping distance from the incident and the need, if necessary, to drop everything and move on to another more serious emergency. Finally, these tasks plus many others were carried out amidst great noise, haste and tension. There are many RAF Fireman who have undertaken just such tasks, some have received bravery awards but every RAF Fireman trains for that eventuality.

Some may never enter an active flame mass or extricate an incapacitated aircrew or extinguish a raging inferno but all RAF fireman accept that responsibility and can, if need be, deal professionally with any potentially life threatening situation.

During my time at Honington the crew, still led by the indefatigable Sergeant Burns, would train ceaselessly, particularly at weekends. Sergeant Burns would call practice crash after practice crash, both daytime and night-time exercises. Often hoses would be run out over great distances and water relay systems set-up and the next practice would involve ladder drills or rope lowering exercises. At the burning area, an aircraft would be set on fire and Fireman would practise under hot conditions. For a young and keen fireman, these were great times, wonderful learning experiences which – I didn't realise then – were going to stand me in good stead for later days. I was at this time still a LAC and had not yet completed a driving course. There is a huge difference between a Fireman driver and a Fireman. Once a driving course is completed there is, without doubt, greater responsibility and more demands made. However, there was no shortage of volunteers for driving courses. After all, a heavy goods vehicle licence was a useful qualification to have in Civvy Street.

The prospect of me going on a driving course whilst I was at Honington seemed fairly distant but, during my time at Honington, Sergeant Burns let me drive under supervision on the airfield at weekends. At every opportunity I would have a go at driving, usually with Sergeant Burns instructing. One regular weekend task was to check the airfield crash gates – nothing special but it required a driver and vehicle to literally drive round the airfield perimeter and check that the crash gates were accessible. I would always volunteer and any driver would welcome the opportunity to be chauffeured around for a few hours on a Sunday. Once the runways at Marham were resurfaced, it was time to return home, so to speak. I returned to Marham a much more accomplished Fireman and Airman and I had no problems settling back in. I was almost the complete airman; I was a bona fide member of the Pigs Bar. I could, if need be, go ten pints without a pee, I could relate a tale of sexual conquests and I had, during my time at Honington, played football for the station team. The one thing I hadn't done which all my contemporaries had was an overseas tour. All on our crew had done overseas tours and the names of those overseas tours regularly came up in conversation; Germany, Australia, Singapore, Hong Kong, Aden, India, Egypt, Malaysia, Libya, Cyprus, Malta, Gibraltar, Kenya and many more but so far the furthest I'd been was Wales. Funny thing was, there was never any talk of the culture or landscape of those countries – talk was always of the bars and the red light areas.

Shortly after returning to Marham I was placed on PWR (Preliminary Warning Role) for overseas service. I half expected it and could hardly wait. Initially I was informed I was off to Borneo. I was duly inoculated and commenced all the other preparations. Prior to departure, I was instructed to attend at RAF St Athan for a driving course. Returning to a training station after my time at Marham came as a bit of a shock. Bull nights and parades, but one soon adapts. I remember the Thursday morning pay parade at St Athan as quite an ordeal – hundreds of Airmen and Airwomen parading and marching out to receive their weekly pay. If you failed to salute correctly or came out of turn it was to the back of the queue you went. The infamous Warrant Officer Clint controlled the driving school in those days. I'm sure he was a nice man really but he put the fear of god up thousands of trainees. Nevertheless, I survived quite well really; I passed all the various tests, four tonner, land rover, car and fire trucks at first attempts and returned to Marham a fully-fledged Fireman driver. RAF St Athan has a special place in my heart not because of my time as a trainee, but I was to return there many years later with my wife and family to a very nice married quarter. However, as a trainee I well remember the NAAFI dances and the coach load of women bussed in from Cardiff; there weren't many Welsh Rarebits (Cardiff Virgins) amongst that lot.

I returned to Marham and, after a few weeks embarkation leave, I was all set to depart for a twelve month tour in Borneo when I was summoned to SHQ (station headquarters) to be informed that I was now going to RAF Masirah, a tiny island in the Indian Ocean off the coast of Oman. I was quite looking forward to Borneo but, such is service life, you just get on with things; adaptability is the key. There is always a sense of sadness, or joy in some cases, leaving an RAF station. Each posting has its own memories and the leaving of friends and the security of familiarity can bring its own anxieties. However, as I was to learn later, there is nothing but sadness as you leave behind your wife and children and set off on an overseas tour or detachment.

I had no special affinity for Marham other than my admiration and respect for Sergeant Burns and, to a lesser extent, Jock McCart. Sergeant Burns was a very firm but fair man, an ideal role model in any profession. I never met Sergeant Burns again until I attended a RAF Fire Service reunion in 2003. This was thirty-seven years after I last seen him and, as I went to the bar, I heard this voice that straight away evoked something in the deep recesses of my mind. It was Sergeant Burns and I was lost for words. I looked at him and he looked exactly as I remembered him – dapper, debonair and, even though he was then into his seventies, he looked as fit as ever. Although I always thought he stood about six-foot when in fact he was smaller than me (five foot eight), I was so pleased to see him and he remembered me as Junior and I suggested to him that Junior was probably inappropriate for a man in his late fifties, but Junior I was. I have met many individuals of varying degrees of stature, culture and character but Sergeant Bob Burns was without doubt one of my favourite character of all time. Although I was sad to leave my crewmates and my girlfriend in Swaffham, I knew I probably wouldn't return or keep in touch so I accepted the inevitable. I was now more preoccupied with how I would cope overseas. After the pleasantries of a leaving do and other fond farewells, I set off for Gatwick airport. I had just turned twenty years of age, never been abroad before and was about to set off on a journey into the unknown.

2. Arabian/African Odyssey ~ Masirah & Mombasa

Rock of Aden, Woe is me;
Let me take myself away from thee,
Let me count the days to go;
Till I may my kit-bags stow,
Then may I thy beauty note,
From the 'blunt end' of the boat

As is customary in the Royal Air Force, a posting means that you go off alone, make your own way and sort things out for yourself. Sounds easy enough, but when you are travelling thousands of miles, burdened down with kit, requiring important documents and timetables, you need your wits about you. To get to Gatwick I had to travel on London Underground for the first time – not a pleasant experience. I was pleased when I arrived at Gatwick with a few hours to spare. I booked in, was told to wait to be called forward and sat down, ready for a long wait.

My deliberations were interrupted by the actions of a group of men who suddenly burst into the terminal and made towards the departure desk. The group were singing and appeared to be in an inebriated state. However, they soon calmed down and all but one left. I had an idea this person was a serviceman. Like me, he had short hair, a rare phenomenon in 1960s men, and he was smartly dressed, another rare phenomenon in the 60s. I could hear him booking in at reception and asking for the Aden flight. After conciliatory words with the receptionist, he was told to go and wait near me. As he sat down next to me he asked in a broad Lancastrian accent, "Are thee going to Aden?" almost as if I was waiting for the next bus home. "Yes," I replied and that was it, the two of us became great friends over the next five years. Phil Sinnot was also a fireman, en-route to Masirah. Phil was two years older than me, had been in the mob a couple of years longer and was posted from RAF Rudloe Manor. For both of us it was our first overseas tour and we were both unsure of what lay ahead.

Travelling on the VC10 aircraft was an experience. I'd never flown in anything other than chipmunk aircraft and this was Phil's first ever flight. A nine-hour flight to Aden was a good way to overcome any flying anxieties.

After a brief stop at Cyprus it was off to Khormakser Airport, Aden. I can remember the changing atmosphere as we drew nearer to Aden; this was, after all, a war zone and we were receiving information about what to do on landing. When we did land and taxied to the terminal, the cabin doors opened. Anyone who has ever flown into Aden will remember the smell, the noise and the heat! Even on a still night, as this was, the heat was unbelievable; it was like being engulfed in steam. Sitting there on the aircraft, I suddenly became soaked in sweat, and I was a young, relatively fit and healthy young airman. I couldn't believe it. What followed next was even more unbelievable. RAF Policemen entered the aircraft and gave instructions about departing.

"As you leave the aircraft collect your luggage, follow the security patrol and run between the columns of water drums." The airfield was under attack. In a few seconds, we had to gather our thoughts. As I stepped out into this new world I could see tracer and hear gunfire in the distance. The combination of the heat and prevailing chaos caused Phil and me to run for our lives.

I had left the safety and comfortable surroundings of Marham far behind and was now on my own and listening to every instruction very carefully. Names were called out and people came forward to welcome new arrivals and lead them off to join their ship, unit or squadron. Phil, a few others and I were left until last and given instructions to return to the airport in four days time to catch the next Beverley to Masirah. Meanwhile, a coach was waiting to take us to the Red Sea Hotel. I had never stayed in a hotel before and imagined this would be something to write home about, but the Red Sea Hotel was hardly the Adelphi or the Ritz; it was just a building in the middle of Aden used as a transit billet.

As we waited to depart, layers of clothing were being peeled off and we all made for the soon-to-become-familiar water-coolers. How Phil and I managed to carry our bags to and from the coach I will never know. In addition to our normal service kitbag full of jungle greens, khaki drill and civvies, we firemen had an extra kitbag full of protective clothing, including a helmet and boots.

At the hotel we had to carry our kit up endless flights of stairs and report immediately for a security briefing. A very calm, cool and smartly dressed RAF Policeman gave the briefing.

"There have been a number of incidents this evening; a soldier has been killed by a sniper and several Arabs were shot in the returning fire. A fuel depot has been blown up and there is a major incident occurring in the Crater district. Do not under any circumstances go near any windows and leave the premises at your own peril."

"Where's the bar?" asked one of the old sweats, and off we all trooped. Tiger beer, a long flight and the recent experiences were all a young airman needed for a good night's sleep, but the night was still young. As is customary in the services, no matter how bad things seem, there is always worse to come, and Phil and I and a few other first tourers were regaled with numerous hair-raising stories, some of which were probably true, but I am sure there was an element of exaggeration in many. Ironically it is usually those furthest from the action who tell the greatest tales. Decapitation, castration, mutilation – take your pick – this, we were told, was the fate that awaited us. Someone shouted, "What about masturbation?" but no-one laughed.

Waking up in this strange land for the first time was almost as startling as the doors opening on the VC 10. There I was laid on a bed naked but still soaked in sweat; I couldn't really see me ever adjusting to this searing heat. A coach was available to take us to Steamer Point, a secure area, with a safe beach-apart from the sharks. Off we went to Steamer Point calling in at the RAF fire section located there. There were quite a few firemen who I knew from Marham and Phil and I were made welcome; almost a sanctuary amidst all this bedlam. We were even offered a trip round Aden on one of the domestic fire trucks. Phil and I declined once we were told we would have to wear protective clothing, carry weapons and ride on the roof of the vehicle as shotgun. "No thanks. I'd sooner watch John Wayne in Stagecoach than have a go myself," at least not until I was acclimatised.

The Red Sea looked more inviting and off we went like lambs to the slaughter or chips to the fryer. It was a dull, humid day; how could we possibly catch the sun on a day like today. We had been well warned not to spend too long in the sun but the sea was warm and refreshing and Phil and I were both good swimmers. That night, back at the Red Sea Hotel, the duty officer on seeing us sent for an ambulance and we were on our way back to Steamer Point, this time it was to the hospital. Reluctantly we climbed in to the back of the ambulance and after a short while it stopped. The driver came round, told us to lie on the floor because there was a gun battle ahead. As we entered the hospital there was further activity, medical staff rushing to and fro. Phil and I would have gladly gone back to the hotel but, after an age, a medic finally had a look at our red and pink bodies and, in no uncertain terms, told us how stupid we were.

"You must be blue jobs (RAF types); there are soldiers dying in here from gunshot wounds and you two pitch up". The next day, covered in calamine lotion, we were taken back to the hotel. After a few days inactivity, it was time to make our way back to the terminal for our flight up to Masirah. As we struggled with our bags, added to by the addition of a few gifts bought in the soukh, the pain from the sunburn was excruciating and it is true, things can only get worse. If we thought we had difficulty arriving at Aden we were in much worse state departing. Not the comfort of a VC10 seat, we were now ensconced in a net seat feeling every bump, bounce and turbulence as we set off on the long journey 'up country'. The weekly Beverley flight known as the RSM, after three stops Riyan, Salalah and Masirah was to become a familiar and welcome sight but on this occasion I was glad to see the back of it. On arrival at Masirah the whole station, about sixty men, turned out. New arrivals were something of a novelty and as the Moonies arrived, old sweats were going home. There was also a fair bit of good-humoured banter but, on reflection, it must have been really tough on the married men, putting up a chart, pictures of their family and counting down from 365. It didn't really bother Phil and me – we were both single and we had joined the RAF to travel. The fact that Masirah was an island thirty miles long by three miles wide, thousands of miles from anywhere and devoid of women was of little concern then.

When the SNCO i/c the fire section (Flight Sergeant Paddy Gibson) greeted us he looked rather sternly at us and said, "You haven't been exposing your bodies to the sun have you?" Phil and I both made the effort to stand up straight and say "No." "Good" he said shaking our hands and patting us on the back – ouch! After exchanging pleasantries with those returning to the UK, we were taken to our accommodation, a four-man room that became home for the next twelve months. Phil was in the next bed to me. Across the way was an older man, John Lightfoot, known affectionately as Heavy Clog or Prof as we all called him, only because the he read the Daily Telegraph. In the other corner was a lad known as Chilly; his surname was Will so it had to be Chilly Willy. Once the Beverley departed, life reverted to a relatively quiet, peaceful existence. It was none-the-less strange watching the link home disappearing for another week. Phil and I were given time to unpack and told to report to the fire section the next morning.

RAF Masirah fire section 'team meeting'.

The fire section was different than that I had just left. The crew was young men; almost all-first tourers and many of them had been through training with me. Old sweats so they told me, avoided twelve months unaccompanied tours like the plague and would volunteer for any of the many accompanied tours. Nevertheless, I took to Masirah immediately; it wasn't as humid as Aden, although it was still hot, damn hot – certainly couldn't walk on the sand in your bare feet.

The fire section was a modern building, the domestic accommodation was clean and bright, the Turtle club (the NAAFI) was great and the whole atmosphere on the station was friendly. I was allocated to my crew. The crew chief was a pleasant, softly spoken man – Sergeant Blencoe – who made me very welcome. The daily fire section routine would be vehicle and equipment checks first thing and then the rest of the day was spent playing volleyball, table tennis or, in my case, playing football. Inter section sport was a highly competitive business and I'm sure it did much to improve moral and defuse potentially stressful situations, both personal and collective.

Those who didn't partake in sport would come along to cheer and attend the celebrating parties. Firemen always excelled in certain sports, certainly volleyball – we did have the advantage of regular practice and I can recollect games in a fire section that have lasted eight hours or more. No wonder I now suffer with an arthritic back! Swimming was another regular, almost daily activity whether that is taking a chance in the Indian Ocean with a watchful eye out for sharks, manta rays or any of the other fearsome looking local fish or basking at the station pool.

'Bondu bashing' was a new activity for me but one I became quite adept at. It simply meant a walk out into the desert. Phil and I both enjoyed a good Bondu bash and would, on our day off, leave camp after breakfast and return in time for evening meal. We would have

Author and MK7 fire truck, RAF Masirah.

with us nothing but a water bottle and no thought of where we were going, no careful planning, just off into the Bondu and we never once got lost. Mind you, it never rained, there was no low cloud and there was little chance of getting lost on a small island.

Very few other airmen shared our enthusiasm for Bondu bashing; many never left the confines of camp at all, returning home the same Moonie colour as they left the UK. Some did panic tan near the end of their tour in the hope of convincing their wife that they hadn't spent their tour in the Turtle Club bar. Invariably Phil and I would end up at one of the various beaches, surf beach, millionaire's beach or jelly fish beach and after a ten mile hike in the Bondu, we were prepared to dive into the sea and take our chances with any sea creatures. Masirah Island was, and still is I suspect, a breeding ground for turtles. Turtles would come ashore bury their eggs and disappear leaving their offspring to fend for themselves in a very hostile world. In the first place, local Arabs enjoyed turtle eggs and they would search out the eggs. Those baby turtles that weren't collected hatched into a waiting array of crabs, flies and other predators. It was a remarkable sight watching the turtles scurrying to the open sea and relative safety. Quite often Phil and I would come across 'stragglers' – baby turtles that had become disorientated heading inland instead of seawards. We would spend the best part of our days off ferrying these lucky creatures to the sea and as the day wore on and we were returning to camp we would convey baby turtles in a fire bucket, back to our room releasing the turtles the following day. Given the longevity of turtles, there are many turtles plying the oceans of the world that remain indebted to Phil Sinnot and George Edwards and I hope they remember to include us in their prayers.

As a Liverpudlian born down by the docks and with many relatives who had gone to sea, the sea always fascinated me. Certainly the Indian Ocean held my imagination. Seeing Arab Dhows for the first time, watching a manta ray lift out of the water and somersault and the eeriness of a shark's fin darting through the water captured my imagination. I also was captivated by the desert, walking though a wadi or a sandstorm, being spat at by a camel or just missing out on a snake's deadly bite were real charmers for me. I had also taken to reading stories about Lawrence of Arabia and the forerunner of the SAS, the Long Range Desert Group. Consequently the desert and its people intrigued me. I was also picking up the odd word or two of Arabic apart from the usual *"imshie"* used to reply to a request for *baksheesh*. Phil and I had met several Bedouins out in the Bondu and they were always extremely hospitable and friendly. Masirah was, however, far from the outside world and political unrest and turmoil had not spread its tentacles to this very remote corner of the world. However, having said that, during the early part of my tour, Arab extremists came on to the island and blew up the water distillation plant; this caused discomfort for both the indigenous Arab population and the service community. Local politicians, most of who worked for and appeared to welcome a British presence, resolved the matter.

The fire section routine was a fairly pleasant business; twice a week the Beverley aircraft would deliver mail, rations and personnel. The duty fire crew would be ordered by Air Traffic to man-up, that all encompassing term used to bring firemen to a state of readiness. Kit would be donned, vehicles manned and radio contact made with Air Traffic. Man-up in those early days meant carrying out all these obligatory duties about an hour before the aircraft's estimated time of arrival. The heavy fear-nought suits and heat in the cab of the fire tenders soon made one feel dehydrated. I often used to think if we were called into action we would be shattered even before we started.

However, the flight sergeant at the time, Paddy Gibson, deemed it appropriate and who was I to argue. This twice-weekly interference with our volleyball, table tennis and water skiing activities was a tiny cross to bear. In the unlikely event of an aircraft ditching into the sea, the fire section was tasked to respond using its zodiac inshore rescue craft. We were all trained up in its use and it was a useful piece of kit, both for its legitimate use and its more leisurely purposes. Friends of the fire section, usually the catering section, were given jollies out in the Zodiac and it was certainly very popular – almost an honour to be selected for a trip out. Part of our legitimate duties was to practice pick up drills. A dummy would be thrown overboard, the Zodiac was to circle then, making a slow approach, crew men would lean over, grab the dummy, push it down. On its upward return, the dummy would be hauled into the Zodiac. That was the theory of it; more often the coxswain would get his approach all wrong and the dummy would end up getting mangled in the engine propellers. When the new Flight Sergeant (Gordon Ditchfield) took over the fire section he was known to be extremely keen, efficient and something of a taskmaster. From day one, he set about testing the fire crews in all aspects of their work covering every potential incident or disaster. He had only been at the section a few days when he called another practice – an aircraft had ditched. The Zodiac crew, myself included, set about launching the Zodiac. Out into the Indian Ocean steamed our intrepid crew led by our highly competent coxswain, Professor Lightfoot. We all knew our various roles and everything was being done very formally and taken very seriously. The Flight Sergeant said nothing until we were about two miles out to sea.

"You can swim can't you Scouse?"

"Yes, Flight."

"OK, over you go, I want to see a practice lift out."

At first I thought it was nice of the Flight Sergeant to know my name – don't forget, he had only been here a few days and he hadn't spoken to any of the crew yet. I soon realised, however, he meant business and into the water I went. Treading water in shark-infested waters must be one of the best laxatives known to man. However, as I watched the Zodiac disappear, I was unsure what I feared the worst – an altercation with a shark or, equally gruelling, a mauling from the Zodiac's propeller. After what appeared an eternity, I could see the Zodiac approaching and, despite the crew's willingness to attempt this live rescue, I feared the worst. I do believe in times of great danger surges of energy pulsate through the body and as the Zodiac neared and the sound of the propellers increased, I do believe I raised myself out the water and returned to my seat in the Zodiac without any help from the crew. Flight Sergeant Ditchfield made many changes to our routine but he was the new boss and that was his prerogative. Once he had carried out all his practices and exercises, we soon returned to our previous routine. However, he did dispense with the lengthy 'man-ups'.

In terms of actual incidents, Masirah had very few. I remember when there was a squadron of Hunters transiting though, one took the barrier and we were left to extricate the aircraft. Having said that, Masirah did produce one of the all-time classic incidents in the annals of the RAF fire service. One day near the very end of my tour, come to think of it I was tour-ex King (the one who was the next to return home), I was instructed by Flight Sergeant Ditchfield to standby with the trailer pump, we were going out to a ship on fire. My colleagues, Jock McVey and Ian Easter, and I prepared ourselves for the expected brief sojourn to put out this small fire on board a passing merchant vessel. The Flight Sergeant met us at the jetty and we were ferried out by Rhino, a large platform used by the RCT to unload ships. The journey out was uneventful and quite pleasant. The Flight Sergeant had by now exerted his authority and was, in fact, well respected. I was only days away from going home and was reflecting on an otherwise happy tour of duty. We were all led to believe that we were going out to a small fire on board the MV Daphne a Greek registered merchant vessel. On arrival it was not quite like that. Initially Jock and I lashed the trailer pump to the Rhino while Ian set up the delivery end and waited for instructions from the Flight. It was obvious from the Flight Sergeant's expression that this was not a small incident. "This ship is carrying a dangerous cargo and the fire could well reach it anytime. Get to work."

In times like that training overcomes fear and, almost instinctively, Jock and I set about getting water up to Ian. Flight Sergeant, meanwhile, contacted Masirah and reinforcements in terms of fireman and other station personnel were brought out. Large quantities of foam would need to be pumped into the ship hold, a further indication that this was a serious incident. By the time the reinforcements arrived, Jock and I had found our sea legs and became accustomed to the motions of the ship. Watching the arrival of the additional personnel, many of whom were not firemen and therefore not possessed with those natural fireman qualities of tenacity and robustness, was quite sad.

There really was fear written over many faces and, on reflection, it was quite a difficult and dangerous activity, throwing yourself on to the rope ladder dangling from the side of the Daphne. You had to judge the swell of the sea, go at a wave's zenith and make a dash for it; one slip or slight delay and you were crushed by the returning Rhino. There were some that were simply too frightened to take that plunge and they remained on the support vessel. An additional fear factor was the omnipresent sharks. My mate Phil was one of those to travel out with the support group. I watched from the Rhino as Phil climbed the rope ladder. He was just about to climb aboard the Daphne when I heard the Flight Sergeant say, "You're not joking now Phil". Phil replied, "What did one VD germ said to the other; if I fall now I'll be a right gonorrhoea." The support team got to work hauling compound drums onto the Daphne. Now picture the scene – drums of foam compound being hauled up the side of the Daphne, many drums bursting, disgorging their black pungent, smelling contents into the ocean. Foam compound in those days had ox blood as a constituent part – great manure for the garden but even greater for attracting sharks. Before long, large numbers of sharks were on patrol looking for a tasty fireman. Sounds a bit like a NAAFI dance but these sharks removed the parts that a NAAFI shark would normally caress. Once onboard the Daphne, personnel were put to work assisting in the movement of hose. Jock and I continued with our task. We remained on the Rhino looking after the trailer pump and the suction hose. The sea was becoming quite choppy and there was a possibility we could be washed overboard. Consequently, Jock and I secured ourselves to the Rhino by rope borrowed from the ship crew.

As the evening drew in, the additional personnel were taken off and returned to Masirah their task completed. Jock and I remained all night on the Rhino, occasionally receiving small scraps of food from the ship crew. Our task basically was to keep the trailer pump full of fuel and to ensure the suction hose remained in the sea. In addition we were constantly adjusting our rope lashing and those of the trailer pump. During the night we received a message from Flight Sergeant Ditchfield that the ship's captain was concerned that the Rhino might damage the side of his ship. We were attached to the Daphne by rope and, depending on the swell of the sea, we did occasionally bang into the side of the Daphne.

Rhino alongside the Daphne.

Rhino with missing starboard section in stormy waters.

Trailer pump crew on Daphne – author and Big Jock McVey.

Trailer pump in action.

It wasn't a pleasant sound especially as we were not rising and falling in tandem with the Daphne. We would more or less hit the Daphne then bounce up and down its side. "We're going to have to move you away from the side of the ship" and, although separated only by about twenty feet, abandoned almost on a flat bottomed steel platform in shark infested waters, at night and in increasingly heavy swell is something that doesn't fade from my memory. We continued pumping throughout the night until we received a message that the fire was now out. We were to remain on the Rhino till dawn and then take it from there.

Come daylight we were, I remember, very hungry and very tired but we were a team well trained and well led so that compensates for those discomforts. The Flight Sergeant informed us that the danger of fire and explosion had passed but there was a new danger the ship's hold was full of water and there was a possibility the Daphne may list and sink. Jock and I now had to move the trailer pump on to the Daphne and start pumping out the hold. This was a relatively straightforward task but once the suction hose was lowered into the hold it regularly became blocked. All sorts of debris was swirling about and I had been tasked to look after the suction hose, so it went without question that I would be lowered into the bowels of the Daphne and off I duly went. I spent three days and two nights on the

Daphne, no sleep, little food but content in the knowledge that I had put into practice many of the skills and knowledge gleaned from my training. I also had great faith in the Flight Sergeant. The situation stabilised and the Flight Sergeant, aware that I was shortly to return home, made arrangements to get me ashore. I remember arriving back at Masirah and, would you believe it, the Station Commander who had only been in post a few days was there to meet me in his car and conveyed me to the airman's mess where a meal awaited me. The Station Commander had probably previously never spent more than a few minutes in the company of an RAF fireman but here he was sat next to one who had not washed or slept for three days, who was very tired and probably talking gibberish. He probably still thinks RAF firemen are always like that.

The MV Daphne incident is included in the annals of the RAF fire service folklore. I have met many Airmen who can relate the Daphne incident much better than I; ironically, most of them were many miles away at the time of the incident. Final comments on the Daphne incident, Flight Sergeant Ditchfield was awarded The British Empire Medal, voted Man of the Year and was featured in the 1968 television documentary featuring the Royal Family. Her Majesty was heard to comment on the Daphne incident and mentioned Fight Sergeant Ditchfield specifically. Two years after the incident I was now stationed at RAF Church Fenton when I received an extra £19 in my weekly pay – that was a huge bonus in those days. I duly went to general office and was informed that this was my part of the salvage money relating to the MV Daphne. I became a bit of a celebrity for a while at Church Fenton, especially after embellishing the story a tiny bit to the women in general office.

Some five years later, now stationed at RAF Brize Norton, I met up with Gordon Dichfield. He was now a Flight Lieutenant and I was a Corporal. I was to realise that Mr Ditchield was one of life's gentlemen and not the fearsome task master that we all thought he was. Another feature and personal development during my Masirah tour was my progress in RAF football circles. On leaving school, I went to work down in the south docklands area of Liverpool with my dad. Every lunch-time, thirty minutes football in the Coburg dock complex was mandatory.

My dad, on reflection, must have been in his late fifties when he finally packed in playing. He was always on the opposite side to me and, like every other player, he took no prisoners. My dad was a foreman so many of those playing saw me as an opportunity to get back at my dad and he, in turn, would have no favourites. I learnt very quickly the art of timing and positional play. I have played football at various levels up until I was late fifty I'm pleased to say I was never injured and I think that was all down to my time spent learning how to avoid bad tackles in the Coburg dock. I was also never booked, which I also put down to my early football days. It was pointless arguing with a decision; if I ever did some, burly Liverpool dockworker would slap me round the head.

RAF Masirah station football team 1968.

I think I had only been on the Island a few days when I was asked if I wanted to join the fire section six a side football team. I duly went and became part of a very good section team with a good balance of youth and experience – I was then on the youth side. RAF inter section football is quite competitive and you do get quite a few section players who present as professionals in all but ability and it can be quite amusing listening to their comments and playing along-side them. Nevertheless these were committed players who made a valued contribution to RAF sport. After a few games for the section team, I was selected to play for the station team. Quite an honour really and I was quite chuffed. You may think, why have a station team on a little island. Who are you going to play? Well, we regularly received visits from passing Royal Navy ships and they would always put out a very good team followed by an equally good piss-up after the game. At this time, the British withdrawal from Aden was taking place. Most of that RN task force was returning home via Masirah. I remember playing teams from HMS Bulwark and HMS Hermes, two of the largest ships in the fleet. They certainly had a wider selection to pick their teams from but we had the advantage of playing regularly on sand (I knew every particle of sand on the Masirah pitch) and we were probably more acclimatised. However, these games drew big crowds. Every available body would turn up, some complete with their crates of Amstel or Tiger beers. Believe it or not this small detachment of Airmen would take on the might of the RN and we would beat them, much to their chagrin. I remember RN lads attempting slide tackles – nothing against that on a grass pitch but on a sand pitch it was painful and dangerous. I played in a game when a sailor broke his leg and another game when a sailor tore open the whole of one side of his leg.

Throughout my time at Masirah I remained in the station football team and kept my position as a right half as it was in those days. We used to put out a team against the visiting Combined Service Entertainment shows when they came to the island. One particular game was against a Mike and Bernie Winter's team. They were both quite good and the taller of the two, Bernie, was quite competitive. Ten years after that game I was to write to Mike and Bernie and invited them to put out a team against RAF Llarbruch, where I was then stationed and they were booked to do a show. I'm pleased to say they accepted the offer and put out a team with those two playing. One CSE entertainer who didn't play football during his visit was Carl Denver but he sang a few songs at the fire section for those on duty and unable to get to his show. Boy could he consume alcohol! Mind you, there were many on the island that could match him in that department. Alcohol abuse was, and probably still is, a serious problem in the military. The problems being you are almost encouraged to partake with the demon drink. It takes enormous will power to abstain or even moderate your alcohol consumption. I was no different from any other airman in the drinks department and I could hold my own in any company and, believe me, there were some heavy drinkers at Masirah. My mate, Phil Sinnot, developed a serious alcohol addiction brought about by two factors; one was his ability to sing every dirty ditty and recall hundreds of joke. Consequently, whenever there was a leaving do (a Marsalam in Arabic), people would call upon Phil and insist he came and joined in the revelry. I know at first he was happy to do so but this was no stupid individual. Phil was a bright lad and he realised he was becoming addicted and tried to abstain but the pressures were too much. Secondly, Phil experienced what we all anticipated and dreaded, that message from home that a loved one was ill or dying. One evening an officer called to our room and one instinctively knows something is wrong. Phil's dad was in hospital and arrangements were being made to get Phil home. Don't forget this was in the days of no telephone contact with home and letters took about a week to reach us.

There was also the problem of getting Phil off the island. To catch a UK bound aircraft, he would have to be routed through Aden or Bahrain. Phil left the island not knowing what was wrong with his dad and when he would make it back to his home in Southport. All our thoughts were with Phil in this difficult time and it always reminded one of our remoteness and also that things like this can happen to us all. Phil returned after a few weeks, informing us that his dad had died and been buried by the time he got home. I can remember to this day Phil coming back into our room informing us of what had happened, putting his bags down and walking over to the Turtle Club. We all offered our condolences as best we could but that was the catalyst for Phil's alcohol problem. It is worth remembering that Phil Sinnot was a non-smoking, teetotaller when he joined the RAF. He was, in fact, a train spotter and came from a very well known Southport family; there is actually a block of flats in Southport called Sinnot House named after his father. Phil was, several years later, discharged from the RAF, under some Queens Regulation, as airman, whose services were no longer required. Service life can be harsh and brutal, mental toughness is a more valuable virtue than physical toughness and, for a man like Phil who was basically a gentle benign individual, alcohol cost him dearly. .

There used to be men at Masirah drinking daily pints of Pernod, brandy, whisky, anything really and the cost was minimal. I never took to the spirits but could knock back quite a few cans of Tiger. Everyone knew the hard drinkers; one in fact was a well-known cook. You would go to breakfast in the morning put your plate out to receive egg and bacon and you would have to move your plate round in circles trying to keep up with the cook's shakes hoping the breakfast would land on your plate and not the floor. No-one took no notice and I used to think then that perhaps they should receive counselling or be repatriated but I was informed that if that happened then anyone who wanted out would behave like that, so it became accepted practice for many. We also had a fireman who thought it was about time the local Arabs were converted to Christianity and off he would go with his bible under his arm, boldly marching into the Arab quarters denouncing Allah. Surprising how quickly he was despatched off to the psychiatric ward at RAF hospital Wroughton. Another airman decided he was going native and dressed as a local Arab, ate in similar fashion i.e. sitting on the mess floor legs crossed eating without the use of knife fork and spoon. No one took any notice of him and he completed his tour and was given the relative luxury of his own room.

On reflection, Masirah was a wonderful tour. Waking up almost everyday to glorious sunshine and a relatively stress free day. I swam almost every day in the warm Indian Ocean played football twice a week, table tennis daily and often spent five or six hours every day playing the number one fire section sport, volleyball. Idyllic times; however, if I was married at that time I probably would have found it a difficult experience. Nevertheless I had some wonderful mates and the NCOs and the few officers on camp were also nice people. In fact, the station commander, a Squadron Leader Spiers, regularly came to the fire section and chatted with us all.

I also remember at the fire section we had a local Arab man who worked as a cleaner and his name not my choice but believe it or not, was Sambo. Not only was Sambo the fire section cleaner, he was also the executioner for the indigenous population; don't forget corporal and capital punishment was an accepted practice in some Arab cultures. He was, amongst the Arab community, a very important man as indicated by the fact he had three wives.

I got on well with Sambo; I used to practice my Arabic with him and took a genuine interest in his lifestyle and culture. I was one of only a few to have visited him at his home and, as the photograph shows, his home consisted of a few oil drums. I remember one day Sambo coming to me clearly in pain; he had done some damage to his wrist – I could see the swelling and he put his arm on the floor and insisted I stand on his wrist. I refused but offered to take him to the medical centre, which he was not all that endeared with instead he went off and found someone willing to straighten his damaged wrist. I also remember Sambo once telling me in his broken English that his number one wife "mush taman (no good), she is leaking." I always took that to mean she was experiencing her periods.

Sambo, RAF Masirah's Fire section cleaner,
who was also the island's executioner!

One thing for sure, you never went near the few Arab women that were on the island – that was an unwritten law. I cannot think of any of the RAF lads even thinking of doing that. Having said that, all the women from the age of puberty wore either the abaya, the black gown that covered them from head to toe, or the yashmak face veil, and one could only imagine what lay under those veils. Invariably the thought was of a very old woman. That was not the case with the images of the other women in my thoughts and probably everybody else's. We had no television and an open-air cinema showing U rated movies. Consequently when the CSE shows came, watching the supporting dancers always raised pulses.

One clandestine and illegal activity did take place – only the once – and that was the watching of a 16-millimetre naturism film. No one claimed any responsibility for the film but word spread it was going to be shown and the venue was going to be our four-man room. The projector was set up and a new record for the most airmen cramped into one room must also have been created. Bodies were everywhere and from amongst the crowd came those immortal words "Has anyone seen the sheriff?" (the only RAF Policeman on the Island). I obviously thought there was some concern that the sheriff may come and confiscate the film and arrest a few of us, but no. A voice from atop one of the lockers shouted "I'm up here," so the film duly commenced. It is surprising how a few women prancing around naked can captivate an audience of grown men; you could hear a pin drop and I bet there must have been much under the sheets activity that night.

During my tour at Masirah, I was given the opportunity of either three weeks leave back home in the UK or a three-week trip to Mombasa. Much as I would have liked to see my family, the idea of three weeks in Mombasa was more tempting and that was the chosen option. I had a mate in general office, an Irishman who played with me in the station football team, and it was his job to sort out these matters. He was really helpful booking flights and arranging accommodation. My mate Phil Sinnot was also given the same option and it was agreed that we would travel together. Sad to say, shortly before our departure, Phil was notified that his father was seriously ill and rushed home. Several weeks before our planned departure Phil and I had been saving what we could and even packed in drinking alcohol. Our holiday generated considerable interest on the island. Most men stationed at Masirah were married and it was only right that those men return home to their families. Comments were made about African women and the night-clubs but, generally speaking, I took no notice and thought I'll just make my own mind up and see what happens when I arrive. The time duly arrived when it was time for me to leave. I was sad my mate Phil was not with me but he waved me off and wished me well. I think it fair to say that all station personnel were aware of my destination and, in the small close knit RAF community, I suppose it was something different than the normal routine of an isolated desert outpost.

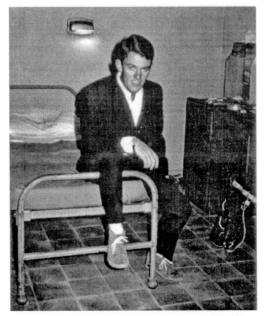

The author awaiting transportation to Mombasa.

I was leaving Masirah after six months on the island flying in an Argosy aircraft en-route to Aden. I left the island full of apprehension and excitement. I was acclimatised and familiar with the area; consequently, I had none of my earlier trepidations. Having said that, my arrival at Aden was no different than my previous visit. If anything, this time it was a more tense and hostile situation. Small arms fire could be heard all around the town and there were more aircraft movements, which was understandable as the British withdrawal from Aden was at its height. However, this time I had no overnight stay in the Red Sea Hotel, I was transported over to a civilian aircraft and flew initially to Nairobi and then on to Mombasa. On arrival at Mombasa, a coach awaited all those military personnel commencing their R&R (rest and recuperation). Most personnel were either Royal Marines or Army. I was the only RAF. All but me was dropped off at the Silver Sands leave centre about five miles north of Mombasa. I remained on the coach and asked the driver to drop me of at the Angel Hotel in Mombasa town centre. I was aware that my mate back at general office in Masirah had booked me into a hotel and I'm sure he thought he had obtained a quality hotel but little did he or I realise that my hotel served other functions, namely those of a house of ill repute.

As I entered the hotel my bags were taken to my room, while the manager, a very cordial and affable African escorted me to the bar. The place was empty and strangely quiet apart from about ten young African women sat together. They all looked towards me and started to giggle and I thought no more of it. I asked the manager why it was so quiet and was duly informed that nothing happened until evening time when all the British soldiers arrived from their leave centre. I did feel somewhat isolated and thought for a brief moment that maybe I should have booked into the leave centre. However, I was given a free drink, sat down and three women came and sat down with me.

I was fairly naïve in these matters and I remember more than anything else their stunning beauty and excellent use of the English language. They asked me where I had travelled from and, ever conscious of security, I was a bit reluctant to answer any military questions. However, I did explain I had just come from an island in the Indian Ocean and they asked if it was Masirah and when I said it was they started laughing and gesturing.

"No women at Masirah – you wankie-wankie all time" and then started to tease and caress me in a most erotic manner. One pushed her breasts into my face while another put her hand on my leg and started to rub my very erect penis. Here was I, a virile young man who had not seen a woman for months, suddenly finding himself in the company of three very attractive women who were obviously skilled in their chosen trade.

Right there, only a few minutes after arriving at the hotel, I experienced the first of my many ejaculations in Mombasa. I was, to say the least, embarrassed when a distinct wet patch suddenly appeared for all to see on my white cotton trousers. I made my apologies, which only heightened their amusement and they followed me up to my room. I thought I would be left alone to sort myself out but they were having none of it. All three women assisted in the removal of my stained clothing whilst, at the same time, removing their own brief attire.

I had no time to compose myself; the women simply threw me on the bed, one beauty grabbed hold of my erect penis, which disappeared deep into her throat. The other two women were teasing me sucking each other's breasts and standing over me pushing their midriffs into my face. One of the women kept saying, "You like African women?" to which I replied, "Very much." It was only a matter of minutes before I ejaculated once more only this time there was no embarrassing stain.

I thanked all the women profusely for what they did but they were still in a playful mood, pushing their breasts into my mouth and their hands were all over me. Needless to say there was another stirring in my loins and my third erection in less than half an hour surfaced. This time the women insisted I have sex with one of them and, careful not to offend, I left the choice to them. When I penetrated the chosen beauty it really was exquisite and her body movements were quite sublime. This woman, like all the others I met over the next three weeks, had what I can only describe as fantastic muscular strength in the lower body region. It was impossible to try and delay my ejaculation – I was simply and exquisitely sucked in then blown out in a matter of minutes.

This was my third ejaculation in almost as many minutes. I hadn't yet unpacked, eaten or finished my first drink but I'd had enough sexual activity for one day, or so I thought. I asked the women where I could get something to eat and, realising that I was knackered, they took me back to the bar.

I enjoyed a pleasant meal in the company of the women who were telling the other women of our sexual exploits. All present were laughing and coming over to speak to me. One of the older women called me Chico and that was my name throughout my stay in Mombasa. I finished my meal, had a few beers and tried to get to my room for a kip but the women insisted I danced with them. There was a jukebox full of mainly Beatles records and I was delighted to dance with beautiful women to my then favourite music. An interesting aside about that jukebox, there was a record by Screaming Lord Sutch called 'As I was digging in the cemetery up jumped a man who was all black and hairy'. Since leaving Mombasa, I have never heard this record played. However, I shall always associate Lord Sutch with Mombasa and that record. As I danced with the women they would say, "You nice happy boy, you not rough with us." I would laugh and say to them, "I'm not rough but you are very rough with me." Eventually I managed to get to my room, unpack and collapse for a few hours before the evening entertainment commenced.

I was woken by a woman shaking me. I was, as is customary, naked and in those days I would usually wake with an erection. I could hardly avoid that fact and, once more, my penis was gripped and called in to further action. That done I was given a rub down in the shower, dressed and made my way down to the bar. The bar was totally different in the evening; the place reverberated to the sound of loud music and loud British troops and young African women looking to entertain those troops – for a price.

The thought did cross my mind about the price I would have to pay for the services already rendered and I went to ask advice from the hotel manager. To my surprise, he informed me that my hotel was all-inclusive and had been paid for by the military and that included the use of the women during the day who worked his bar. He also went on to say that all the women were talking about me and making reference to my sexual prowess. In all modesty, I was no different to any other young heterosexual who had just spent six months without the company of women. I joined in with the general melee that was taking place and made friends very quickly with some Royal Marines, one of whom lived in Liverpool; he was known by all and sundry as Boots, as were many marines.

He was a big, athletic individual and carried a cane with a screw top. Unscrew the top and he would extract a long blade and I guess he would use it if the need arose. The talk generally in the bar was of Aden and in particular the incident in Crater when the Northumberland Fusiliers were trapped. I, along with everybody else in the Middle East, was aware of this incident but now I was receiving first hand accounts of what happened. Apparently the Northumberland Fusiliers were enticed into Crater and, once inside, their means of exit was denied. According to my sources, the Fusiliers were captured and appalling atrocities were inflicted upon them including crucifixion. Apparently there was a rescue planned but the High Commissioner did not grant permission and the fusiliers were left to their fate. It was then that the famous Mad Mitch incident took place; he went against orders and marched in with his Argyll and Sutherland Highlanders to the skirl of the bagpipes.

I was aware that whenever the High Commissioner's name came up in conversation, men would spit; such was their disdain for his actions or lack of action. In later years, I served in the Armed Services Recruiting Office in St Helens and a colleague, Staff Sergeant Alan Whelan, was a Northumberland Fusilier and had served in Aden. We had in the RAF Careers a Sergeant Danny Techeney of Arab descent and Alan would not or could not remain in the same room as Danny. It takes a long time for wounds like Crater to heal, if they ever do.

Perhaps because I was the only RAF lad and generally younger than most, my newfound mates took me under their wing and I toured the bars and dives of downtown Mombasa with them. We certainly saw some sights and shows on those trips; strip shows, sex shows and many servicemen hurled abuse, cigarettes and bottles at the various artists. At first I used to watch in amazement and I will always remember the first time I saw a coke bottle disappear into a stripper's vagina only to return and the hoards of squaddies would clamour to drink from the bottle. Throughout the night we drank, danced and a few sexual activities were thrown in for good measure. Come the early hours of the morning, the men were making their way back to the leave centre whilst I was returning to my hotel. I entered the hotel and it was very much the calm after the storm; women were relaxing and counting out their night's takings. It was a relatively pleasant atmosphere and I had my last can of Tiger beer before retiring to my pit. As I made my way upstairs one of the women who I had seen earlier in the day came over and informed me that she was my guardian angel and was coming to bed with me. I explained I was tired but she insisted and came with me and subtly said, "You will be safe with me, no-one will harm you." I didn't realise until then that I was in quite a dangerous situation, I was accommodated in a sleazy hotel in the back streets of Mombasa. Remnants of the Mau Mau and other insurgents were known to be in the area but here I was young, innocent and very immature. I went into my room with my woman friend and she insisted we had sex before I went to sleep, during the night and again when I woke. I hadn't been in Mombasa twenty-four hours but I had lost count of the number of sexual encounters I had experienced. Nevertheless, my morning was spent in the company of the working girls who also slept at the hotel. I certainly looked out of place but was quite happy in their company and they took an interest in me, where I lived in England, etc...

After breakfast I went for a walk around town. I probably went to places I should not have but in those days I had no fear. I did see some appalling poverty and beggars of all descriptions followed me everywhere. I was not aware that black people and white people were supposed to walk on different sides of the road and used different shops and restaurants. There was a very distinct apartheid system until it came to sexual relations and then we are all equal. I did my own thing and went about my own business freely. I could not, even in those days, tolerate discrimination and I got some very strange looks from some white gentlemen... I was a working class man and proud of it and I could not consider myself superior or inferior to others. I had black friends in the RAF and at home in Liverpool and one of my favourite people then was Cassius Clay.

After my ramble around Mombasa I returned to the hotel ready for a Tiger beer. I could in those days knock back quite a few beers no problem. I never suffered hangovers but I put that down to the generally high level of fitness I enjoyed. I wasn't getting my usual high level of sporting activity at Mombasa but I was getting more than my share of sexual activity. That afternoon I consumed a few beers, danced with the girls, went to my room for some more group sex activities, had a few more beers and then I joined in the evening activities with the incoming servicemen. They arrived rested and ready for action whilst I had already enjoyed a full day's drinking and fornicating. I managed to survive another day and night's frantic activity and spent the night in bed with my guardian angel. This woman, it transpired, looked after the other girls. She was very attractive, not as young as the other girls but she seemed to have some influence in the hotel. Day two came and I was beginning to tire but I was young, fearless and reckless. I was also determined to make the most of my holiday.

I drank more beers, visited some seedy bars and returned to some more frolicking in the afternoon followed by another wild night. I was in the company of another Royal Marine and we were watching these two beauties performing a striptease show. Somehow and I can't remember how, we copped off with these two women and spent the night with them in a very seedy hotel. I remember waking up and trying to climb out of bed but this woman was wrapped around my body and I was unable to extricate myself. As I lay there under a makeshift mosquito net I was trying to work out how I ended up with this woman and what was happening to me when she awoke and another sex act took place. Later that morning I returned to my hotel and my guardian angel was quite angry that I had stayed in another hotel. She kept saying, "You be careful, many bad people about." It made sense what she was saying but as soon as you have a drink and an African beauty propositions you, that's a different matter. That afternoon I drank at my hotel bar and was out again in the evening.

That night I was in a bar with a large group of Marines. As I went to the toilet a woman came up to me, put her hand down my trousers and asked me to come with her. I knew I shouldn't but I was half inebriated and suitably aroused. As she led me outside, a group of Africans appeared from nowhere and were trying to force me into a car. As my young life flashed before my eyes I struggled as best I could and, before being whisked off to an indescribable fate, the Royal Marine lads burst out of the club and dragged me back inside. It was a very scary incident and I was beginning to realise that I was living very close to the edge.

During the evening of the fourth day I fell into a very deep and disturbing sleep and I shall always remember this one and only nightmare. A combination of alcohol abuse and wholesale debauchery are a fatal cocktail and I can visualise now being summoned to meet the grim reaper himself. I remember trying to walk backwards on a descending escalator but, try as I might, I descended. As I reached the bottom the gates of hell opened and there stood Satan ushering me in. Sure enough, there was a roaring fire and, as I was about to be thrown in, I awoke from my nightmare lathered in sweat and shouting for mercy. That was it; I needed to move out of my hotel and the associated surreal atmosphere and seek sanctuary in the leave centre.

That morning I made my way on foot to the Silver Sands leave centre and on arrival I pleaded with a very sympathetic Army Major to allow me in. He could never understand how and why I ended up in the hotel and secondly how I had survived so far. The RAF always have to be different quipped the Major but I was in no state to argue and readily accepted his offer of accommodation for the rest of my holiday. I must have slept all day and woke with the rest of the lads in the billet and went into town with them on the bus provided. This was much better; I was going into town about 8pm refreshed and raring to go.

Once in Mombasa I made my way over to my hotel ready to grovel to the manager for the few bits of clothing I had left in my room but he was pleased to see me. He told me that the RAF had already paid for my accommodation so he never lost any income. He also stated he was pleased to see me safe. I also saw my guardian angel and she was pleased to see I was safe. The last time she saw me she informed me that I was very drunk. She insisted I come back to her at the end of the night and I usually did. This was a much better system – we would party all night then make our own way home, either by taxi or wait for the first bus which left about 8am. Ironically, that first bus came from the leave centre conveying those service personnel who were not out on the town every night, those service personnel invariably were WRENS, WRACS and WRAFS. In Aden where they had come from they were in the minority and even the ugliest female service person would be a beauty in the eyes of the vast majority of troops. I was embarrassed a few mornings as I waited for the bus to take me back to the leave centre after a night on the tiles. I would be stood at the bus stop in just my shorts – in those days, items of clothing could be exchanged for services rendered or entrance fee into a club. The service women would look at us with due contempt but when they returned back to their bases they would once again have the upper hand but, for the time being, they played second fiddle to the African women.

I had also made some friends from a Royal Navy warship the Ghurkha, which was visiting Mombasa. There were some rum lads amongst that crew and they certainly knew how to party. I went onboard the Ghurkha and had a meal with a mate I befriended. He used to get up to all sorts of pranks and I remember him arriving back late and being sentenced to seven days nines as they called it – seven days loss of pay seven days loss of leave and more important to him seven days loss of grog (rum ration). I remember the RN shore patrol exerting their power and authority in the bars and dives of back street Mombasa but they bore no resemblance to the American Navy shore patrols that carried huge coshes and would, without hesitation, use them gratuitously. I had a wonderful, never to be forgotten experience in Mombasa.

Throughout the holiday I remained in daily touch with my guardian angel, who I thought genuinely liked me. She certainly did not like me for my money because I ran out of money after a week; it was only my clothes and my personal possessions that kept me in the lifestyle that I become accustomed to during those hectic few weeks. When the time came for me to return to Masirah, I was ready. I don't think I could drink any more beer, dance any more dances but most significantly I was sexually exhausted. The thought of going back to my desert island for a rest and recuperation was quite appealing.

Author at the monument to the men of the SS Baron Inverdale.
The inscription reads: 'In memory of the men of the Baron Inverdale who were
massacred at this point in the year 1904'.

When the time came for me to depart, who should be at the bus station but my guardian angel. She had, of her own volition, taken time out to come and bid me farewell. She gave me three leaving presents: the first was a big bite on my shoulder saying "tell your friends that your guardian angel gave you that". The second present was an elephant hair bracelet, which I wore for many years – apparently a sign of fertility! The last present was very unusual and was presented to me in an envelope. When I opened it I didn't recognise what it was; however, inside were several of her pubic hairs – to remind me of her, she said. I did show a very few close friends the latter present but I'm afraid they were disposed of after a short time... On my return to Aden I flew, like almost everybody else, in a tee shirt, trousers and flip-flops. Everything else had been sold or given in exchange for services rendered.

My arrival back at Masirah was like the prodigal son returning to his family. Word had spread that I had moved into the leave centre; word had also got back that I had done a good job upholding the high traditions of a Royal Air Force airman. That night I entered the Turtle Club to a full house, all present keen to hear of my tales of daring–do in the flesh pots of East Africa.

How different my libido is these days and I think the following RAF ditty, courtesy of Harold Bennett's wonderful book *Bawdy Ballads and Dirty Ditties of the Wartime RAF* (Woodfield Publishing) very aptly encapsulates the ageing process...

Nemesis
My days of youth are over, my torch of life almost burnt out.
What used to be my sex appeal is now my waterspout.
Time was when of its own accord t'would from my trousers spring
But now I've got a full time job to find the blasted thing.

It used to be amazing the way it would behave
As early every morning it stood and watched me shave
But as old age approaches, it fair gives me the blues
To see it hang its withered head and watch me clean my shoes.

Another of my favourites from the book is:

Aircrew Chum
A poor WOp/AG lay a-dying
At the end of a bright Summer's day,
His comrades were gathered around him,
To wash all the blood stains away.
Take the bullet from out of my shoulder,
And the shrapnel out of my brain,
And the pom-pom from out of my liver,
And patch up the turret again.

I'll be riding the clouds in the morning,
No more this gun turret to cuss,
So please patch me up in my shroud,
For I'll not be needing this bus.
So hold your glasses steady,
And let's drink a toast to the sky,
For here's to the dead already,
And here's to the next man to die

There is an obvious sense of morbidity to the ode but I like it because I had friend (now deceased) who was an Air Gunner. I like to remember him in this cavalier style and this is how he would want to be remembered. I also consider this ode to be a fine testament to the courage and fortitude of the Bomber Command crews who encountered death on a daily basis. They dealt with this occupational hazard by adopting this cavalier and ambivalent attitude. I bet however that they were still terrified every time they went to work. I do think Harold Bennett's book is a wonderful, historical record of the RAF way of life, especially for those who served in the Second World War. I would however recommend it to all RAF personnel past and present. It is a fine testament to our predecessors and I am sure some of the ballads are still being sung to this day.

Like the vast majority of station personnel I had on my wall a chuff chart a chart counting down the days to do. There used to be one airman, a Jock lad whose nickname was 'Nugget; every time you came into contact with him the first words he would utter in a broad Scottish accent were "no got long to do." I was coming to the end of my tour and it was a wonderful feeling. In these situations rank has no relevance. The most important person amongst the ranks is the

Tourex-King in fact there was a crown available for those willing to don it. I had grown to like Masirah very much. I loved the heat; the daily swim and I enjoyed my job and the comradeship. Of course, I was looking forward to going home to see my family but I knew that most of my friends in Liverpool had moved on with their lives and my friends now were in the RAF.

I arrived at Masirah as a Leading Aircraftman but left as a Senior Aircraftman and a fairly accomplished one at that. It is a fact that I actually sat and failed my Senior Aircraftman's exam at RAF Marham. I sat that exam totally unprepared; all my mates were confident I would pass. Consequently I believed them and never bothered to revise. That was a lesson well learnt. I never again entered any examination unprepared and I never again failed any of the many examinations I subsequently sat.

World Jury shipwreck off the coast of Masirah.

When I first arrived, I was one of only two LACs on the island. The other, as it turned out, worked in the communications centre and he became a good mate of mine and, like me, he was a member of the station football team. I also had my twenty-first birthday on the island. My mum in fact sent me a twenty-first birthday cake; unfortunately the cake became a victim of the 1967 Gulf war. As the cake was passing through the Suez Canal the canal was closed for a time.

Subsequently my cake melted; none-the-less it arrived several months later looking like a dump of camel dung. I did, however, take the cake over to the Turtle Club and it proved to be an excellent opportunity for another piss-up. I have to confess on that occasion I knowingly told my mother a lie. I did write and tell her that the cake arrived satisfactorily but I knew she would have been upset if she thought otherwise. I also received from my mother a twenty-first birthday request on the British Forces Broadcasting Service. That record was the Tony Bennett classic 'May Each Day in Your Life Be a Good Day'. It was with a sense of joy tinged with sadness that I left Masirah and, even all these years later, I remember vividly those halcyon days spent at RAF Masirah.

RAF Masirah 1967 (The lonely outpost).

3. Glory Days ~ Church Fenton & the Royal Tournament

I returned home a much wiser man but in the first instance I had to accustom myself to my home life. It was strange waking up at home having been away for twelve months. My parents loved all five of their children so it was important they never made to big a fuss of me but my dad was himself ex RAF and he was clearly keen to listen to my (censored) tales and my RAF mates were always welcome at our home. My mum was more concerned that I was being fed properly. I loved my family dearly but I was missing my mates the banter the job and lifestyle. I also arrived home a much wealthier man I had saved and had quite a healthy Post Office saving book (POSB was the abbreviation for the savings book but it was also a term used to describe anyone who was considered to be a miser).

I could have saved more but I had enough money to pay cash for a car. My dad, a friend of his and I went to look at a few cars and I came across this bright green Austin A35. Subsequently I paid £65 and became the first in my immediate and extended family to own a car. During those first few days of my disembarkation leave, I would take my family for days out in my car. I had, however, agreed to see Phil and after a week at home I contacted him and we met at Exchange Station, Liverpool and embarked on a night out in Liverpool City centre.

It is worth remembering that, at this time, we were both tanned, fit, had a few bob in our pockets and were looking to make up for time lost. I also had developed a good line in patter and I could quite easy embellish my tales of time spent abroad in the service of Her Majesty. I also had my elephant hair bracelet on my wrist and, once again, this generated considerable interest – another excuse for a yarn. That night I met and chatted up a woman while Phil cracked a few jokes to some blokes at the bar. Anyway, I agreed to meet this woman the following night. This was a strange encounter and one that was destined not to last long. I duly met her and she took me to a party at Liverpool University campus. I was introduced to her circle of friends, most of whom were members of the University Officer Training Corps. Some thought it might be fun to ridicule this poor benighted heathen of an RAF fireman but I soon drank them under the table and came away with the belle of their ball. I obtained my just rewards and she was suitably impressed – not so when I didn't turn up for our next date. Instead I contacted Phil and back into Liverpool City centre we went.

Phil and I had an unusual relationship; he was older than me only by a few years but he was much brighter, full of useless information and great company; he liked a pint and a few jokes. He had an interest in sport and was in fact a great supporter of the Sand Grounders – Southport FC. He was also quite a handsome chap and, given all his creditable personal qualities, he really should have had no problem pulling the women but that was an aspect of Phil's life that he was not very good at. This problem became a big concern for Phil and all his mates. Most of us would go out with the sole intention of meeting members of the opposite sex and Phil was no different but all the years I knocked about with Phil he only ever had the one female acquaintance. That acquaintance was Clare.

After my experience at Liverpool University Phil and I went into Liverpool town centre and I made conversation with a young, attractive woman who was with her mates. Phil was part inebriated and part shy and he was reluctant to woo any of the women. I made a date with my newly found acquaintance and asked her to meet me the next night and bring a mate for my mate. I had stern words with Phil about going easy on the drink and he duly scrubbed up and went with me on the date. My new acquaintance duly arrived, complete with the only one of her friends who was prepared to go on this blind date. Phil's date was big; in his own words, "It's a baby elephant!" However, I convinced Phil he should give it a go, if only to have a sexual encounter – something he hadn't had for a long time. Phil needed no excuse to get pissed and he duly did that.

He started off the night so well, full of good intent, telling a few clean jokes before the rude ones came out. Nothing happened on our first date but we agreed to see them the following Saturday. I would pick them up in my car and take them to Southport. During that week Phil stayed over at my house and my parents and siblings thought the world of him. He really was a decent, well brought up lad but developing a drink problem. My parents never saw that side of Phil and he was too much of a gentleman to behave inappropriately in front of my family.

We had a few quiet beers during the week; Saturday came and I insisted we didn't go for a drink during the day, then off we went to meet our women friends. My new acquaintance was a pretty thing and I was later to find out that she was that year the Queen of the Liverpool Orange Lodge. Phil's woman was quite a pleasant thing and she appeared keen to make a serious go at establishing a relationship with Phil. I should imagine she never went on many dates and Phil was a good catch.

We had a pleasant evening telling a few stories and behaving with all the decorum one would expect from an RAF Airman. I did make some gentle advances but was told, "I'm not a woman like that," which was fair enough. Phil's woman friend was much older than mine and she was behaving very much like a chaperone and keeping an eye on me. She suggested we meet again, only this time we would go the pictures. I would have abandoned ship there and then but Phil was keen to meet up again and for his sake I agreed to go the pictures. Our relationships developed but I must admit I was getting restless and concerned that this was becoming serious. Clare made it plain she didn't like me; she told me she thought I was a bad influence on Phil!

After a few days, Clare asked if we would like to have a weekend at her aunt's caravan in Rhyl and off we duly went, having first met her aunt, who gave us the once over. It soon became apparent that Phil was consummating his relationship while I was restricted to a grope of my woman's lovely breasts. I was concerned for Phil; despite his maturity, I thought he could be set up for a shotgun wedding. I asked him if he was taking precautions. He laughed and said, "Yes, I tie myself to the bed". He was happy in his relationship and my friend was a pleasant individual who I had grown to like, quite a bit. Phil and I started going out separately; I would go to my friend's house meet her parents and she came to mine. Both sets of parents were impressed and, within a short space of time, we became very attached. Time came for me to report to my new posting, RAF Church Fenton. I promised my girlfriend I would telephone as soon as I knew my shift arrangements and off I went.

If RAF Masirah was a desert paradise, it turned that my new posting was a paradise in a beautiful part of Yorkshire, located between the two fleshpots of Leeds and York. This was a wonderful tour for me in every aspect! On arrival, word had it that I had played football for RAF Masirah and that first week I played the first of my many football games for the station team. At the fire section there was a Corporal Tom Sawyer and anyone associated with RAF football in the sixties and seventies would remember Tom. He was a very talented centre half – nothing got past Tom. Not only did he have good skills on the ball, he was a powerful header of the ball but he was also a fearsome looking individual with his flat nose and muscular build. I was to take up my position as right half alongside Tom. He was lacking a bit of pace when I played with him but he would tackle, win the ball pass to me and away I would go.

All Tom ever talked about was football. I did not become aware that he was a married man with children until much later. He was not only captain of the station team but he also played for the local village team, Ulleskelf, on Saturday and then on a Sunday he played for the Avon Cosmetics factory, which was located nearby. I had no say in the matter – Tom told me I'd been selected for those two teams also and I duly turned out with Tom as instructed. It goes without saying we developed a good partnership. Service football is not too rough but playing in the local leagues could get a bit hairy. When things did get rough, Tom would normally deal with those situations in his own inimitable style – a set too. I also very quickly made some wonderful mates of my own age with similar interests.

The station was fairly small in numbers and all the single men lived in one big barrack block. This was in the days of the big dormitory, thirty-five in each dormitory with a bedside cabinet and large wardrobe separating you from the next man. I was quite happy with this situation there was a mixed bag of tradesmen in our dorm and we usually went the NAAFI together and then there would be those similar to me who frequented Leeds and York and other flesh-pots on a regular basis.

I had mates who were firemen but I also had mates from all sorts of trades. If I ever needed a job doing on my car my MT mate would do that. I had a good mate who worked in clothing stores; another was an admin clerk and a few mates from air traffic. However, returning to my woman friend in Liverpool, I did phone and she was writing to me but it was difficult to get home because of my football and social activities. I did go home and my friend, encouraged by her parents, suggested we get engaged. I did think about it but, no sooner had I arrived at Church Fenton, I went out with some lads and met a woman who was very willing and able to cater for a young airman's sexual needs. I had to do the honourable thing and tell my Liverpool girlfriend that I didn't want to get engaged and therefore it was best if we went our separate ways. That was a very difficult thing to do but I was still a very young man and my lifestyle was not conducive to settling down just yet. My social life by now was very full; almost every night we were out on manoeuvres. Friday and Saturday night would be either Leeds or York although I much preferred Leeds. Sunday night was NAAFI night and then Monday and Tuesday were spent either at Pontefract Wakefield or Knottingly. We used to be made very welcome at the workingmen's clubs in these areas, we never had to pay an entrance fee and the beer was always very cheap and usually some decent fellow would buy us poor servicemen a drink.

The main reasons, however, for visiting these places, on these nights, was because it was Ladies' Night. The men stayed at home, the ladies went out on their own looking for some respite from housework and domestic chores. Who better to oblige than a dozen or so airmen? It was a strange situation; we were made welcome but the local menfolk would not dream of going to a ladies night – that was sissy. Call us RAF types sissy but these were happy days and even the ugliest airman had a chance of copping off.

I met a woman at a Pontefract Ladies Night who became a weekly acquaintance. She was about ten years older than me but very attractive in that she had an exquisite body. At our first meeting we retired to the back of my car and cemented our relationship. I then went to her home and experienced a more comfortable sexual activity on her living room floor. This was a very pleasurable relationship; there was nothing involved other than sexual activity. She never asked to see me or wanted to know anything about me, which was nice.

One night I pulled up outside her house and she asked me to follow her. I had no idea where I was going or what I was expected to do, so I steeled myself for the worst. As we walked past this church she pushed me in to the church doorway and insisted we have sex there and then. It was quiet, there was no one about and I duly obliged. Another time I arrived at her home and there was another woman there. My friend asked me to have sex with her and her mate and I happily obliged.

Whilst I was involved with my Pontefract woman, I met a nurse from the nurses' home in Leeds. A visit to the nurses' home was a monthly activity. We would go to parties at the nurses' home and the nurses would be bussed to our NAAFI dances. This was a mutually satisfying activity the nurses generally just wanted a good laugh and a dance. There was no way in the world that I would have any sexual activity with this woman; like most of the nurses, they were from Southern Ireland and devout Catholics.

We used to have some good laughs at the nurses' home; they would put on a buffet and disco and we would do the same for them at our NAAFI dance. I was asked one time by a sergeant if I could arrange for some nurses to come to a Sergeants' mess function. I was given a minibus by MT and duly collected and returned the nurses. No disrespect to the SNCOs, but the nurses refused to return to a Sergeants' mess do again. Another interesting tale about the nurses my nurse friend used to come up to the NAAFI dance; we would just dance the night away and I would drive her home in my car. At the end of the night I would get a peck on the cheek or a handshake.

On one occasion the nurses were being bussed up and I had, along with a few others, been banned from the NAAFI for one night and it was the night of the monthly nurses visit. I had to wait outside the NAAFI and explain to my woman friend that I couldn't go in the NAAFI and the reason for this is as follows. One of our motley crew was posted so we had been out all day and returned to the NAAFI in high spirits. The NAAFI manageress, Miss Tuson, was a lovely woman and we always used to have some good-natured banter with her. On this occasion we all burst into the NAAFI on broomsticks looking for the wicked witch of the North, Miss Tuson. She thought it amusing, especially as she closed the bar. We soon apologised profusely and she reopened the bar. Nothing more was said about this incident until we were all summoned to our respective Flight Commanders. I had to appear in best blue before SATCO, a Squadron Leader Groboyski. He asked in his Polish accent why I call NAAFI manageress a wicked witch and ride round NAAFI on a broomstick. Unfortunately I was unable to convince the SATCO that it was just a joke. He banned me from the NAAFI for one night and a similar punishment was meted out to all involved. Apparently, a very observant off duty RAF Policeman witnessed the event and decided it should be reported. As it was, even before we were aware action was being taken, Miss Tuson received a sincere apology and flowers from her favourite customers. I used to like Miss Tuson a lot. I would sit with her in the NAAFI and have a cup of tea and tell her any problems I may have had. She was the archetypal NAAFI manageress; a caring matriarch and none of us would have seen her upset. Anyway, I never went into the NAAFI that night and neither did my mates. As I waited outside I could see the RAF Policeman lurking; he must have thought we were planning a sneak attack.

Many Polish officers served in the air traffic control branch so we had fairly frequent contact with and usually got on very well with, certainly Mr Groboyski was a real gentleman. Steve Davey tells a tale of the time a new Air Traffic Control Officer of Polish origin arrived at RAF Fairford. Angry because there was a fire truck encroaching 'his' airfield he demanded to know every movement of fire trucks and why they had to move. Ever obliging, the crash crew informed air traffic of every movement, inconsequential or significant. After about two hours of this the Polish Officer exploded and shouted through the squawk box "I don't want to know when you go for bloody piss" and that was the end of that practice.

My relationship with the nurse was a pleasant interlude from all my other social activities. We used to go to the pictures or go for walk and when I was with her I never drank. I did, however, meet another young woman in Knottingley. She was sexually active but in a different way to my friend in Pontefract. At this time I was seeing all three women in the same week so I had to be careful to get the names right and to behave in the appropriate manner for each woman; all the world really is a stage and each man in his time will play many parts! Well, I was playing many parts at Church Fenton. In between my sporting and social activities I got myself a part time job working at a local chicken farm. The corporal in charge of our crew – the one and only Paddy Collins – worked there and he got me a job. It was hard, dirty work but we were paid five shillings an hour and worked four-hour shifts.

In those days a pint of beer cost a shilling a pint so it's easy to work out the relative value of five shillings. Four hours work was sufficient to pay for a few pints and a packet of fags. We could, on one of our all day benders, knock back 'quite a few' pints and with no trace of a hangover the next day. Our job at the chicken farm entailed in the first instance bringing out all the dead chickens, digging a small hole and putting them in. The stench was quite awful. I'm sure current health and safety legislation would not allow such a shoddy practice. Then we would drag a wheelbarrow full of feed into the cauldron of the chicken shed and fill up the feeders. When I first started, I used to tread gingerly, trying not to harm the chickens but after a few shifts I followed Paddy Collins' example and hurtled through, pushing chickens out the way. After we fed the chickens, off to the Junction Pub we would go or maybe off to complete a shift on fire section duty. So good were we at our job that the owner of the chicken factory suggested that Paddy and I consider leaving the RAF and working full time for him. There was no chance of that – the thought of working full time in a chicken factory did not appeal to either of us. We used to get prisoners working on the farm they were supervised by prison staff – some were lifers. We used to give them cigarettes and I would tell them tales of what I got up to. This may have been an incentive to them to avoid offending behaviour and stop wasting their lives – I hope so. I enjoyed this work to an extent. I looked upon it as a good workout and the money kept my car on the road and went some way towards paying for my hectic social life.

Our fire section duties, which were more or less secondary to our social activities, consisted of either a morning or afternoon shift with one full twenty four-hour duty sometime in the week. It was certainly the best shift pattern I was ever to work. The station was a flying training school and chipmunks were the aircraft. The fire section had a beautiful Mk 5 fire truck; it really was a glean machine. We had a dry powder aircraft rescue truck (ACRT) and a DPI. Whilst at Fenton, I went off again to St Athan and RAF Catterick to complete the Mk6 course. The M6 was probably the finest airfield crash tender ever built. It was built on a Salamander tank chassis and had independent suspension in all six wheels. The driver sat in the centre of cab with two crewmen either side. Vehicle checks included unwinding the tension in the wheels and to do this the vehicle had to be driven over a rough course. If this did not happen the suspension would seize consequently the rough course was a must. However, it was not always possible and driving on and off the roadside kerb was sufficient to unwind the wheels. The rough course was quite an exhilarating experience and I have taken many non-firemen over various rough courses. Two funny Mk 6 stories included the tale of the MK 6 being driven over a manhole cover at the same time as a workman came out the hole. Apparently the workman was very angry, chased after the Mk 6, pulled open what he thought was the passenger side the door and dragged out what he thought was the driver, little realising that the driver was in fact sat in the centre of the cab.

RAF Church Fenton football team 1969.

Another tale I heard was of a young airman who made a complaint about a corporal using foul and abusive language. The corporal was reprimanded but the complainant was subsequently roped to the crash bar on the front of the MK 6 and driven over the rough course, a very scary activity in anyone's book. Night flying was a rarity. The fire section lads were all well known on the camp, not least through Tom Sawyer's reputation, but Paddy Collins was also a character of some distinction.

There was usually a fireman or two in the pig's bar in the NAAFI most nights and our spiritual home was the Junction pub in Church Fenton village. We usually began or finished our exploits at the Junction; the manager, a man named Fred, was a great friend to all the RAF lads. His wife Barbara was a lovely person. She did, however, try to improve the image and decor of the pub but once a few regulars drifted away she soon changed her ways. If we were ever short of cash, a sub from Fred was commonplace. "Don't tell the missus," he would say and he would always buy us a pint. I remember having difficulty paying back some money I borrowed. He wouldn't take if off me and that was the same for most of us. I learnt some years later that Fred passed away. I was very sad when I heard that news but he left this mortal coil safe in the knowledge that he was a kind man, much loved and respected by many airmen. We had some wild nights in his pub and the stay behind on a Friday and Saturday was the rule rather than the exception.

Airmen's civilian attire, 1960s style.
Left to right: the Author, Eddie Kopka, Phil Sinnot, Larry Lamb.

During the three years I spent socialising in the Junction there was never any trouble. We would get quite raucous and there were regular sing-a-longs but no aggravation of any sort. I enjoyed a very pleasant experience at the Junction. I had for some time been trying to woo the deputy NAAFI manageress but she was having none of it. However, I persisted and she agreed to a date. This woman was attractive in a peculiarly sensual way. She was small and petite with a lovely soft complexion. She wore little make-up and she had a very full bosom. All the Pigs bar regulars were always trying to impress but she had probably heard it all before and was content to lead us all on and drool we would. I would disappear for a few nights and when I returned she would ask me where I had been and what I had been up to. I told her the truth and she must have been impressed with my honesty and realised that I was not like the rest of the Pigs Bar regulars – I was going out and actively seeking enjoyment rather than drooling at her all night.

"Some women like a tough to treat 'em rough, but you're my cup of tea," I quoted to her and that must have impressed her because she agreed to go out with me. She was thirty-five and I was twenty-two and I could sense this was going to be nothing other than a mutually satisfying one-night stand and I had a plan. I asked Fred if he could provide a room at the Junction. He was, as usual, ever obliging but he was concerned that Barbara may object. He suggested I tell Barbara that I was bringing my fiancée from Liverpool to meet my friends and Barbara would be all right. Rather than lie to Barbara I left it to Fred to explain. I said nothing to my mates of my plan. I had visions of all the camp turning up at the Junction just to see my friend and who knows what would have happened as I trooped upstairs with the NAAFI sweetheart.

We went for a meal and turned up at the Junction near the end of the evening for last orders and then went up to our room. This was a fulsome, warm-hearted woman who had not experienced a sexual encounter for some time. She was a divorcee and had experienced some form of domestic violence, which was, I suspect, the reason why she avoided involvement with the many airmen who would have gladly crawled three miles over broken glass just to receive a peck on the cheek from her. But she was fantastic in bed... She certainly wasn't rough like some I had known and she was game for a long night of passion. I remember Fred bringing breakfast up to our room the following morning. He had a coy grin on his face and I, in turn, had a huge grin on mine.

Some time later, Fred and I were talking about sexual experiences. He said in passing that he remembered, in his distant past, making love for an hour. Not being in anyway boastful I said, "I made love nearly all night in your pub" and that was another tale for Fred to tell his customers about me when it came time for me to move on.

The Junction pub holds a very special place in my heart. In my current occupation I often travel across the country. Sometimes, when I am feeling in a reflective mood I will make a detour and sit in my car outside the Junction. I visualise the young airmen coming and going, the many happy hours spent in the bar, the people I drank with and the jukebox with its fantastic selection of records. I think of those two kind people, Barbara and Fred, and of course my night of passion. Memory is the one gift of god that old age cannot take away.

Another well-liked character we would take with us on some of our escapades was a 'knight of the road' – a tramp who travelled round Yorkshire living a nomadic lifestyle and was well known in the local area. He was a proper tramp who lived in hedgerows or barns with permission and certainly not as we know them today. He was a giant of a man, very well spoken and a wonderful raconteur. We would take him out for a few pints and he would never over-stay his welcome, never got drunk and always returned to his hedgerow or barn. We all liked him and even Fred and Barbara would make him welcome. During the winter months he would hibernate somewhere in York but we always knew summer was on its way when our friend arrived in the village on his old bike. We learned one night that he had been killed in a hit and run accident, which upset us enormously. He had quite a lengthy and laudatory obituary in the Yorkshire Evening Post and it transpired that he had a distinguished military record, something he never mentioned to any of us; modesty is a wonderful virtue. We did, however, posthumously dine him out from the Junction and there were a few beers drunk that night in his honour.

The fire section routine was very pleasant, certainly compared to what was to come in later years. We would spend most of our time on standby, usually cleaning the vehicles and the section. There were few tasks to complete; there was no barrier or rhag to worry about and very little night flying. The chipmunk was a relatively simple aircraft and I seem to remember it carried eighteen gallons of fuel, two less than the Mk 5 and there was no leg locks armaments or ejection seat. We used to man-up only when one of the student pilots went solo, I used to be glad I was only watching as the chipmunk invariably bounced on and off the runway. We occasionally practised a lift out drill; that entailed the fire crew responding to an emergency called by air traffic and we were tasked to lift out the pilot. It was always an instructor selected for this task and some would try to make it as difficult as possible but as soon as we withdrew our quick release knife the pilot became most co-operative. One fire section task we did have to undertake during the summer months was to spend a week at RAF Rufforth, a relief landing ground for Church Fenton.

RAF Church Fenton's all-conquering five-a-side football team.

Four firemen would drive over in the morning and we basically sat in a caravan all day with the ambulance driver and medic. Generally we played cards or mulled over the problems of the world and discussed our previous night's activity and planned for the next. We'd drive through the outskirts of York and when York races were on there was always slow moving traffic. Paddy Collins would always rearrange the windscreen washers on the aircraft rescue land rover. The washer would point out away from the vehicle windscreen and as we were crawling along in traffic he would switch the washer on and water would appear as if from nowhere and soak some poor unsuspecting pedestrian. If they looked in our direction we would look totally innocent and afterwards laugh at their reaction as the person (usually an attractive woman) looked up into the blue sky wondering how they got wet, childish but innocent fun. We also had to drive past Thorp Arch women's prison and, at that time, their most well known inmate was Christine Keiller, so that used to give us something to talk and think about.

The only incident of note during my tour at Fenton (apart from the time Phil put his foot through the wing of a Chipmunk when we were practising a lift out) occurred when the crash one crew were instructed to respond to a mayday call from an over flying American F111 that crashed about five miles from our base. I was the driver of crash one and the SNCO fire section, another wonderful individual Sergeant Ian Priestly (later I understand Squadron Leader), travelled out with us. Apart from a bit of map reading we had little to do, we found the wreckage and crater caused by the aircraft engine burrowing its way into the earth. The American pilot ejected safely but I often wondered if that had been a British pilot would he have ejected and abandoned his aircraft over a densely populated area. No sooner had we arrived – and we were first of the emergency services to arrive – when members of the press arrived and started asking questions. Fortunately we had been instructed by air traffic to inform the press that this incident was subject to a 'D' notice I had no idea what that meant but Ian Priestly did.

During my tour at Church Fenton I was informed that the station Warrant Officer wanted to see me in his office and I was to wear my best blue uniform. I had no idea why but Sergeant Priestly informed me that I was not in any trouble and off I duly went. He gave me quick once over and informed me I was being dispatched as the stations representative to The Royal Tournament at Earls Court. Despite the fact that my best blue had hardly been worn I was fitted out for a new blue, new cap, new shoes, etc and off I went for three weeks to Earls Court.

On arrival I paraded with all the other non-competitors and was given a box to look after; I was now Usher Edwards. My box was just behind the Royal Box and I got to see all the VIPs who used that box. Another service man shared the box with me, and what a man he was. He had been in the Royal Navy for about twenty years, went to sea once, didn't like it and he had all sorts of London based postings. He had in fact been in one of the field gun teams. He was a nice enough guy but he was involved in all sorts of strange goings on. Anyone who has ever completed a tour at Earls Court will know of the bizarre sexual activities that go on and my RN partner was in the middle of it all. Well-known television personalities and other celebrities were literally like flies round shit as they tried to obtain the services of the many servicemen who participated in the Tournament. After the evening performance, those servicemen who were so inclined would sit on the wall opposite Earls Court and Rolls Royces; Bentleys, Jaguars, etc would pull up and off would go a serviceman to supplement his income. I'd previously never known a homosexual, let alone their practices, but there were predatory homosexuals all around.

Much as my RN colleague tried to convince me that this was an opportunity to earn big money, I refused to succumb to any such behaviour, but that didn't stop me getting pestered. Our job, basically, was to collect tickets, usher visitors to their seats and, if need be, point them in the direction of the toilets. In 1969 there was almost no concern for security. People often presented at our box without a ticket and my RN mate would let them in free. I thought this very wrong but I soon found out that the people coming in free were very senior members of the RN. These gentlemen would attend only to watch the Field Gun competition and then they would disappear. On some afternoon performances there was a more senior officer in our box than the one occupying the Royal Box, but more often than not our box was also occupied by some very well-known public figures who were acquaintances of my RN colleague. I would never condemn another person's sexual behaviour or preferences but I used to have to escort some very strange men to their seats in our box. Almost all wanted me to escort them to the toilet, but that I declined. There were, however, many willing to earn extra income, none more so than my colleague.

Every day he would have a tale to tell of how he earned his money. Sometimes he would tell me that he had to urinate on people or beat people and one client made him stand over a sheet of glass and defecate on the glass while he laid underneath – and these are only a few of his tales. He used to say "I can get you a client willing to pay you a £100 a night or wine and dine you in the best places in town", but I refused.

I would go across to the Tournament pub, but the beer was crap and overly expensive and the place was full of wealthy men looking for servicemen, so in the end I would get the tube into Soho and enjoy the sights there. I was very happy to return to Church Fenton and pick up where I had left off. I remember returning to the Junction and relating my Royal Tournament experiences to Fred and the locals, which generated a few laughs and a few free beers.

I was still in touch with my woman friend in Pontefract and my nurse but I was becoming involved in quite a close relationship with my woman friend in Knottingley and she was trying to turn our relationship into something serious, so that was a bit of a problem. In addition my mate Phil had applied for an exchange posting to Church Fenton which was duly granted. Consequently I was bound to spend more time settling Phil into his new posting and introducing him to our merry-go-round. I had another very good mate, Clem Gettings, who was an admin clerk and from Wexford. He left Ireland and joined the civil service but after a few years he was bored and joined the RAF. Now Clem was a Pioneer; he had taken the pledge as a youth and alcohol never passed his lips. You may think, "What a boring fart," but not so. When most of our gang went out and got pissed, Clem remained compos mentis and was able to carry off the best of the women who we encountered on our escapades. We were at the nurses' home in Leeds one night. It was Phil and Clem's first visit to this venue and, half way through the night, one of the senior nurses came to me complaining about Clem and Phil, stating they were drunk and causing a nuisance. I went over with the nurse and there was Clem dancing on a table. I explained to the nurse that Clem was a teetotaller and was simply enjoying himself; she was quite happy with that especially when she realised he was also from Ireland but when I went to find Phil I could not excuse his behaviour. Phil had apparently fallen into the buffet and, as I approached him, I noticed bits of food all over the parts of his body that had fallen into the buffet. Life now at Fenton was fairly hectic for me and I was beginning to question where this was all going to lead me. In all the time I had been at Fenton I never had a quiet night in other than when I did my twenty-four hour fire duty. Six nights a week I was out and my Austin A35 knew its own way to the fleshpots that my cohorts and I frequented. I was not getting home as often as I would have liked and my parents were totally unaware of the life I was leading.

When I did come home on leave or for a weekend, I would bring some mates with me and in to Liverpool town centre we would go. My mates were a motley crew of the stations finest characters, but, such is life, some were falling by the wayside, talking of promotion and settling down. I had no such thoughts, at least that was until I had an unpleasant experience one night in Knottingley. I was in the company of another RAF fireman and we were chatting up two women. They found us very amusing and we were making plans to move on to another venue when in walked a group of local men. The next thing I remember was waking up in hospital with a very severe headache. Apparently amongst the group were the partners of the two women. I still have the scar under my left eye where I was kicked and for a few weeks after the event I had a face full of cuts and bruises. If I needed a wake up call this was it and, as if by divine intervention, I was once more placed on preliminary warning role for overseas. Word had it that the RAF base in Singapore was closing down and airmen were being posted out there for twelve months. I thought perhaps that was where I was going but that wasn't the case. As it transpired, I went off again to the Middle East but this time to RAF Sharjah.

I had quite a few parties to attend before I finally set off for another twelve months in the desert. My very last night at Fenton was spent in the Junction Pub with Fred and Barbara; I was after a quiet night before setting off the next day for Brize Norton. I had sold my car; in fact that went to a civilian MT driver who also had a small pig farm in Fenton village. I knew him quite well and he told me that he intended to convert my old A35 by cutting off the car roof and then using the car to transport his pigs to and from market. Quite poignant really as that is much like I had been doing during my tour at Fenton. However, that last night at the Junction was a fairly sad affair. I really liked Fred and Barbara – they brought some semblance of normality into my hectic lifestyle. As the night drew to a close, I bade my farewells to a weeping Barbara and a few others and was about to make my way back to camp when up popped the merry widow of Fenton village to offer me a lift. 'The merry widow', as she was known by all and sundry, was a very familiar figure in the local area. I knew her to speak to but she was not my type of woman.

I had no desires towards her, although many did. However she knew of my reputation and I of hers. She was aware that I was off overseas the next morning and asked if I wanted to come back to her home. I would, in normal circumstances, have said no, but what the hell... There followed an unusual and bizarre sexual encounter. I don't think we said anything; it was almost a perfunctory act, she doing the decent thing for this departing airman. It is with some pathos that I reflect on the whole range of female relationships I experienced at Fenton. It is fair to say that I had spent time with some very attractive women yet my last encounter was with the merry widow of Fenton. Glory days... they just pass you by.

And so off I went on my next journey into the unknown...

The Mk5 – a quality British built fire truck.

The MK 6 RAF fire truck on the move.

RAF Sharjah Fire section.

4. RAF Sharjah

Just below the borderline Sharjah is the spot
Where we were are doomed to spend our time in the land God forgot
With prickly heat and scorpions and black faced natives too
Bang in the middle of nowhere four thousand miles from you
We airmen of the Air Force earn our measly pay
Guarding Sheikhs with millions for a few rupees a day
Living with our millions and waiting to see our girls
Hoping that whilst we're away they haven't wed our pals
These sweltering months at Sharjah are months we wished away

ANON

This rather dated ditty aptly sums up my time at Sharjah. It's hard to imagine that this dump of an RAF base was only a few miles from Dubai, now one of the most exclusive holiday destinations in the world. But it certainly was not a holiday destination in 1971. Reference is made in many RAF publications to Sharjah being best described as a "slum" and for those stationed there in the fifties and sixties, it may have been. During my time there, 1970-71, I wouldn't say it was a slum, but one very quickly became aware of the differences between abject poverty and grotesque opulence. There was no sanitation for the local people and it was not uncommon to see Arab men and women squatting and carrying out their bodily functions before your very eyes. It wasn't uncommon either to see flies land on the results of those bodily functions and then make a bee-line for your lips, nose or eyes... On the other hand, there were Sheiks' palaces with all their grandeur.

The road system was primitive and on the odd occasion we were called to an incident off base, cars would follow us passing both sides of the fire trucks. The only positive comments I can make about my tour at Sharjah are that it was glorious weather and I was able to clock up quite a few miles Bondu bashing. The station personnel and the fire section lads were great lads but this was very much the business end of the RAF and Sharjah had none of that relaxed holiday atmosphere associated with Masirah.

~ 81 ~

In 1971 Sharjah was a relatively large base; the station commander was a Group Captain, accompanied by his lady wife. We had
a Warrant Officer in charge of the fire section (Dan Dare) and two
fire crews, each consisting of ten men. Quite a bit of flying took
place, including night flying. The fire section crews covered incidents both on and off base. Consequently we provided a twenty four
hour emergency service and we also had a Zodiac inshore rescue
craft. The fire section routine consisted of a three-shift system: an
afternoon shift followed by a morning shift – 07.00 till 13.00 – off
that afternoon then back for the night shift followed by a day off. It
was not too difficult a shift system but the night shifts could be
tiring, especially if we were interrupted during our sleeping duty. I
remember we used to get called out to brustey fires; these were no
more than fires in local Arabs' homes. It was a fairly simple, straightforward incident. There were no electrical appliances to worry about
and a burst from the first aid hose reel would normally suffice.
However, each brustey had its own well attached. Consequently a
slow approach to the fire was important and an even more cautious
approach once we dismounted from our tender. We had four local
Arabs working on the section as cleaners. They only worked days
I'm pleased to say. I well remember one of the Arab cleaners assault-
ing young Taffy Edwards. We were carrying out our vehicle checks
one morning when this almighty scream came from the crew room.
We all dived in thinking that Taff had scalded himself or something
similar but, to our disgust, one of the cleaners had jumped on Taff's
back like a dog trying to mate a bitch. We had a hard job removing
the Arab from Taff's back but that incident terrified Taff and he was
never alone again and refused to leave the camp. Poor Taff – he was
a blonde haired, blue eyed individual and we soon learnt that some
Arab men had a predilection for such types. Shortly after my arrival,
it became common knowledge that the camp had been earmarked for
closure under the defence cuts of that year. Situations like that only
serve to demoralise the troops and one tends to think, "What's the
point, we're not wanted so we might as well go home". As it was, I
served a full thirteen-month tour with a month leave at home in the
middle of my tour. As usual, there were the normal purveyors of
doom and gloom amongst the ranks but I tended to avoid those and
try and make the best of any situation – ever the eternal optimist.
Before long I was playing football for the fire section team, the wing

team and the station team. Sometimes I would play twice a day and given the good nature and comradeship of RAF firemen, I could always get someone to cover my duty. There was a large floodlit sports stadium on camp and evening games were always well attended.

RAF Sharjah fire section volley ball team.

RAF Sharjah fire section football team.

The stadium was used for intersection finals and all station games. While I was at Sharjah we had detachments of Scots Guards and Greenjackets. Consequently games against the Army were quite high profile and very competitive. I had played against Army teams when I was at Fenton in the Yorkshire services league. I always found Army teams very formal, "Your ball, sir", "Over to you, Corporal" and all that but not so in RAF sport. When it came time to play one of the Army regiments there was always a lot of pre game hype and I remember the Army lads would do nothing else but train and practice whilst we went about our normal duties. The Army team would arrive as a team fully kitted out in matching kit whilst we would arrive straight from work in our own shorts and socks and handed our shirt on arrival. RAF spectators would drift up to the ground with a crate of Amstel under their arm whilst the Army spectators would march up to musical accompaniment. The only musical accompaniment we had was the chorus of boos and catcalls directed at the squaddies. Despite the fact that we never trained together or practised any set pieces, we usually won and that is some testament to the individual skill and talent of the RAF lads. There was a Corporal fireman, Spud Murphy; well, he was a character and a half. Everyone on base, including the entire civilian workforce, knew Spud, even the station commander and his lady wife. Spud when sober was a decent fellow but when inebriated he was totally different. Unfortunately he was inebriated most of his tour.

Well, Spud took a liking to me and never missed any of the football games I played in. When I played at the stadium he would be there waiting in the VIP seats, complete with his crate of Amstel. Once the game started any opposition player who came within a few yards of me and Spud would be on the pitch threatening harm, and god forbid if I was tackled badly. There was no mercy shown to the perpetrator. My mates used to say, "Old Spud thinks he's your dad" and I would say, "My dad would behave entirely the opposite. He would tell me off for getting caught in a tackle". Spud did become a serious embarrassment and I remember asking him one morning what he thought of the previous night's match to which he replied, "What match?" Spud was taken off shift duties at Sharjah because he was coming on night duty smelling of alcohol. Consequently he was a given a day job but was coming to work in the morning smelling of alcohol. He was subsequently taken off all duties and left to fester in the Pigs Bar with several other old sweats who shared Spud's alcohol problem. I remember once our rooms were being painted and we were instructed to allow access for the Pakistani workers to our rooms. Come the day, we all tried to rouse Spud but he was out for the count. The Pakistani workers threw a sheet over him and carried out the work around him. Several hours later, the job done, Spud woke and disappeared trying to find his room. Now that the room was redecorated, he obviously thought he was in the wrong room. A final Spud story, we knew he never wrote home but he received letters from home. We were informed that Spud's wife wrote to the station commander seeking information about her husband. The CO's wife apparently kept in correspondence with Mrs Murphy and, being a good CO's wife, I'm sure she accentuated the positive about Spud but there was not much the good lady could say other than Spud is still alive.

In addition to football, volleyball was a major feature of this tour. We would play for hours on the section and the off duty lads would come in just to play volleyball. It goes without saying that the fire section volleyball team was all conquering, as was our five a side football team. We used to do well in the drinking competitions as well. In addition to the NAAFI, there was a Malcolm club, which was a pleasant place to drink – a bit like a lounge bar as opposed to the Pigs Bar at the NAAFI. We had to behave with a modicum of decorum as there were two Malcolm club women working there. RAF lads would be drinking with Army lads and then, come last orders, the Army Duty Corporal would come in and say, "Scots Guards, time to leave". Up stood the Guards and retired gracefully. Occasionally a brave RAF corporal entered suggesting it was time for the RAF lads to retire. Cans, bottles and abuse would hurl his way and then one of the Mally women would say, "Time to go boys" and not a word was said other than "Good night miss" and off we would go. When I first arrived at Sharjah I was told to make sure I was by my room window at 9am. That was the time Raquel (after Raquel Welch, heart-throb of that generation), one of the Mally women, went by on her way to open the stim (soft drinks) bar as we called it. On my day off I duly came to the window at 9am and waited excitedly for Raquel to pass by. I was not impressed. She must have been in her late fifties but she did become increasingly attractive as the months went by.

Unlike Masirah we did get to see women especially at one of the beaches we frequented. Transport was available every afternoon or we would use one of our own fire vehicles to travel to Carne Creek beach. It was all lads off camp but every now and again an American woman would parade up and down the beach stepping over our bodies or rubbing lotion all over her body. Believe you me it was torture! I made friends with one of the civilian Air Works air traffic controllers, a fellow Liverpudlian, and his very attractive and pleasant wife accompanied him.

Sometimes they would pick me up from our accommodation and take me to the beach or to their home. His wife was a lovely woman but I really believe she never realised the impact she had upon the lads. When it became known that I was being picked up, all my mates and many more who I didn't know would come over to our accommodation, not to speak to me but to catch a glimpse of this lovely woman. Complete strangers would come up and rather rudely ask if I was having sexual relations with this woman. I certainly was not; that's not to say she wasn't a very attractive woman.

Despite the air of gloom prevailing on the station, we still used to have some wild nights in the NAAFI or the Mally. Being a big station, individual sections would form their own groups and we would take it in turns to out sing each other with ribald songs. In addition beer cans would be flying between the warring sections. I remember one wild night in the NAAFI the film Jungle Book had been on the cinema that evening. Later in the evening there must have been a hundred or so of us who marched to the tune of the elephants' dawn patrol. Nothing got in the way and any immovable objects were climbed over. Those not marching were hurling cans whilst we were, in turn, returning fire. Surprising really those well-trained mature men could behave in such a manner but we did. We had wonderful nicknames for some of the firemen; there was Midland Red, he was from the Midlands and thought he was a bus driver. There was the Cringe, Catweazle, and the Mekong Delta (this was a man who had a rather large amount of veins protruding on his forehead). There was Budgie, the great Davie Trayner who never stopped talking and the usual Taff, Paddy and Geordie.

We also had our own sick note, a Liverpudlian by the name of Phil Southern. Most mornings one would meet Phil as he was on his way to the medical centre to report another illness. "Morning Phil.

How are you?" "Not so good," he would reply. Well, thirty years passed and I was on parade at a Liverpool Remembrance Day parade and whom should I meet but Phil Southern. "Great to see you again, Phil after all these years. How are you?" I enquired. "Actually I'm not so good", he replied! We had a wonderful Sergeant in charge of our fire crew, a Paddy Fleming. He was a cheerful man and tried very hard to play volleyball to the standard of some of the section star players but he was no match. We used to play little tricks on sarge and wind him up. Come the volleyball game, we'd decide to duck a few balls and blame sarge. "Your ball, Sarge", we would shout for impossible retrieves and he would go for it. Having missed hopelessly, we would say, "Come on Sarge, you're not trying." He would rise to the bait and then we would all say "We don't want you in our team anymore". He'd sulk and we would say, "Sarge, you really have to try harder next time!" but he was a great crew chief and a lovely man. One time we were playing volleyball and sarge went for a ball but he misjudged it badly and it broke one of his fingers. As he was jumping around in pain we were all offering to help and as we each had a hold of the break he screamed in pain while we all called him a big baby. Sad to say but he is another I heard died a few years ago.

We also had a very good five-a-side and eleven-a-side football team on the section and competition for places was quite strong. OC Regiment was a member of the team and I seem to remember we were inter section champions in both sports. We used to have a Jock firemen named Dougie Fleming who played with the flare and fire of a Scotsman. He was very competitive and if he could curtail his fiery temper he would have made the station team. I remember we used to play football against the Arab taxi drivers' team. They played football barefoot and Dougie was not averse to standing on toes and squaring up if he felt aggrieved. Dougie was involved in a very unsavoury incident with a taxi driver. Dougie was returning from a rare night in Dubai and apparently he became embroiled in an argument with a taxi driver. It was alleged that he hit the taxi driver and allegations were made against him. Very quickly rumours spread that Dougie had caused serious injuries to the driver and we were aware that such an incident has massive implications. Some sort of compromise was reached and no charges were made but we were all very concerned, as was Dougie. As it was Dougie returned home safely and later became an instructor at the fire school at Catterick. Tragically Dougie was killed in a car accident on the A1, another dedicated RAF fireman I was pleased to have known and called a mate.

One of my most high profile games of football was played at Dubai in the town stadium against the Dubai town team. This was an emerging football nation and the team was semi professional and even then there was a lot of money being poured into the local and national team. As far as the local population were concerned this was an international match. We travelled to the stadium in our kit, disembarked off the coach and went straight on to the pitch and into action. There was a full house but no Brits in the crowd. I remember a lot of noise and seeing some fearsome looking spectators, some wearing their ceremonial daggers or carrying bandoleers and firing skywards. We were beaten fair and square but we were certainly made to feel unwelcome both by the crowd and the opposition.

Another particularly unsavoury incident comes to mind. We would on occasions drive down or walk to Carne Creek in the morning, shift pattern permitting. One morning Dave Traynor, Roy Bennett and I walked down to Carne Creek and there were just the three of us on the beach – not another soul in sight. We would go out for a swim and one of us would remain on the beach to look after our personal possessions. Roy and Dave were out swimming and I was laid out sunbathing watching our kit. As usual a little nap was in order and I was awoken by the presence of three Arabs who were sat next to me. I thought straight away this is very strange Arabs don't sunbathe but if these three wanted to do so they had miles of unoccupied beach to choose from rather than right next to me. The eldest Arab asked if I was from RAF Sharjah and made reference to my friends swimming so far out. I had heard of servicemen in the Middle East being high jacked and there is a well-known Arab torture known to all servicemen – apparently Arab women were very skilled at cutting your balls off. A million and one things flashed through my mind, not least self-preservation. There was no way Roy and Dave could get back in time to assist in my salvation and, as it was, they were not aware of the Arabs' presence till they came ashore. Anyway, the eldest Arab spoke excellent English and started asking me what military aircraft were at Sharjah and general military questions I laughed very politely and kept saying I know nothing about them things I am only a simple fireman. He was becoming increasingly more assertive and forceful in his questioning and then went on to explain that the youngest of the three was a soldier from Aden. He asked if I had heard of FLOSY (the front for the liberation of South Yemen). Of course I had, but I said no. He kept saying I looked a very fit man and suggested that I was Special Forces. I laughed again but I was panicking a bit by now. He asks me why Great Britain remained in the Middle East and went on about Israel. I just kept saying I am a fireman trained to save life. I think in the end he probably thought I was stupid but I lived to tell the tale.

When Roy and Dave came ashore the three men got up and walked away. "Who were they?" asked Roy and when I got my breath back I told him what happened. On returning to camp, I contacted the RAF Police and they took me to meet a security person. I related my experience and photographs were produced and there they were, the three Arabs. They were known insurgents and the younger one was in fact a known terrorist. I had a few beers that night to calm my nerves. Steve Davey, that well-known RAF Fireman raconteur, tells a wonderful tale of FLOSY. That goes as follows. Based at Aden (circa 1967) there was a RAF Regiment (Rock Apes) squadron providing a specialist reaction force to the increasing threat from FLOSY terrorists. From time to time the "rocks" would search the areas of the camp including the large number of Aden Arabs and Ethiopian civilians employed on camp. The fire section and air traffic compound was surrounded by a chain link fence, barbed wire with a guarded gate entry. One day the Regiment descended on the compound in force and made all the civilians stand against the fence with arms up and legs spread. Fire vehicles used to be equipped with a battery powered loud hailer. Taking in this scene one fireman grabbed the loud hailer and, hiding in the crash bays, made a broadcast. "As you can see by the bodies on the fence we run a tough camp here". The Regiment Squadron Leader was not impressed. Incidentally, talking of Special Forces, occasionally a light aircraft would land at Sharjah. It was thought that aircraft was carrying Special Forces and they were undertaking some clandestine operation out in the desert. Individuals would deplane and then disappear into the bondu. Then, out of the blue, that same individual would appear in the NAAFI bar and they would be left alone at the bar. They had clearly been off base for several weeks and were generally in a very unkempt condition. They never made any effort to speak to us and we would leave them alone. That is all except a fireman Corporal named Johnny Holden. Johnny stood all of five foot five and weighed about nine stone and he wasn't far off forty years of age. For reasons best known to Johnny he went over and harassed this character and, before we could intervene, Johnny was throwing punches. However, the recipient of Johnny's blows simply put one hand on Johnny's head and with his other hand he carried on drinking his pint – it was very comical. None of John's blows made contact but he must have thrown hundreds. I'm pleased to say it was taken in good spirits and before long we were all chanting, "Johnny, Johnny!" The man with no name smiled and walked away. That night, John made his way back to his room and apparently he lost his key. He attempted to enter his room via the small window above the door. Someone must have given him a bunk up because the window was about six-foot off the ground! When we returned to our room we could see John's legs dangling from the window whilst the rest of his body must have been dangling inside his room. When we arrived, however, he was asleep and we left him like that. I remember going the toilets in the early hours and he was still dangling – he must have been stiff the next morning.

I had another scary incident at Carne Creek. Most of the firemen were quite good swimmers and we would stay in the water for a long time. Phil Sinnot for instance would swim for hours. I would swim across the Creek, a distance of about a kilometre. I was doing just that one-day when I spotted a dhow coming towards me. At first I thought nothing of it and kept on my course but I noticed that the dhow was changing direction and suddenly came towards me. The crew must have seen me and were clearly intent on causing me harm. I trod water and waited as the Dhow came straight at me and, with only a few seconds to spare, I dived as deep as I could and could feel the water turbulence as the Dhow passed over me.

Just over half way through this tour I returned home on leave for a month. This was the time of a national postal strike; hence my parents were not quite sure when I would be home. That turned out be no bad thing as it took me three days to travel from Brize Norton to Liverpool. I travelled by train from Swindon and made it to the buffet car and, as expected, downed a few cans of beer. I noticed this extremely attractive woman. She was, in fact, a model and I had no hesitation going over to her and explaining where I had been for the last six months and all the privations and deprivations I had been through. She never spoke and looked the other way but I thought there was a chance she may take pity on me when she asked if I wanted a beer – I knew that I had cracked it. That was it, I spent the night in a Manchester hotel with her and we were both mutually satisfied. In the morning I went to Piccadilly station expecting to catch a train home but I noticed the York train was about to depart and I took that train instead. I made my way to the Junction Pub and spent a most enjoyable night there with many of my old mates, both service and civilian. I travelled home the next day and, as I wasn't asked when I landed in England, I had no need of any excuses for my delay. It was difficult sometimes coming home. I always remember the song from 'Paint Your Wagon' sung so elegantly by Lee Marvin, "I was born under a wandering star". Well that was me, then but things change. At home my two brothers were courting and my mates at home were doing the same. It was only natural therefore that I would contact my RAF mates and that I did. I used to meet Phil Sinnot in Liverpool and he would stay at ours and me at his home.

I had another good mate named Chuck McKinley. He was a fairy by trade (air traffic control) but he had all the personal qualities of a RAF fireman – he could certainly go ten pints without a pee. Chuck, Phil and I went into Liverpool for a night out and ended up at Liverpool's most famous dance hall, the Grafton Rooms. Well we had been drinking heavily and we tried to cop off with a group of three women but to no avail. They thought we were mad and would have nothing to do with us. I thought no more of that incident till six months later when my Sharjah tour was completed and I found myself back at The Grafton Rooms. I was on disembarkation leave and had agreed to meet Phil but he missed his train and never turned up. I went in to the Grafton Rooms alone and whom should I meet but the same three women I had met six months previous. I recognised the woman I had been trying to impress and went over and asked her for a dance. She refused at first and danced with her mates but I tried to apologise for my previous behaviour and she accepted my offer of a dance. She remembered my two mates and me and I suppose, if I had been in the company of my mates, she may not have danced with me. I probably would have consumed a few pints of beer as well but as it was I was sober. We danced, she much better than me, and I told her the tale of where I had just been. I asked to see her again and by the end of the night she agreed. I met her a week later and we drove out to Southport in my newly purchased Vauxhall Viva. This woman two years later became my wife and my whole world changed (for the better) from that first date.

5. Love and Marriage ~ Lindholme & Brize Norton

My tour in Sharjah completed, I was posted to RAF Lindholme, which is a few miles outside Doncaster. This was a different world for me now; I was madly in love and my only interest in life was getting home as often as I could. Unfortunately the shift pattern at Lindholme was a complicated business. We would go on duty at 7 am and could remain on duty till midnight – it all depended on flying. I was one of only a few of the Mk 6 drivers on the section. Consequently there always had to be a Mk 6 driver on duty. Although there was no flying at weekends we had to provide domestic fire cover. On reflection, there was never any mention of the average working week. We could be on duty all weekend and then put in about ten hours each weekday. Days off were rare and that was the same for weekends off. We knew we were undermanned but lo and behold Lindholme was closing down so additional manpower was highly unlikely. I had an additional problem at Lindholme. I was asked to play for the station football team and once the SNCO i/c the fire section (Flight Sergeant Gerry Nicholls) found that out, he was very keen I did. "Good for the reputation of the fire section", he would say. To ensure I was able to get the Wednesday afternoon off, I had to arrange cover for my duties. Consequently I had to return the favour. I had a great mate at Lindholme, a fireman by the name of Bob Lowe who later became a Warrant Officer. He was, at that time, single and would always cover duties for me.

Lindholme was not my favourite posting although, with all my postings, I made no enemies and made the most of the situation, at the same time picking up valuable experience. RAF Lindholme station football team was by far the best football team I ever played in. Located at Lindholme was Northern Radar, full of fairies (air traffic controllers). Consequently the station football team was made up mainly of fairies plus a cook, a shiny (admin. clerk called shiny because the seat of their trousers were always shiny), a blanket stacker (store man) and myself. We played in the Lincolnshire Services league and I still have the medal I received for being part of the team that won that League in 1972. We played the old fashioned five forwards, three in midfield and two fullbacks. I played right half and at left half was the very talented Eddie Brennan. Up front was a Geordie lad who had played professional football for Sheffield Wednesday and there was a Liverpool lad who played alongside Geordie. Both these lads reminded me of the Newcastle United centre forward Malcolm McDonald – big, burly and fearless.

RAF Lindholme fire section night out.

RAF Lindholme station football team 1972.

I had always been quite a good crosser of the ball and I knew if I could land a ball near their heads or feet they would always connect and at least hit the target. When we played inter section games it was my job to mark these two but my mate Mick Green ably assisted me. Mick was the finest tackler I have ever known. He was only about five foot five but his strength and timing in the tackle was something to behold. Mick was an interesting guy; one of a family of eleven children, he was the only male. He was from Preston and, like me at that time; he was courting and trying to get home as often as he could. It was difficult for Mick and I to have weekends off at the same time but we did on occasions meet up in Liverpool, him with his girlfriend and me with mine. One weekend Mick and I were both on duty and I had been having serious problems with my car, a Vauxhall Viva. I had a relative who worked in a Vauxhall garage and he obtained a reconditioned engine for me. Mick volunteered to assist me lift out the old engine and fit the new and, with the aid of a rope, it was quite a successful operation. However the time came to start up and, whoosh, the engine burst into flames. For one split second Mick and I ran away intent on finding a phone to summon the duty fire crew till we realised we were the duty fire crew. We put the fire out using a BCF extinguisher, rectified the fault and I drove a few thousand miles before finally disposing of what was the worst car I ever had. Another occasion I was returning to camp late one Sunday night I had three other RAF lads in the car with me and just outside Liverpool on the East Lancashire road the accelerator cable snapped. I struggled to repair the problem as best I could. I reconnected the cable but I put it on back to front. In other words, when I accelerated I had to take my foot off the accelerator and when I needed to decelerate I had to press down on the accelerator.

Talk all the time at Lindholme was of the impending closure of the camp. I was in a way looking forward to it but it was a worrying time for the married lads. It meant more upheaval, another change of married quarter and school change for their children. The closure duly arrived; all but one of the firemen was posted, complete with fire trucks, to RAF Lossiemouth. I remained at Lindholme on my own and was given the task of categorizing all the fire extinguishers on camp. I had to either scrap them if they were beyond reasonable repair or service the useable ones.

It was a relatively straightforward task and I had been given a month to complete that task before I was to move on to my new posting, RAF Brize Norton. I never knew why I remained but I was very happy. The thought of moving further away from my girlfriend did concern me. However, it was a strange experience – one day I was living in a room with four other airmen in a barrack block with about a hundred more airmen and the next day I was all alone. Lindholme was, during the Second World War, a Bomber Command station and at the end of one of the runways was the infamous Lindholme Bog. Rumour had it, that quite a few Bombers crashed in the bog and, were never seen again until, that is, their crews re-appeared as ghosts of the bog. Most RAF airfields have some sort of ghostly history but Lindholme's was quite plausible and certainly the elderly local people talked of nothing else. Being all alone in that barrack block I thought of nothing else I heard every creak and every door banging and I'm sure you can understand why I left the lights on all night. Many years later I returned to Lindholme Prison, as it is now, in my capacity as a Probation Officer. I was visiting an inmate. Despite my relative lack of any affection for the camp, I felt a tinge of sadness as I saw the state of the place. What was once a happy and thriving RAF community with a first class football team is a prison and, in my opinion, not a very good one at that, but that may have changed. It was quite poignant seeing my old room and the station soccer pitch but one has to move on, and off to Brize Norton I went.

What a contrast: Lindholme with its Hastings aircraft and homely atmosphere to Brize Norton with all the hustle and bustle of a modern and strategic operational air base. The place was huge with VC10, Belfast and Britannia aircraft operating round the clock all year round. There were two station commanders when I arrived – one administration, one operational – and there must have been a few thousand RAF personnel employed on the station. It was like moving from a small rural village to a major city. I was, to an extent, a big cog in a small wheel at Lindholme but at Brize I was a very small cog in a very big wheel. There were 160 RAF firemen although many of them were deployed to RAF Fairford providing fire cover for Concorde. I was accommodated in the Fireman's barrack block, the one closest to the runway and, despite the fact that the aircraft took off and landed only a few hundred yards from our block, I soon became accustomed to the noise. I was allocated to one of the four eighteen man crash crews and after a brief introduction to the layout of the airfield, I was soon driving one of the major foam trucks on the many and varied tasks undertaken by the crash crews. One of the most boring of tasks was to standby when a VC10 was carrying out engine tests. We would sit by the aircraft in a major foam truck for hours on end whilst the aircraft engines were tested to maximum throttle.

RAF Brize Norton Fire Section inspection.

Duties became fairly routine and the night shift could depending on aircraft operations, be a long tiring duty. I remember the Turkish invasion of the northern part of Cyprus in 1974. Twenty thousand British dependants were evacuated, and most of them came home via RAF Brize Norton. The fire crews, provided assistance to personnel as they disembarked from the many aircraft that flew in and out over that period. RAF fire crews always provided assistance to the medical staff, who brought back from overseas, the sick and wounded to RAF Brize Norton. An interesting, but quite sad aside. I currently supervise an offender who is an ex soldier. Interviewing him for a Court report he told me the tale of how he was beaten up in Germany in 1974. He and his two mates had been drinking heavily all night. They returned to barracks and one of the three soldiers went berserk. He killed one of his friends and beat up the other with a pick axe handle. The survivor was left severely disabled and was hospitalised for many years. Since that incident, the survivor has been registered disabled, and life has been quite miserable and sad for him. As I listened to this tale, I remembered this incident and realised that I was at RAF Brize Norton at the time. I was part of the fire crew who helped carry this casualty off the plane. A little funny story about this offender. I assisted him obtain accommodation. When I asked, about previous accommodation, he told me that there had been problems.

"What are they?" I asked.

"Problems with noise.

"What sort of noise?"

"The noise I make with my blow up doll," he replied.

RAF Brize Norton Fire Section on parade 1973.

At Brize there was the largest aircraft hanger in Western Europe, at least that was what we were told. As a crew we would regularly carryout fire practices at the hangar and attend for briefings about opening and closing the hanger doors in event of a fire. All very important stuff. One evening we were listening to a engineering Warrant Officer explaining, very elegantly, how to open the doors, however, not just anybody could open the doors it had to be at least a Warrant Officer such was the importance of this operation. Apparently, it took about twenty minutes to open the doors and even longer to close and if there was snow on the roof, doors were not to be opened. We all listened 'intently' and making our way back to our respective vehicles suddenly the doors started to open and the engineering WO started to jump. As we all turned round there was a very young LAC Fireman looking at his sticky out index finger, banged to rights as they say in my new trade. I have heard many RAF firemen swear but the engineering WO beat then all hands down.

At Brize we operated a four-watch system. Two-day shifts, two-night shifts, followed by a wonderful four days off. It was a fact of life at Brize that most of the firemen had part time jobs during their four days off. I was no exception and as I was still madly in love and travelling home for my four days off, I obtained employment with a Liverpool employment agency called, Rent a Man. I would report to their office and they would send me out to a haulage firm and I would drive whatever vehicle came my way.

After a few weeks working for the company, I was asked to report to a food distributors in Runcorn. On arrival I was informed that all the company drivers had been dismissed: apparently a large amount of corruption had been taking place. I thought no more of that, collected my lorry and delivery destinations and off I went. What I didn't know was that there were pickets on the departure gate and as I went to leave they climbed all over the vehicle cab and threatened me serious harm. I made my way through the pickets and off I went delivering food to hotels, hospitals and restaurants throughout North Wales and the Northwest. It was quite a pleasant little job and the money was most welcome.

One of my delivery drops one day was to a canteen at Liverpool docks. I dropped of my delivery and was making my way out of the dock when a man carrying a clipboard approached me. He stopped the vehicle went through his notes and suddenly declared that the firm I was driving for was blacklisted and informed me that I was scab labour. Men appeared from all directions and it was a very tense situation. I explained that I was only a serviceman trying to earn an extra few bob and in the end I was allowed to leave. There are always at least two sides to every dispute and in this situation I had my own opinion. My father and grandfather spent all their working lives on Liverpool docks, apart from war service. They were not supported when times were very hard – quite the opposite – and militancy, in my opinion, served no purpose other than to drive employment opportunities away. My conscience was clear – I was working to supplement a relatively meagre income, I was saving money to provide for my family and I was saving a business from collapse. As I became more familiar with the job I would take my future father-in-law out with me on my deliveries. He was then a redundant Liverpool dock worker.

He used to look forward to our travels and he had no complaints about my actions. Not all Liverpool Dockers or Liverpool people are militants but in the seventies that was often the way they were portrayed. I remember one delivery to a factory canteen; the canteen manageress came over and enquired if I had any surplus items. If I did she would pay in cash or in kind. I had neither items left over nor the inclination to part with them if I did – whatever the reward.

A year after arriving at Brize I married my fiancée Anne and we moved into our first married quarter, 14 Devon Place. It was our first home and will obviously always have a particular affection in our life. It was nothing special, quite small really, but we made it as comfortable as possible. Anne is from a family of seven children and they are a very close-knit family, consequently it was a big wrench for her moving away from home. However, her parents would visit regularly, as did her brothers and sisters. My own family also visited regularly so we were never completely isolated from our families.

Anne obtained a good job in Witney, which she enjoyed, and I had obtained very well-paid part time work as a cement-mixer driver. I used to enjoy this work and it was rather pleasant travelling all round Oxfordshire and Wiltshire. We also enjoyed a good social life. Anne made some very good friends in the married patch and at her work. I was doing well at my job and, for the first time, I was beginning to consider promotion. I sat and passed all my promotion exams and was selected for the mandatory RAF fireman five week advanced course at RAF Catterick.

As with all my firemen courses, I enjoyed this. There was usually an element of academic work but in the main the courses were of a practical nature. A year after we were married, Anne gave birth at RAF hospital Wroughton to our son, Peter. I still believe to this day that a newborn child is a minor miracle and our little miracle changed our lives completely. Every other family on the married patch seemed to be giving birth and it brings families closer together with lots of shared interests. In October 1973 I was promoted to Corporal and posted to RAF Waddington. I was making arrangements to move when I was summoned to see the Officer in charge of the Fire section. He informed me that there was a vacancy for a Corporal Fireman at Brize and I could remain at Brize but with a transfer to another crew. Additionally there was a four month detachment to RAF Sydenham in Belfast that was about to happen which would have to be staffed by firemen from Brize. Remain at Brize and I would be transferred to another crew and I would be expected to complete a four-month detachment in Belfast. I agreed to the offer put before me. The day after promotion, I reported for duty complete with my brand spanking new Corporal tapes on my arms.

There were men on this crew who had been in the RAF much longer than me and consequently they were intent on making my first few days fairly difficult. I was quite a young NCO fireman and resentment raised its ugly head but I knew I had worked hard and done all that was asked of me, and more. Primitive instinct in these situations suggests you either fight or flee and there was no chance of me fleeing. It didn't take me long to settle in to my new role. I had seen good and bad NCOs; consequently I had my own perception of what made a good NCO. Not long after promotion, I duly set off for a four-month detachment to Sydenham, Belfast. Apparently there was no fire cover for the station and the task of providing that cover was given to Brize Norton. It was a wrench leaving Anne and my son but Belfast is a lot closer to home than some of the places I had already been.

Sydenham was an unusual posting in many ways. In the first place we were billeted on HMS Maidstone, a Second World War battleship that was berthed in Belfast docks. Prior to our use the ship had been used as a prisoner of war ship. However it was condemned as unfit and unacceptable for prisoners but fine for us Matelots and Airmen. The accommodation was very basic; the twelve on detachment were located in one cabin with literally no room to swing a cat. Despite the generally poor state of repair of the Maidstone, we were expected to keep our accommodation tidy and behave in a civilised manner. We were subject to regular captain's rounds and, believe you me, Royal Navy inspections were much more thorough than any I experienced in the RAF. There was a Master at Arms billeted very close to our cabin and he was a very powerful individual – his word was law. I befriended a Navy killick (leading seaman) and what a character he was. He was demoted and promoted twice during my four-month detachment. We had some wild drinking sessions both on and off the Maidstone. It became quite competitive between our small detachment of Airmen and the equally small detachment of Matelots. Workwise, we had little to do although I do remember a shout to a cylinder store fire on board the Maidstone. We extinguished the fire and then had to cool the cylinders. Fairly straightforward, but we never knew whether the cylinders would blow or not.

Sydenham was, on reflection, quite a good learning experience. Back at Brize I was part of a crew of eighteen men and the junior of the four NCOs on the crew. Now I was in charge of a four man crew and could plan our day's activity and deal with the many everyday occurrences. I also shared accommodation with the crew so was, in effect, responsible for them off duty as well. We would always go out together – the few places we could safely go that is – although, even in the Belfast Docks area, I was determined to go for a walk, something I always did and always have done wherever, I may be.

It was a bit scary at times, especially when a car would drive slowly behind me. The fact that we had to grow our hair long before this detachment was of no comfort. We still stood out like sore thumbs. The local people who worked on the base were, however, great with us and they gave advice about places to avoid and, for that matter, people to avoid... I survived this detachment unscathed. The fact that I managed to get home for a couple of long weekends helped but, generally speaking, it was a good learning experience for me. I returned to Brize and continued where I left off on crew and with my part time job. Looking after my relatives when they visited was also like a part time job – not many weeks went by without visitors. This would involve trips to Burford, Stow on the Wold, Oxford, Lechlade and many more wonderful Cotswolds locations. Out of the blue, I was informed I was being posted and a few weeks after notification I was on my way to Gutersloh in Northern Germany. Anne and baby Peter were left to hand over our quarter and I was to return to barrack room life again.

6. Germany Calling ~ Gutersloh & Laarbruch

I was posted to RAF Gutersloh in the January of 1975. The station was a formidable looking place with all the paraphernalia of the cold war. All sorts of NATO aircraft flew overhead, Rapier missile batteries were constantly manned and RAF Regiment lads provided ground defence. Gutersloh was, in fact, only a few minutes flying time to the Eastern Bloc border. It didn't take long to realise that this was no training camp or maintenance unit, this was the very sharp end of the cold war and, if you did forget, there were enough signs about to remind you that, '**the purpose of this station is to prepare for war**'. It was difficult to comprehend the enormity of the situation especially if, like me, you had young children and they played with their little friends or went to nursery oblivious to all around them.

There was no time for familiarisation or acclimatisation, especially under the command of the Fire Section Warrant Officer, the redoubtable Mr Morrell MBE BEM. He was known to most station personnel as a man to be avoided but to the station firemen he was known affectionately as 'Uncle Jack'. He was into about his sixth year at Gutersloh and he just oozed confidence and power. He was a station celebrity, well known to all station personnel and it was not only Firemen who he tormented but also any unsuspecting airman or officer for that matter. He would have no hesitation bawling at some off guard personnel who maybe inappropriately dressed or not walking properly. He was also heavily involved in all aspects of the Taceval (Tactical Evaluation Exercises) that were so common in RAF Germany. He appeared to be on a personal crusade to ensure that his section and his station always satisfactorily completed a Taceval. Senior Officers lived in fear of him. We on the other hand, tried to avoid him. One has to remember that to get a poor Taceval result was tantamount to losing a war and could result in all sorts of recriminations. Witch-hunts began to find out which section on camp performed badly and then the individual apportioning of blame process commenced. There really was no hiding place and individuals could be sent home with their otherwise promising careers ruined if they let the safety and security of the Western World down. At least that is how important the situation was made out to be. The Fire Crews were constantly on a state of readiness so we were slightly better prepared than some unsuspecting shiny or store man. We were also familiar with Mr Morrell's bark and bite; consequently his raucous voice and choice of language never offended us.

I was posted to Gutersloh at a time when the powers to be in the RAF Fire service decided that, given the cost of the new major foam trucks, only corporals could drive and corporals also had to operate the monitor. Also, instead of Sergeants in charge of the crew, it was now deemed more appropriate that Flight Sergeants took control of each crew. All this happened almost over night and a whole clutch of SNCO and junior NCO firemen arrived at Gutersloh at the same time. I gather that Uncle Jack was not at all happy with this situation. He could well have encountered some difficulty with this new collection of men at his section. He was, after all, in complete control and there may well be a dissenter or an individual prepared to make comment on his totalitarianism but none of us, despite our combined years of service, saw fit to rock the boat. Uncle Jack thought nothing of lambasting our Flight Sergeant and as for the eight Corporals on each crew, well he just treated us with total disdain. When the new staff arrived there were insufficient married quarters, consequently we were accommodated in a barrack block only a few yards from the section. Uncle Jack was never far away from us when we were off duty, but that didn't stop us enjoying a pint or two.

On arrival I was allocated to my crew which was led by a Flight Sergeant (Roy Kinder) who called himself the Poisoned Dwarf but that turned out to be too nice a description for him. Whereas Uncle Jack was a hard taskmaster who had no favourites and cared not what we thought of him, this man was wicked and tried to curry favour especially if we met him off duty. Whereas Uncle Jack was a smart, assertive individual, this man was scruffy and untidy. Despite Uncle Jack's formidable manner, he was a credit to the RAF Fire Service; consequently one grew to admire him. One never grew to like the poisoned dwarf; we treated him with contempt. Each shift we would be lined up, all twelve of us and we would be detailed off to our respective duties. There was a pecking order on parade; the senior Corporal on the right and so on down the line to the most junior crew member. On arrival I was the junior member of the crew and as the Poisoned Dwarf swaggered down our line detailing off duties, he came to me and informed me that I would be in charge of the broom cupboard.

"Thank you Flight Sergeant" I said. "I can assure you it will be the best broom cupboard in the Royal Air Force."

It went over his head but a few weeks later I heard Uncle Jack shouting at the Poisoned Dwarf, "what's happened to the broom cupboard" and the Poisoned Dwarf sent for me.

"Explain to Mr Morrell what you have done to his broom cupboard," said the Poisoned Dwarf. Pleased it seemed that I was about to incur the wrath of the boss. "Well sir the Flight Sergeant gave the broom cupboard to my charge as an extra duty and I did inform him that I would ensure this would be the smartest broom cupboard in the RAF." I was relieved of my broom cupboard duties but I had also come to the attention of Uncle Jack.

A few days after that little occurrence, I met a station officer who I had played football with at Church Fenton. He was now a Squadron Leader and one of his secondary duties was that of station football officer. He insisted I come along to train with the station football team. I explained that would be very difficult given Mr Morrell's attitude to sport. "I will have a word with Mr Morrell," he said. A few days later I was summoned to Mr Morrell's office. He was none too pleased with the visit from the Squadron Leader but I was able to convince him I had not set this up. "I'm keeping an eye on you" he said and I thanked him for that and left. He did keep an eye out for me and, in a way, I think he realised I was no malingerer, which was his favourite description for almost everyone.

I had no problem with the physical demands of the job at Gutersloh but it was very arduous; we were in and out of our vehicles all day and night. We had plenty of real emergencies to deal with and then there were Uncle Jack's practices, which he called any time, and then we had the Tacevals. If we were off duty and the Taceval alert sounded we had to be in the section within a matter of minutes, or else. It wasn't so bad if we were in the barrack block or the NAAFI bar but when I obtained a married quarter which was five miles from camp and with no car, I had to push bike it back to the section pretty dam quick. Whilst we were on crew we were never allowed to be idle. We had to be seen during the day to be carrying out some tasks or other. Afternoons we had to undertake classroom lectures and Uncle Jack would often sit in. The lecture room was located on the second floor of the section, consequently there was a fireman's pole connecting the two floors. It was a fairly regular occurrence to be in the middle of a lecture either presenting or "listening" and then the emergency alarms would sound and away we would go down the pole, often landing in a heap on the floor. I remember Flight Sergeant Dolman hurtling down the pole in front of me during one shift only to hear a cracking sound come from his ankle; he never made it to that incident. Tom Dolman was my crew chief for a while and what a character he was. Tom was a very blunt speaking, no nonsense sort of fellow, ruthless on the volleyball court and ruthless with his language. I liked being on crew with Tom mainly because he was good at his job and never shirked anything. If he thought he and his crew were being messed about he would say so; I heard him many times berate Air Traffic Control.

My son Peter on sentry duty at RAF Gutersloh 1975

One activity Uncle Jack did permit on his section was volleyball, although he would always warn us that any injuries incurred would be deemed self-inflicted. I remember one game during that hot summer of 1976 we were all engaged in a very tensely fought volleyball match. Suddenly a huge bang and then a huge fireball appeared from one of the reheat pans. A Lightning was tied down on the reheat pan; a common occurrence and the engine would be tested to maximum capacity. There was always a lot of noise when this sort of servicing took place, one of many sounds you were familiar with on duty. What made this sound so different was the loud bang and fireball and this was the result of the aircraft bursting a fuel pipe during the reheat run. I remember to this day being very focussed on the volley ball game and then turning to face the direction of the bang. There was a momentary pause and then we all shot off to our respective vehicles and crew positions and set off to the burning aircraft. In these sort of airfield incidents there are no instructions passed between the crew.

There isn't time but fortunately RAF Firemen are well trained in these sorts of incidents. Men will know exactly where to position their vehicles, how to produce foam in an instant and firemen will enter the flame mass confident that they will have back up. The particular problem with this incident was the fact that the engineer, on hearing the bang and seeing the flames, had shot out of the aircraft without switching off the fuel delivery system. Consequently, when we arrived, fuel was still being delivered to the fire. We didn't know it then but as a crew we knew without prompting that we would have to locate the seat of the fire and, more important, we were unaware whether there was still a body in the cockpit.

By this stage in my Gutersloh career I had moved on from in charge of the broom cupboard to second in command of the crew and a position on crash one. Consequently I was part of the three-man immediate rescue team. Our job was to enter the flame mass, make our way to the cockpit safe in the knowledge that the major foam trucks would be laying down a foam path simultaneous to our entry into the flame mass, that's the theory. We did manage to gain an entry into the cockpit and would, if necessary, have extricated the engineer but he was recovering in another place. We managed to extinguish the fire which was a combination of the foam mass and the fuel ceasing to flow to the seat of the fire. Emergencies like this happen in an instant and crews move from a very relaxed state of readiness or even a sleeping duty to a major incident in an instant. It is a fine testament to the fire crews of the RAF that this is the sort of work they excel at.

As ever we had no time to sit back and recover from our exertions. We had to replenish our vehicles as soon as possible as other aircraft were in the circuit waiting to land. Once again, firemen are not told what to do, each driver will proceed post haste to replenish and resume his normal stand by position. Gutersloh was probably the busiest of all RAF airfields at this time. All sorts of aircraft operated from the station, Lightning's, Harriers, Wessex, Hercules, and Belfast's to name but a few. In addition a variety of NATO aircraft flew in and out of the base and we had to be familiar with a whole host of aircraft escape systems weapons systems and cockpit layouts. An example of a situation where things could go horribly wrong happened one afternoon on crew. We were deployed to a F111 aircraft. En route we were instructed by air traffic control that the pilot was to carry out a defector drill. We were familiar with this scenario and our instructions were to surround the aircraft and deny any exit and capture the pilot.

As per our plan of action, the major foam trucks surrounded the aircraft whilst the crash one crew went straight to the aircraft cockpit. The senior corporal removed the crash one ladder and pitched it against the aircraft canopy. He then climbed the ladder, removed his pistol and instructed the pilot to leave the cockpit immediately. I watched from my position as a driver of one of the major foams as Corporal Tagg Whippe berated the pilot, who seemed reluctant to leave his aircraft. Tagg was waving his pistol and I could see the pilot waving his hands. However, Tagg was a fearsome looking individual and the pilot opened his cockpit. An F111 aircraft has a hinged canopy that opens to the side not the normal sliding canopy that we were familiar with. As the canopy opened it was hard not to laugh as I watched Tagg and his ladder fall backwards to terra firma. F111 aircraft were known throughout RAF Germany as widow makers, many simply fell out the sky during my Germany tour. Tag's dear wife could herself have been another F111 statistic that day but, in true fire service fashion, Tagg simply picked himself up, dusted himself down and started all over again.

Stationed at Gutersloh fire section was one of my all time, great RAF firemen and RAF characters, gentleman Flight Sergeant Steve Davey. Steve was totally different to the Poisoned Dwarf; the two had nothing in common. Steve was respected for what he was not what rank he held. Everybody liked Steve and, without any prompting, he could get the best out of his subordinates. Steve was a very rare breed for the RAF fire service he was as rough and tough as the rest of us but he had a very high intellect I say that because he was a regular contributor to the station magazine, Zietung 47. His articles were always interesting, amusing and articulate but his written word was exactly like his spoken word.

He was a very positive role model for us all and I like to think that I at least worked with a model professional in every sense of the word and I hope at least some of Steve' s leadership style influenced my behaviour. I have in my collection of memorabilia, some of Steve's old articles and in one he details a day in the life of a RAF Gutersloh fireman. He selected a date at random, which happened to be the 22 June 1976 (I was on shift this day) and from the fire section daily occurrence book he gave a vivid account of a typical shift. On that day the duty crew deployed to twenty-three separate airfield incidents, including two major emergencies. He also published the fire and other emergency incidents for that year, which were sixty-two domestic fire incidents and four thousand and fifty four airfield incidents.

By any standard, fire section incidents at Gutersloh were on a par with any other RAF or civilian counterpart. The shift pattern we worked was a fairly gruelling routine; we worked a day shift, night shift and a day off. Having said that, the day off commenced at 8am at the end of a long night shift. On our day off we had to arrange for any of the multitude of domestic chores one has to undertake in the service, medical and dentist appointments, clothing stores appointments, range practice etc. We had one weekend off in three and we had a taceval or mini-val on average about once every two months. Having said that, morale on the fire section was generally very high most people had volunteered for Germany, as there was a financial incentive to do so. Leave, according to Uncle Jack, was a privilege and family commitments were the responsibility of your wife.

During this tour, Anne gave birth to our second child, Christine at the Army hospital Rintell, which is in that well-known German town of Hamlin (Pied Piper). Anne had a few complications during child-birth and was admitted to Rintell several weeks before the anticipated birth. Rintel was a one hundred-mile round trip from Gutersloh and my son, Peter, now two years old and I would as often as possible travel to Rintel. On many occasions I would arrive at the hospital to be told there was an infection on the ward and visiting had been cancelled. We would see Anne at a ward window and like me she was trying to put a brave face on things but it was a very difficult few months for our little family. Fortunately we had some wonderful neighbours and Peter spent many a night with my next door neighbour when I was on night shift. Steve Davey, once he heard of this situation, suggested I visit Uncle Jack at his home and ask if I could alter my shift pattern and I duly went one Sunday afternoon and called at Uncle Jack's married quarter.

Uncle Jack made me very welcome and, whilst his wife enter-tained Peter, Jack informed me that he was unable to alter my shift and that was the end of that. I carried on managing my family affairs and working shift work. Fortunately the birth went OK but I have a deep disdain and mistrust of Army Doctors. Things may have changed, but I got the distinct impression some Army doctors lack empathy, compassion and medical skills. I still have to this day the medical wristbands worn by Anne when she gave birth, the band simply states 'WO Cpl Edwards'; translated means wife of Cpl Edwards. Anne was never addressed at all by the doctors, neither was I for that matter. Any information was passed to "nurse" and then passed on to us. RAF medical staff in my experience, were, completely the opposite, kind, compassionate and professional.

Anne and I will always be eternally grateful to a RAF medic who lived next door to us at Gutersloh. Christmas day 1975, I was on day shift. All training and routine work was cancelled. We were on standby for emergencies only. Just after our crew Christmas meal, one of the emergency phones sounded and I answered. It was the station medical officer, a Wing Commander and he asked to speak to Corporal Edwards. He informed me I had to report to the medical centre straight away. Steve Davey was our crew chief that day and I passed on the message to Steve and off I went to the medical centre. On arrival I was taken to the treatment room and there in his Christ-mas day clothes was my son, Peter, asleep on the treatment table with Anne holding his hand. The medical officer informed me that

Peter had a convulsion that morning and he had been brought in by ambulance. Anne then told me that she was sat with Peter on her knee when she noticed his eyes roll backwards and he stopped breathing. She ran next-door to our friend and RAF medic who gave Peter mouth to mouth resuscitation. This one-off experience, I'm pleased to say, had no long-term effect on Peter. But it took Anne and I a long time to get over the shock of that event.

Socially, Anne and I enjoyed a fantastic time at Gutersloh. We lived in a large block of flats (6/3 Lubeckerstrasse Harsewinkel) with our own children's play area, our own cellar bar and great neighbours. Anne was making better progress than I with the language I suppose she had to because she shopped in the local village. Although I had been in Germany a few months longer than Anne she could speak much better German than I. The first few words I learnt were those immortal ones known to all military personnel in Germany, *"Ein grossen beer bitte"* (one large beer please). I bought a new car, took the German driving test and days off were spent touring the local area which really was beautiful. Anne and I have always been regular attendees at church so we had friends at Church, at the fire section and friends in the married patch. We also had some very good friends amongst the German firemen who made up about half of the section. Some RAF lads, for whatever reason, didn't make any effort to communicate with our German crewmates. I started playing squash with a German fireman, Alvis Teal and he invited Anne and I to his home many times. We got on extremely well with Alvis and another German fireman, Heinrich Bunte. Henry as we called him did not live far from our married quarter; he had quite a large dairy farm, which he and his elderly mother managed between them. We were invited to Henry's and this soon became a regular occurrence. Peter would play in the cattle shed and I found this fascinating. As I had never previously been in a cattle shed myself I enjoyed it as much as Peter. Henry's mother loved to nurse Christine and, in her broken English, she would say, "Christine Deutscher kinder (German baby), which she was and like all British military births in Germany, those children have dual nationality. Often Henry and I would have a few schnapps together and I would end up getting a lift home. Such was our friendship that Anne and I were invited to Henry's wedding.

Gutersloh continued to be a difficult and demanding tour of duty. Nonetheless, Anne was very happy there and had lots of friends. We were more or less resigned to a contented three-year tour and were making arrangements to bring both sets of parents out to Germany on holiday. As if from nowhere news came that the fire section at Gutersloh was being reclassified. In other words, all those firemen who were posted out in haste to man the new fire trucks were no longer needed and redeployment of staff would have to take place. Not one to delay matters and to act before any form of discontent set in, Uncle Jack decreed that the last to arrive would be the first to go and that was non-negotiable. I was one of the last to arrive and informed I was on my way to RAF Laarbruch, another front line RAF Germany base, only this time it was a Jaguar and Buccaneer aircraft base. Anne, like myself, began to accept such interruptions in our life as every day events in life's rich tapestry. I was not given much time to prepare my married quarter for hand over and, as usual, Anne was left behind to complete that very onerous task while I set off to commence my tour at Laarbruch.

On arrival at Laarbruch I was allocated to a fire crew and set about familiarising myself with the base, the aircraft and most importantly my new colleagues. Laarbruch fire section was a world apart from the one I left at Gutersloh. For a start, the section was led by one of life's real gentlemen, Warrant Officer Dennis McCann. He was totally different in every way to Uncle Jack.

Dennis was a softly spoken, quite benign individual with none of the aggression manifested in Uncle Jack. One could tell straight away that Mr McCann was well respected by all and sundry. If ever there was an individual to fit the adage that it's not the uniform that makes the man, it is the man in the uniform, well this was he. After a few weeks on crew Dennis informed me that the day Corporal, a man named Jim Curry, was about to be posted on promotion and Dennis wanted me to take on this role. At first I had my doubts, the day corporal, a familiar term on most big fire sections, was usually the longest serving corporal on the section and the one keen for promotion. It also would take me away from my crew mates, with all that entails the comradeship, daily banter and the basic day to day role of responding to incidents and emergencies. I sought advice from my crew Sergeant and he thought it would be a good idea and, after speaking to Jim Curry, I took the job. Basically my job was to act almost as a personal assistant to Mr McCann. I would discuss crew deployments, the good, bad and indifferent aspects of the fire section and its personnel. I would also be required to carry out fire training for all station personnel, give lectures and practical fire demonstrations to all sorts of groups; wives club, families club, school groups and local German groups. I had rigged up a portable cooker and I would demonstrate for instance, the right and wrong way to deal with a chip pan fire.

RAF Laarbruch Wilkinson Sword of Peace parade.

I was also required to take one of the Mk 9 trucks to the very popular German fire service rallies. The German fire crews would proudly show off their trucks and fire skills and along I would come in a huge crash tender, demonstrate how to produce foam on the move, always the highlight of the show. I also visited many German fire stations and gave presentations on how to deal with armed aircraft incidents, ejection seats, etc. I was also required to ensure the vehicles at the section were serviced regularly and this took a lot of my time. Negotiating with the motor transport section could be a delicate issue, MT would accuse our drivers of recklessness but at the end of the day I had to ensure there were sufficient serviceable vehicles available otherwise flying would cease and that was out the question. Another major function of mine was to be a part of the station taceval team.

RAF Laarbruch charity football team.

I was aware of the taceval team at Gutersloh but this was the prevail of senior station personnel. At Laarbruch, the fire section day corporal was very much a part of this team. Our role was to plan and operate our own station exercises in preparation for external evaluation or the real thing. We would meet, set a date and time and decide who was doing what and then we would carry on with our normal duties until the exercise start date. We were sworn to secrecy and much as people tried to obtain information from me, there was no way I would be forthcoming. Wives and families were familiar with a taceval. They created a huge interference in our normal routine. For a start, exercises always commenced in the early hours of the morning and could last up to four days; longer if things went pear shaped. If we hadn't had an exercise for a few weeks, station personnel got very twitchy and the talk all the time was of the impending taceval. My next door neighbour would try all sorts of tricks to cause me to slip up; I was often invited round to his for drinks and, at the end of the night, he would slip in those immortal words, "any news on the next taceval". People would be watching my every move and some fire section SNCO's would resort to bullying tactics to glean some information from me. However, wild horses wouldn't have obtained any information from me. Even Anne was never privy to any information I had. Once the exercise started, all hell broke loose, Police vehicles were driving around the married patch and around the local village town sounding their emergency klaxons. Sirens on base were screaming and the base turned from a sleepy hollow into a war zone in a matter of minutes.

RAF Laarbruch fire crew and day staff.

Once the exercise started, I collected my vehicle and put on my nice white armband with the words DS (directing staff) emblazoned on it. It meant I was on the side of the baddies and, as ever the odds are stacked in favour of the baddies. The goodies, the station personnel, had to abide by a set of rules and to operate in an atmosphere of mayhem and confusion. We meanwhile were immune to air attack, bomb blasts, fire, snipers, missed meals and lack of sleep. We knew exactly what was happening and who was going to be the next unsuspecting victim. My role was to enter a building, or not as the case may be, and pass on an inject. The inject was no more than a piece of paper that stated for instance, 'your building is on fire or, your communications systems have been destroyed'. I would then record all actions. I had unlimited access to any station building, vehicle, or aircraft for that matter. I could put a sticker on an aircraft confirming the aircraft had been sabotaged and rendered unservice-able and therefore, out of the game. The object of the exercise was to generate as much confusion as possible. Personnel were generally being deliberately messed about. I tried to be as civil as possible to those I stung but it was difficult. I remember one armoury Warrant Officer attempting to throw me out of his armoury complete with my piece of paper torn into little pieces. I knew this man quite well; the armoury was a place I frequently visited during my normal duties. I remember the Warrant Officer once telling me the tale when, as a young airman during the war he had to collect weapons off dead servicemen.

His wartime experiences, thirty years' service and here I was, blowing up his armoury with pieces of paper and inconveniencing his men. I could have returned to our command centre and made out an adverse report but I was able to come to a compromise. I agreed to return in an hour and blow-up his armoury once more when his men were better prepared. As the exercise wore on, personnel wore out and tempers could flare. I knew from my own experiences at Gutersloh that tacevals were knackering. Little sleep, meals out of tins, no washing facilities, unaware of what was happening at home or when this whole charade would finish was an ideal recipe for a few heated words. I remember another inject when four of us were sat in a land rover outside the station operations centre, the home of the goodies and their leader. I was unaware of this inject; we each had our own and on this occasion, I was to observe and take notes. Just like the film, High Noon, the clock ticked down and Gary Cooper (aka the station commander) came out to meet his fate. As he came into view I was passed an inject and on it were the words, You have been shot by a sniper. "Give that to the station commander," said the senior DS, a Squadron Leader. I had no choice but to leave the relative security of the land rover and stop the station commander in his tracks. Initially he refused to accept my inject but I insisted and reminded the Station Commander I was a member of the taceval team and all station personnel were expected to respond to injects. "Follow me sir," and I escorted the CO to the land rover. Within those few brief minutes of me receiving the inject and executing the action, the land rover had emptied and my taceval colleagues had left the vehicle and were in hiding. I tried to act as professionally as possible in front of the CO but I felt very isolated. "Am I allowed to escape?" "No sir you have been shot dead and I am about to take you to the holding station for all those who have suffered a similar fate". I can understand the logic in removing the leader but it was a tense stand off between the two of us. Later that day I met up with my DS colleagues who were anxious to hear of the station commander's reaction. "He was very disappointed," said I, "he thought he could at least have been injected by an officer" and left it at that. An interesting aspect of this station commander and service life, prior to the arrival of the station commander my little family always attended mass at the station RC church. There was probably about twenty of us each Sunday and my family sat near the altar. This CO was a practising Roman Catholic and joined our small congregation. By no fault of the CO our congregation swelled and we were relegated to the cheaper pews.

Whilst at Laarbruch I became involved for the first time in secondary duties. Dennis McCann was the chairman of the NAAFI committee, a liaison body between NAAFI management and staff and the service men and women who used the facility. Dennis nominated me for the post of entertainment secretary and I was duly appointed. This was a fascinating extra duty and a role I thoroughly enjoyed. It was my job to book all the artists either through the NAAFI's own entertainment organisation or through the local entertainment agencies. The NAAFI tended to have the monopoly but there was nothing wrong in using local resources. One advantage of using local resources was I got to see all the acts before booking. I would travel down to Venlo, just across the Dutch border and the artists would perform for me and I always took another committee member with me. We mainly watched and listened to rock bands but there was normally a female stripper to cast an eye over. This was a purely professional business and I was required to negotiate a price for all the acts. The situation was open to corruption but I was a young, conscientious Corporal and there was no way I would put my career at risk. However, watching female strippers went with the job and it would be wrong to say I didn't enjoy this extra duty. On function nights it was also my job to collect the entrance fees and pay the artists, who, unless they were the occasional big act like Mike and Bernie Winters, were paid through their agent. There would be some really wild and boisterous nights in the Double L club, especially when there was a female stripper on the bill. At times fights broke out between the Army, RAF and RAF Regiment lads and between individual sections. Tables, chairs and other moveable objects would be smashed the odd window put in and not forgetting the odd cuts and bruises to the warring parties. These situations were accepted as almost normal behaviour and I was to learn very quickly that the powers that be turned a blind eye and much preferred the NAAFI to be smashed up than the local pubs and bars. After each function, I would meet with the NAAFI manager, he would present me with a bill for damages and I would make my way to the respective military accounts officer and seek recompense.

Repairs were carried out, the NAAFI spruced up and that was it until the next function. I well remember one night I was at the NAAFI entrance collecting entrance fees when Jack Lawson, a gargantuan RAF Fireman and his wife entered the reception area. For no apparent reason, some Army Field engineers pushed past Jack and his dear wife. All hell broke loose, Jack was engaged in a brawl with about ten Army Engineers when he suddenly disappeared under all their bodies as kicks and blows rained down on him. To even out the odds Jack's dear wife waded in with her handbag flying. It was like a scene from the Keystone Cops. To his credit, Jack and his dear wife successfully beat off the attack and it was a sight to behold watching the beaten and dejected Army engineers retreat to lick their wounds.

Not long after that altercation Jack was involved in an incident of a different sort. He was a member of a RAF Fire crew that responded to a fire in a married quarter block of flats. I arrived on the scene just after the first response vehicle and by that time the situation was under control. Apparently an airman kept a chemistry set in the block cellar and this had spontaneously ignited. The fire spread throughout the cellar and was making its way upward through the different floor levels. The prompt arrival of the fire crew prevented a major incident but heavy obstacles hindered the crew. Jack, apparently of his own volition, set about moving these very heavy obstacles and the crew were able to reach the seat of the fire and thereby extinguish the fire. Jack demonstrated a feat of extraordinary strength and courage; no plaudits, no accolades, simply all part of the job for Jack and his crewmates.

Activities at the Double L club took up a lot of my own time but I had many friends and acquaintances with this activity. On one occasion, the entertainers Mike and Bernie Winters were booked for three shows at Laarbruch; one at the Officers Mess, one at the Sergeants Mess and an appearance at the Double L Club. I wrote to their agent explaining that I had played football against Mike and Bernie ten years ago. I asked if they could speak to them both and ask if they would like me to organise a charity football match between their entourage and a Double L club team. I received a positive response and it was agreed a football match would take place. After my enforced suspension from football at Gutersloh I was now at Laarbruch back into intersection football and the station football team. I knew all the station footballers, the good, the bad and the indifferent. In fact one of my Laarbruch mates (Bill Neal) played centre forward for the RAF team and was probably the number one footballer in the RAF... I knew I would have some difficulty selecting a team but Dennis McCann fully supported any decision I made so I decided to select a reasonably good team and also put out a select team of Double L club members including a few females. We selected a charity, produced advertising leaflets and the NAAFI manager sorted out a bar-b-q and bar. It was all going very well until I received a telephone call from a RAF Officer, otherwise unknown to me, who decided he was taking over this event. He wanted to put out a team of officers and SNCO's and was of the opinion this was to high profile an event for the lower ranks to manage. It is surprising really in the forces how little influence junior officers have in the general scheme of things (see page 120).

~ *Out of the Blue* ~

Group Captain
Leaps buildings with a single bound
Is more powerful than a locomotive
Is faster than a speeding bullet
Walks on water
Gives policy to God.

Wing Commander
Leaps short buildings with a single bound
Is more powerful than a tank engine
Is just as fast as a speeding bullet
Walks on water if the sea is calm
Talks with God

Squadron Leader
Leaps short buildings with a running start
Is more powerful than a bull elephant
Is able to avoid speeding bullets
Walks on water indoors
Talks with God by appointment

Flight Lieutenant
Can just clear a small hut
Is stronger than a bull
Can handle a gun
Dog paddles
Talks to animals

Flying Officer
Runs into buildings
Looks like a bull
Is not issued with ammunition
Can stay afloat in a Mae West
Talks to walls

Pilot Officer
Falls over door steps
Smells like a bull
Wets himself with a water pistol
Stays on dry land
Mumbles to himself

Warrant Officer
Kicks tall buildings out of the way
Leads bulls by their noses
Catches speeding bullets in his teeth
Freezes water with a single glance
He is God!

No sooner had I received my message and passed it on to Dennis McCann than I received an apology and was instructed by a senior officer to carry on with our original plans. As it was, the day turned out to be a resounding success apart from the fact that Bernie Winters decided not to play football but his brother Mike did and entered into the sprit of things very enthusiastically.

Another Double L club event that springs to mind was the Shag Connors and the Carrot Crunchers show. These were a great bunch of lads who did a wonderful cabaret act. They asked me would I be a stooge for them and when they sang one of their ribald songs they would chase me across the stage. I agreed and thought nothing of it and the show commenced. Half way through their act they came across to me and chased me across the stage to musical accompaniment. Doesn't sound much like an act now but there was a lot of cheering and booing, a bit like a pantomime. As I stopped in the wings they said, "If you don't mind dropping your pants we will run back across the stage chasing you again, only this time we'll be carrying your pants."

That worried me a bit because only three days previously I had had a vasectomy at the RAF hospital in Wegburg. As part of the pre-op I had to shave from my neck to my ankles and my delicate parts were encased in a pretty little net bandage that protected the stitches. I agreed to run back across the stage but with my back facing the audience. Shag Conners thought it hilarious when he saw the state of my lower regions. Fortunately, I managed to survive that show without too much embarrassment. I know of many people who have had a vasectomy but I think those of us who had the op at Wegberg in the 70s will remember the trauma associated with shaving every conceivable piece of hair from the neck down. The ward sister would inspect our shaven parts and instruct us to shave again. I think she thought we were all sex perverts and we only wanted the op to increase our sexual prowess. In my case, Anne had had two caesarean sections and was informed, wrongly as it turned out, that she could not have any more children.

The Army doctors at Rintel even considered a hysterectomy for Anne after Peter's birth. Another unforgettable experience relating to my chop, about a month after the op I had to complete a sperm test. I had to collect the sample bottle at the medical centre at 7.30 am and return it by 9am for onward despatch to Wegberg hospital. The medic told me in sick quarters that the sample had to be no more than an hour old. This meant I had to take the sample bottle to work, sneak into the toilet and do the business into the bottle. No sooner had I walked into the toilet than another fireman entered the next cubicle. In between passing wind and belching, he exchanged pleasantries. Then the tannoy called out Corporal Edwards report to the control room. Any pleasant thoughts I had soon evaporated and I had to respond to the tannoy. When I reported to the control room I came in for some abuse from a Sergeant Fireman (Terry Tate) for not responding quickly.

"You're all wankers," he said; never a truer word was ever said. I managed to return to the toilet after my little interruptions and tried again to at least put something in the sample bottle. By now the first aircraft sorties of the day were airborne and the toilet shook as they flew over the building. I managed to squeeze out a sample and return to the medical centre just in time to hand in my sample before the transport left for Wegberg hospital. I handed over the bottle to a medic, and at that moment two female medics who were on the committee of the Double L club came over and asked me," is that all you could squeeze out". "That may appear a little bit to you but it took me three attempts and a great deal of sweat and anguish just to get that little bit" said I.

Laarbruch produced its fair share of incidents for the fire section, both domestic (none aircraft) and aircraft incidents. One morning I was in the process of moving vehicles around for regular servicing when one of my mates called out, "Look at this Jaguar coming in to land…" All the crew looked and without any prompting they all ran to their respective crew positions. The Jaguar was about to land wheels up. Apparently this was a simple mistake by the pilot, who we were later to learn was the senior Jaguar pilot in the RAF. The aircraft crash-landed directly in front of the fire section and by good fortune it never caught fire. I suspect the pilot must have had a fair old shock when he realised what had happened. When the incident occurred I could only watch as the crew sped off, not being in crash kit, I was of little use. I did, however, have to collect back up vehicles from the MT section. The fire section also responded to any incidents occurring in the immediate vicinity; road traffic accidents, house fires and the like, but responses to such incidents depended entirely on the discretion of the Duty Air Traffic Controller. An aircraft about to take off or land had a higher priority and, given the fact that the aircraft were armed, possibly with nuclear weapons, then it was understandable. I remember one road traffic accident we responded to on the base. An airman crashed his car into a tree. Tragically he was killed instantly, sadly the autopsy revealed that he had consumed large quantities of alcohol just before the crash. Drink driving accidents were a common feature of RAF Germany. I have no sympathy for those who drink and drive but a death is a death for whatever reason. When I was at Gutersloh, living in our block of flats was a RAF Police dog handler. It was well known that he was a heavy drinker but he seemed to get away with it. Like most RAF dog handlers, they worked a nocturnal shift. Apparently his colleagues warned him that he was under surveillance and he went on night shift alcohol free. Rumour had it his dog attacked him not recognising his sober state.

During my Laarbruch tour I was detached like many others to Decimanarno, Sardinia. NATO aircraft used the huge bombing ranges located in the south of the Island. I was detached with my mate Bob Parr and we provided specialist fire cover for Laarbruch's, Buccaneer and Jaguar aircraft that were exercising there. There was an Italian crash combine but we provided specialist aircraft knowledge. There were literally hundreds of different aircraft using the ranges from many different NATO countries. Unfortunately or fortunately whichever way you want to look at it there was a fuel strike by the local Italian people and no aircraft could fly. Consequently, we spent the best part of the detachment with nothing to do. When you're away from home bereft of things to do boredom only increases the sense of separation and I was glad to complete that short detachment.

Laarbruch was only a few miles from the Dutch border and we crossed that border hundreds of times. On one occasion my sister, brother-in-law and their three children came for a holiday. I obtained the use of a windowless minibus and a few tents and off we went for a camping holiday in the Moselle region. It was a very pleasant holiday and we were returning home late at night. I stopped at the border crossing and produced all the relevant documents. The border guards asked me to open the mini bus. As they peered into the bus they saw cramped together five children, three adults and an assortment of camping equipment. Other guards were summoned and we were all asked to leave the bus while a thorough check of passports ensued. We must have looked like illegal immigrants. As a family, we camped in the Moselle valley several times but one holiday we all particularly remember went as follows. I was aware that the Nuremberg racing circuit was only a short detour off our route. It was common knowledge that you could drive round the track providing of course there was no race in progress. I was making my way back to Laarbruch in my yellow Ford Escort complete with roof rack. I took the detour and was way out in the country when I noticed a sign for the racetrack. I followed the sign and went down a little track and then I came out onto the racetrack. I must have entered the track at some remote entrance away from the main stand. I was quite pleased with myself chugging along on an internationally known racetrack when suddenly there was an almighty roar and two formula one cars passed by and then a whole host of racing cars flew by. There was indeed a race on and I was in the middle of it.

My son, Peter, thought it wonderful whilst Anne was terrified. Before I knew it I was driving through the main stand area, which was packed with spectators. Above the noise of the passing cars and the crowd I could hear, "Achtung Achtung" (danger danger) coming over the tannoy system. I drove right through the main stand area; I couldn't turn left or right as there were cars flying past both sides of me. As I came through the pit stop area I could see all sorts of flags waving at me and I managed to clear the track through the final pit stop exit. I was directed straight out into the car park and I must admit I have never felt so embarrassed. I parked as far away as possible and walked back to the track. As I mingled with the crowd I could pick up the general gist of the conversation and it was all about some stupid Brit who found himself in the middle of a Formula One race. I did mention it to a few of my mates when I got back to Laarbruch and within a few hours our exploits were common knowledge to all on base. During my Laarbruch tour, the station was awarded the much-coveted Wilkinson Sword of Peace. This must be one of the highest accolades any military unit can achieve. The fire section, however insignificant we may have appeared to many, played a major part in obtaining this award.

Not only did we provide assistance to the local fire service but also we played a major part in local community events and sporting activities. Once the Sword was received at the base, it was decided that there would be a big parade through the local area. Two very smart RAF policemen drove the RAF Germany Commander in Chief's land rover from Rheindalen and the vehicle was prepared to display the sword and lead the parade. I received a message from Dennis McCann that I had been selected to drive the vehicle, accompanied by a RAF Laarbruch, German Fireman, (Paul Recardt). I went to find the vehicle and speak to the two RAF Policemen and explained what orders I had received. They categorically refused to hand over the vehicle. I could only relay this message back to Dennis McCann and within a few minutes the station RAF Police Officer arrived and relieved the two Corporals of their vehicle. It was a wonderful experience driving the vehicle and being a major part of a parade of this nature.

All good things must come to an end and my three-year tour in RAF Germany was nearing completion. My Germany tour was both eventful and interesting. I particularly enjoyed Laarbruch; ironically, Anne preferred Gutersloh. I made many friends in Germany both amongst the local people and within the RAF community.

My family and I left Laarbruch on the 23 June 1978 and drove over night to our next posting RAF St Athan, South Wales. Twenty-five years after leaving RAF Germany, I travelled out to RAF Laarbruch for a fire section reunion, prior to the base closing. That was a wonderful few days and the hospitality and organisational skills of the firemen who organised the event and entertained us was first class.

7. Land of my Fathers ~ St Athan & Coningsby

I was familiar with the layout of RAF St Athan. I had been there twice before but this time I was accompanied by my family. We were allocated a nice little married quarter and had some really nice neighbours. Fire section routine was fairly straightforward and it certainly wasn't anything like the war footing we were always subject to in Germany. St Athan was a huge base in terms of area but little went on in the way of flying. Aircraft flew in for major servicing. However, in terms of the risk of fire there were many buildings that contained hazardous substances. In many ways, St Athan was no more than a collection of factories and training establishments. There were hundreds of civilian employees on the base, including several Ministry of Defence Firemen who worked alongside the RAF Firemen. There were big discrepancies in pay between the two, especially in relation to overtime and weekend working payments. Some RAF lads used to get themselves wound up about such things but it didn't particularly bother me. I could hardly fall out with the MOD Firemen; I had two on my crew, along with two RAF firemen.

The work of the fire section was mainly of a fire prevention nature. I had little in the way of major incidents whilst at St Athan but I had a particularly unpleasant incident. One evening we received an emergency call to the NAAFI. Smoke was seen billowing out of one of the television rooms. The NAAFI was a very large building with many hazards. On arrival, I sought out information regarding the exact location of the fire and whether or not there were any casualties. I soon realised that there was a smoke filled room and a search would have to be carried out. I instructed two of the crew to put on breathing apparatus and off we went to the fire ground. As we approached the scene, a group of trainees pelted us with snowballs. They obviously thought this very amusing; they wouldn't if they had ever donned a breathing apparatus. Inside that facemask, all sorts of things go through your mind. You quickly become disorientated and extremely hot. As you start to sweat, visibility becomes difficult and hearing and speech is practically impossible. You start to think to yourself whether you checked your apparatus properly when you came on shift and then would I have enough air to complete the task. The two firemen were about to enter a flame mass, unsure of what lay ahead, so to be pelted with snowballs was, in my opinion, a heinous thing to do. I radioed for the RAF Police and pointed out the individuals I saw throwing snowballs I wanted them charged but that never materialised. The two firemen entered the television room and the cause of the fire was a colour television. The fire was easily extinguished but the room was full of smoke. The two firemen used a cropper's bolt to remove the padlock and chain, which secured the television to the wall, and they were then able to remove the television and carryout a thorough search of the room. This was a very unpleasant incident but, on reflection, these were trainee Airmen; qualified and experienced Airmen would have reacted totally different.

St Athan was special in that my son started school during this tour. He would travel by coach to a small school in Barry, about nine-miles from St Athan. Fortunately there were no problems with school tears; Peter went on to the bus willingly and cheerfully. We understood from the teachers he was the same when he entered school. One winter evening, Anne was waiting for the school bus to return when a RAF Policeman arrived to inform parents that there had been a snowstorm and the children may not be returning home that night. As it was the bus finally made it through the snow and the children were none the worse for the delay. St Athan was a good posting in many ways for families. The beaches of the Gower Peninsular were not very far away and Barry Island was a pleasant enough place for a day out. My parents and Anne's parents visited regularly during our relatively short time at St Athan. Consequently, Peter and Christine were very familiar with their grandparents; some service families have little contact with their relatives.

During this tour, trouble flared in Iran, which is a long way from South Wales. However, many station personnel were placed on emergency standby. I watched as many of my mates were inoculated and kitted up for this emergency. I had only returned from Germany a few months previous so theoretically I was exempt this deployment. Normal practice states you had to be home at least six months before you could be put on emergency standby. I watched as busloads of station personnel set off for an unknown destination. Personnel were being transported to a holding station (RAF

Innsworth) near to Brize Norton airbase. This was in the middle of a bad winter, road and rail routes had been disrupted and consequently, personnel were deployed closer to the airhead.

Two days after the deployment I was sat at home watching TV with Anne when there was a knock on the door. I answered and there was an RAF Policeman informing me that I was to collect my things and go with him to the medical centre. Anne knew exactly what was happening; many of her friends' husbands had already gone. Off I went to be inoculated and checked out for any serious illnesses and I was transported to the holding place. When I arrived and stepped into the huge hangar full of military personnel, including RAF St Athan personnel, a huge roar came up. In my opinion that's all part of service life and I found myself a camp bed and blended in with everybody else. There were some moans during that ten-day standby period. Many of those deployed were support services and, unlike Firemen they were not used to a camp bed or a few discomforts. Firemen were quite used to these sort of situations, most of us had always worked shifts and could, when necessary, sleep on a clothes-line. I remember one Warrant Officer (an administrator) writing from his camp bed to his Member of Parliament complaining about the food. As RAF fireman we regularly ate food out of tins and at all sort of times. I did say to the Warrant that we could hardly expect silver service under the prevailing world situation.

I returned to St Athan and settled back into my normal family and work routine. One day I received a telephone call from my senior subordinate commander, a Squadron Leader Smith, asking me to report to his office. I had met the Squadron Leader a few times but never for anything of note. Off I went unsure why he wanted to see me and, on arrival, he had my record of service before him. He obviously thought it quite good. We had a long discussion about my future plans of which I was unsure. He suggested that I maybe interested in a commission. The thought of becoming an Officer had never ever entered my head. I was surprised, to say the least, but I quite liked the Squadron Leader; he seemed a pleasant down to earth fellow and I agreed to at least look at the process and what would help my possible application. Then he mentioned that he was looking for someone to take on the role of reporter for his squadron, someone who would submit articles for the station magazine. I could hardly say no and I became a news reporter and I quite enjoyed it. I was also asked by Squadron Leader Smith to pay a visit to the education centre and see what I could do about obtaining the necessary academic qualifications for a commission. This I did and I had a meeting with another pleasant and enthusiastic RAF officer, a Squadron Leader King (the station education officer). After that meeting I enrolled for my next set of RAF education examinations. These I duly passed and was considering undertaking O levels, when completely out of the blue; I was promoted to Sergeant and posted to RAF Coningsby. My commissioning thoughts and plans were put on hold. I now had much more important things to think about. We had been at St Athan only a year and we were on our way again. Another school for Peter and Christine, another home for Anne and for me a big step up; I would be a member of the Sergeants Mess and I was about to become an RAF fire crew chief on a very busy airfield.

Lightning nose-wheel collapse at RAF Coningsby.

Any newly promoted person arrives at their new job with a certain degree of trepidation. I was no different. As a newly qualified Sergeant, there is a lot to assimilate very quickly. For a start, there is the move into the Sergeants' mess; some would say one of the most exclusive clubs known to man and woman. There is a huge difference between life as an Airman or Junior NCO and life as a Sergeant. There is also a big difference between the Sergeants' mess and the

Officers' mess. Members of the Sergeants' Mess arrive there by dint of a lengthy service career and a fair bit of effort. Officers' Messes, meanwhile, accept the uninitiated both at an early age and bereft of any service experience, apart from the few SNCO's who aspired to Officer Status.

Without wanting to court controversy, in my experience a Sergeants' Mess is much more refined than an Officers' Mess and I have been in a few of both. Inappropriate language would be a mortal sin in a Sergeants' Mess, in an Officers' Mess it was not uncommon. Good behaviour and good manners are a must in the Sergeants' Mess; some junior Officers, meanwhile, behave akin to behaviour I witnessed when I was student at University. Childish pranks, wanton waste and stilted language are fairly common in some Officers' Messes'. What possible entertaining tales could a young Rodney (RAF slang for an Officer) have to tell his mess colleagues? Now a Sergeants' Mess member arrives at the hallowed sanctuary of the Sergeants' mess with a plethora of experience and amusing anecdotes. He or she will be respected by mess members who would have been through the same lengthy process, Officers' Mess members arrive straight from school, university, or straight off the street, so to speak. I have resided in many RAF Officers' Messes over the ten year period I was a RAFVR (T) Officer and I found them all bland, impersonal places similar to the new breed of fast food pubs. A Sergeants' Mess has character and charm.

I arrived at Coningsby as a new qualified Sergeant and was initiated into the ways of the Mess by my Flight Sergeant (George Masterson) and his lady wife, Pat. My dear wife also had to be introduced into the ways of the Sergeants' mess. After the familiarisation period, life in the mess was fantastic. We had some wonderful functions and were always guaranteed good company.

I do remember later in my Coningsby tour I was tasked to host a Wing Commander at one of the Mess formal dinners. This was a new experience for me and Anne but my early nerves soon settled when the Wing Commander informed me that this was his first ever visit to a Sergeants' Mess. As it was, he was a really nice person and once he overcame his early anxieties we settled down to an entertaining and enjoyable evening together.

RAF Coningsby fire crew 1980.

RAF Scampton – a fairly typical 1960s RAF V bomber fire section
(photo courtesy of Smokey Fairhurst).

Settling into my role as a crew chief (the term used to describe a fire crew commander) was much more difficult than settling in to the Mess. I knew when I arrived that there would be firemen at Coningsby who had served in the RAF a lot longer than me. New arrivals at any fire section can expect a bit of banter and good-natured ribbing; new NCOs could also expect similar antics. It's all about testing out the new person. I have seen NCOs arrive and start laying down the law as soon as they set foot on the section. We had one SNCO at Brize Norton who arrived complete with a whistle. He lined us up and explained to us all that one whistle meant this, two whistles meant that, and so on. As a crew we soon remedied his whistling. The next day we all came in with whistles and had a whistling competition. I knew I could possibly face some serious envy from the old sweats on the section but it never materialised, I think that was partly due to the fact that we were a very busy section dealing with real emergencies on a regular basis. I was also fortunate that the crew were well organised and well motivated. I was aware, however, that I had just left a relatively sleepy RAF station and was now at one of the few front line stations left in the RAF. Coningsby was one of only four, I think, QRA (quick reaction alert) stations in the UK. This meant the station operated round the clock all year round. Every aspect of the station was geared to ensuring the aircraft could be scrambled at a moment's notice. The station operated Phantom Aircraft, which was a relatively new aircraft for me. I had to learn very quickly the aircraft escape ejection seat, and armament systems. I also had to familiarise myself with the airfield and domestic sites, as well as getting to know my crew. The crew were keen to get to know me, especially as I was quite young for a Sergeant fireman; certainly much younger than the other three Sergeants already at the fire section (Sgt. Stamp, Sgt. Taff the fire Jones, and Sgt Pownall).

Almost the first day I arrived it was pointed out to me that the crew played five a side football and volleyball on a regular basis, "But you don't have to play Sarge", I seem to remember someone saying to me. "What time and where and I will be there", came as a surprise to some and I could hear little schemes being formulated as to what would be the best way to nobble the new Sarge. I met up with the crew at the station gym as arranged and I could sense the crew was planning a surprise attack on what they thought would be an unsuspecting old Sergeant. They had no idea that they had chosen a sport that I relished and, with all due modesty, was quite good at. Tougher, fitter and more devious footballers had tried to unseat me from my throne over many years and I had survived so far and had no intention of losing this little battle. I let the lads pick the teams and, as expected, there was a good team and a woeful team and I was in the woefuls. The game got off to a good start, they scored, my team lost interest and it was left to me to rally my team. We equalised and a few wild and malicious tackles came my way. The lads failed to realise that a wild tackle executed badly can caused injury to the perpetrator and, as each lunge came in, I side-stepped which caused them pain. They were also tiring much quicker than I and wanting to call time out but I insisted we played on till one team had scored ten goals. It goes without saying our team of woefuls won comfortably. Game over, all the lads were knackered and to their amazement I asked if anybody wanted to join me in a five mile run. There were no takers so I went off on my run and agreed to meet the lads in the Castle Pub in about an hour.

That was it, I had won over the hearts and minds of my crew and I was to remain their intrepid leader for the next two years. One of the opposition players was a fireman named Bowden who the lads all called Muppet. I took to Muppet very quickly. He was a lively, enthusiastic individual with a good sense of humour, ideal lad to have on a crew. Muppet failed to report for duty one day and failed to notify me with an excuse. This was, in my experience, a very rare occurrence. Two weeks went by with no contact and I was instructed to instigate the absence without leave procedures. In the first instance paperwork has to be generated and then I had to attend at his room with an escort and itemise all his kit and record it on a formal document. It is quite a laborious and impersonal task. Five pair of socks, three pairs of underpants, seven dirty magazines etc, etc. That done, shortly afterwards I received a telephone call from Mrs Bowden who informed me that her son was in a Hull hospital. He had just been diagnosed with a rare form of leukaemia and he had not long to live. She asked if he could return to his crew for the last few weeks of his life. After consultation with the appropriate people, it was agreed that he could return to the section but not travel out with the crew as we went about our emergency duties.

All the lads were heartbroken when I had to tell them the news. Muppet died about three weeks after he returned to work and as a crew we attended his funeral. At his funeral, so-called rough, tough RAF firemen were reduced to tears; it was so sad and something and someone I have never forgotten.

Life on the section was physically and mentally quite demanding. As soon as you accepted responsibility for the crew and handover was completed, you were totally absorbed in your job. I soon became familiar with the sound of the Phantom aircraft, any little change in engine noise and your mind automatically went into a state of readiness. As it transpired, the Phantom was my favourite aircraft apart from the Hunter. Even at the end of a long shift, every time I heard those now familiar sounds of a Phantom it gave me a little adrenaline rush. However, I never got those rushes when I was chasing one, or on full readiness for one returning with a malfunction. One of the more calamitous experiences I witnessed at Coningsby occurred when one of the Phantoms suffered a double utility failure, basically lost all power on take off. The aircrew ejected and the aircraft crash landed at the end of the runway. The fire crews responded immediately but, given that it was dark and the whereabouts of the aircrew was as yet unknown, Air Traffic Control instructed the crash combine to stop. The second MK 9 truck (Crash Three) drove straight into the back of the first Mk 9 truck (Crash Two). Both vehicles were written off. It was a catastrophic error. Fortunately there were no casualties except a hugely embarrassed fireman driver and his crew chief. Fireman drivers were always taught and constantly warned of the dangers of driving too close together and this was exactly the reason why. I was off duty when the incident took place but reported to work the following morning totally unaware of the incident. I was confronted with two broken Mk 9s and a dejected and demoralised crew. More importantly, I was left to deal with a tirade of very angry aircrew that could not fly because there was no fire cover. For many aircrews this was probably one of the few occasions when they were aware of our existence. It was not a pleasant day and it took a long time for the fire section to recover some credibility.

Every shift at Coningsby was eventful. Aircraft emergencies of all descriptions occurred on a regular basis. Engine fires, wheel fires all sorts of fires and suspected fires. Some incidents needed no more than a cursory check others could involve major fire fighting actions. Whatever the need, it goes without saying that RAF Fireman react to any emergency ready and able to put into practice well rehearsed action plans. If need be, firemen would enter a flame mass and attempt a rescue, however intense the fire or difficult the task. In my entire service career, I never met a RAF Fireman who questioned a decision or thought twice about his responsibilities at the fire ground. I knew a few who could moan and groan for England but never when at a state of readiness. I never personally knew of any RAF Fireman seriously injured in action but I have heard of several RAF firemen who were killed or injured on duty. It is a potentially dangerous job especially on a busy airfield working long hours and under great pressure. I remember one of my very first tasks as a crew chief was to standby for the RAF's last remaining Lancaster as it returned to Coningsby with an engine malfunction. I must have been a Sergeant only a few weeks and here I was on standby for a potential major disaster. As I gathered my thoughts and thought of possible actions, I was joined at the crash bays by the station commander. He obviously had concerns and anxieties similar to mine but, if things did go wrong, he would remain where he was whilst the crash crews deployed to the aircraft. As it was the aircraft landed safely and is still bringing great pleasure to thousands on its displays throughout the country.

One aircraft that did not land safely whilst I was at Coningsby was a RAF Binbrook Lightning. The aircraft was displaying a wheels up warning light and, after over flying RAF Coningsby, it was confirmed that the aircraft's nose wheel had not lowered. I understand that the pilot was given the option to eject and abandon his aircraft or land at Coningsby. He could not return to his own base because Binbrook was providing Quick Reaction Alert cover. We had plenty of warning of the incoming Lightning but there was little we could do but wait and see. As it was, the aircraft landed with its nose wheel up. The Pilot kept the aircraft nose up as long as possible and it was only when the aircraft was coming to a halt that the nose wheel dropped. We were in hot pursuit of the aircraft and, other than assist the pilot out of the cockpit, we had little else to do. It was an interesting experience chasing the Lightning and watching the sparks fly as the aircraft's nose scraped along the tarmac. I always remember the pilot's name, Squadron Leader Piper. As a fire crew we thought it was a remarkable feat of airmanship. I spent the best part of my days at Coningsby chasing real time Phantom emergencies and the occasional practice emergency. Not many RAF Firemen enjoy practice emergencies; especially those called by air traffic control. They were normally unrealistic, convoluted scenarios dreamt up by some fairy (air traffic controller) in their nice warm office. We were always open to criticism or suggestions that we should have done this or that but, when the bells go down for real emergencies, there was never anyone prepared to offer advice or assistance. Consequently we were left to our own devices.

I always remember one station exercise; we were deploying in the early hours of the morning to a Phantom that had just burst a tyre, a potentially dangerous incident. As we chased after the aircraft a vehicle tried to obstruct our route. I made contact with the individual, who informed me that he was a member of the station exercise team and he would report me for driving through a simulated bomb crater.

"Very sorry old chum", said I, (or something similar) "we are on our way to a real emergency and you were very nearly mowed down by the crash combine".

Life away from work was also very interesting and enjoyable. We had a lovely married quarter situated about two hundred yards from Tattershall Woods. Not many days went by without a walk in the Woods or a visit to one of the many local places of interest. Regular visits from Anne's family and my family meant we were never short of babysitters. Consequently we went out for meals quite often. I had also taken up playing squash, which became quite addictive at one time, and I was playing football again, both five a side and eleven a side. I would normally have a night out with my crew about once a month and there was the usual leaving do to attend. I was quite well known on the station, for my involvement in sport but I was tasked to train station personnel in defence support. I had completed the RAF Fire Service Light Rescue Instructors' course and was training station personnel in basic light rescue techniques. It involved a bit of first aid, casualty evacuation, basic fire fighting and a few knots and lashings. This was an interesting activity for me in that it brought me into contact with many non-firemen types. Personnel nominated for training were support trades suppliers, administrators and the like. They were not volunteers so there were the usual moaners and groaners. It was, however, quite a good training programme; lots of practical hands on work which most enjoyed and saw it as different from their normal routine. The DSU (Defence Support Unit) team had access to all areas on base. I would set up a practice scenario for them and they would get to work. They could set up hydrants, run out hose and many other essential tasks all, carried out in full view of other station personnel. They became quite a confident group and developed a good sense of camaraderie. Many became friends of mine and I would see them around the station or in Coningsby village, when the talk was always about DSU matters.

Another of my favourite pastimes was table tennis; I had played this as a lad at home with my dad. We never had a table as such but dad would set up our small kitchen table and we would play on that. I had played table tennis for a few years now in the RAF representing the section and wing at inter section competitions. While at Coningsby we had a thriving and very popular Station Commanders' Cup Competition. Sections competed against each other in several sports and, as ever, it was quite competitive. Fire section teams always did well in this competition, especially at volleyball, five a side football and table tennis. I remember playing table tennis in the competition and I was drawn against the administration section star table tennis player, a Squadron Leader. The fire section had received special permission from the Station Commander no less to play our volley ball and table tennis games at the fire section. We were, after all, unable to close like other sections. The table tennis star arrived at the section in his regulation shorts p/t kit and pumps. I went to the table dressed in my cumbersome crash kit complete with heavy-weight boots. He warned up with all the agility and aplomb of an international athlete and the game commenced.

He sent over a few good serves and I returned those quite comfortably and after a few rallies I knew I had the measure of him. I did have the distinct disadvantage of getting my thumb caught every now and again in my braces and I had one ear out for the aircraft taking off and landing not far from the section. If the bells went down I would have to respond with my crew immediately and therefore concede defeat. As it was, I went on to win the game and went to shake hands with my opponent but he was a very unhappy chappy and informed me that the venue was unsuitable. The noise of the aircraft put him off his game and he was going to make a complaint. I could have added insult to injury and perhaps mentioned to the Squadron Leader that I too heard the aircraft and was hardly concentrating on the game given my primary responsibilities. I never bothered but I knew he would get nowhere with his complaint. As it was, the station commander took a keen interest in the competition and he was very keen that the fire section took part. I remember the station Commander, Group Captain Sprent, who was a very affable gentleman, well known and popular with all the other ranks and

NCOs. All spoke very well of him and I remember meeting him at several sporting events when he would always take the time to and trouble to speak to all present. He was a fairly frequent visitor to the fire section and would have a chat with the lads. He retired during my Coningsby tour and was replaced by a Group Captain who went on to a very senior rank and I remember seeing him in the TV news several times. I cannot make any comment other than he was a totally different type of man and leader to Group Captain Sprent. Life at home; at work and play, was good. Peter and Christine were doing well at school; they had lots of friends and Anne, and I, were settled and content. Then, out the blue once more, a move!

Ladder slide practice RAF Coningsby.

8. Recruiting Duties ~ Stanmore Park & St Helens

Settled and happy as I was at Coningsby, I often thought about my future, not so much for myself but for my family. I had not considered any other career option but a twenty two-year engagement with the possibility of service till I was fifty-five. I still thoroughly enjoyed my job but was aware that I could not maintain the high level of fitness forever and I was finding periods of separation increasingly difficult. I was also increasingly aware that my two children were becoming very attached to their grandparents and relatives back home in Liverpool. Visits home meant contact with a whole host of relatives, who would in their own way, entertain or fuss over Peter and Christine and I could understand their delight at visiting Liverpool. I used to enjoy my visits home too. I occasionally thought of life after the RAF and I knew of many RAF firemen who obtained good, well paid jobs in the Middle East. It was somewhat ironic in a way; most of my RAF colleagues avoided the Middle East during their service but were quick to volunteer on their discharge – money talks I suspect. I often considered obtaining some academic qualifications but shift patterns and a relatively transient lifestyle more or less ruled that out.

In my opinion, life is a mixture of fortune, misfortune, good and bad luck and fate. As if by fate I reported for a night shift on Friday the 22 September 1980 to be greeted by a very solemn looking Flight Sergeant George Masterton. He took me into his office and as soon as I entered, I noticed my name had been erased from the nominal role board. "You're being posted", he said. I thought that couldn't be right. Only a few weeks previous I had contacted RAF records office and was informed that I could expect to remain at Coningsby for at least another three years. I was interested in purchasing a surplus married quarter at, Coningsby but, before doing so, contacted RAF records office. "Do you know where I am going" I asked. "No idea but you have to report to RAF Stanmore Park this Monday for an interview for recruiting duties". At that instance I thought there was no way I wanted to be a recruiting Sergeant and thought I should be able to convince the interviewer that too. George Masterson mentioned that both he and his wife (who worked in general office) had already made representation to the station admin people to keep me at Coningsby but they stated I had to attend for interview as instructed. Over that weekend I thought of nothing else but this forthcoming interview. I was determined that I would be able to convince the interviewer that I was happy at Coningsby doing the job that I enjoyed and was quite good at. I also had some reservations about George and his wife's interference; they really had no right to act as they did without first consulting me. Their motives were purely personal and quite selfish. However, I duly travelled down to RAF Stanmore Park. I attended for interview in Best Blue before a Squadron Leader Wilson.

He had a copy of my service record before him and, as he began, I interjected and, thinking I could save wasting his time and inconvenience, explained why I did not want to be a recruiting Sergeant. I remember the Squadron Leader was a very pleasant chap; he smiled and explained why I was about to start the recruiting course. He certainly had the upper hand; he outranked me but regardless of that, he stated I had been selected on the basis of my exemplary service record. All RAF recruiting staff are high calibre airmen and airwomen and that is why they are considered suitable for the recruiting role. That said, I tried another angle, "what happens if I fail the recruiting course?" With a very wry smile he replied, "all RAF SNCOS are expected to be able to complete the course. You are supposed to have the qualities and aptitude already if you fail the course you may well find yourself being discharged from the service". The matter was resolved. I was destined to return in a month's time to start the four-week, recruiting course. Prior to returning to Coningsby I was issued with a huge file containing pre course reading material.

I arrived back home, informed Anne and, as ever, in her own philosophical way, went about her everyday business of caring for our two children. I meanwhile concentrated on studying for the course and I still had a crash crew to manage until my day of departure. I set off for this new adventure very apprehensive. I was, after all, a robust, pragmatic fireman who was about to embark on a very academic course. I knew, or at least I thought I knew, my limitations and academic study was one. All my previous training courses had been of a very practical nature; I was in my element completing all my fireman courses. The light rescue instructor's course, lowering casualties from a hangar roof was easy for me. Likewise my breathing apparatus instructor's course was most enjoyable, although many firemen found this course very demanding and strenuous; on reflection crawling through sewers with a breathing apparatus on your back can be a scary experience.

On arrival at Stanmore Park I met up with the rest of the recruiting course which was made up of a Squadron Leader, Flight Lieutenant, Pilot Officer, Warrant Officer, and seven Sergeants from a variety of trades. I suspect we were all anxious and apprehensive especially after the introductory briefings from training staff. We were about to embark on a very intensive training course that required excellent presentation skills, good interview techniques and a thorough knowledge of the RAF selection criteria for all seventy ground trades and the officer branches. I probably felt less able than my counterparts; after all, they were officers and technicians and I was a simple fireman. However, my training although non-academic was all geared to confidence and assertiveness and a bit of bullshit. I soon found myself quite comfortable with the public speaking and presentational aspects of the course. Others found this a terrifying ordeal. I had plenty of experience in all sorts of public speaking situations but this was precision stuff with presentations assessed on content but timing was crucial. If we were tasked to complete a ten or a forty-minute presentation it had to finish spot on, an early or late finish, even of a few minutes, was a failure. The first casualty of the course departed for this very reason. We had not been in to the course but a few days and we were making our way back to the classroom when one of our group disappeared never to be seen or heard of again. We were told he had failed a presentation and was considered even at this early stage as unlikely to master that aspect of the course. Another colleague failed a written examination and he too was despatched to an unknown fate. Pressure was certainly on us and every evening would be spent revising or practising our presentations.

There was no time for merriment on this course and even if I had managed a few pints of a night I would have struggled even more in the classroom the next day. Also, as we soon learnt, the training staff would throw in some unplanned and unexpected exercises. For instance we returned from lunch one afternoon expecting a presentation from the staff only to find a note on our desks. Mine read, "you are based at a recruiting office somewhere in Britain. You have just returned from lunch and you have been tasked at very short notice to give a thirty-minute talk to a local school on engineering trades in the RAF. Your presentation will commence at 2pm". I had no time to prepare, I just had to stand up there and then and begin my presentation. Others in the class were also given similar topics and I remember coming to the lectern composing my thoughts and commencing my presentation. As I looked at my audience I realised that they too would have been given a topic to speak about and would be mentally preparing themselves for their presentation. They would not in the least be interested in what I was saying; I could have been talking gobbledegook. However, training staff were listening and watching very intently to what I was saying and how I was saying it and of course the presentations were always recorded on video.

During the early stages of the course, I was instructed to give a twenty-minute presentation on a topic of my choice. I chose to present a stretcher lashing demonstration, something I had done both as a lecture and practical exercise. I obtained a stretcher and rescue rope and placed them near the lectern. I walked to the lectern did my introduction and a short spiel and then moved away from the lectern to commence the practical demonstration. As I moved away, I could hear the gasps of disbelief come from my colleagues. At this stage of training most students clung on tight to the lectern as some form of comfort zone. I did warn the warrant officer that I would select him as the casualty and I laid him on the stretcher and commenced the demonstration. Having secured him to the stretcher, I then pulled out a large safety pin and went to pull out the casualty's tongue. In theory when you secure a casualty to a stretcher he or she is unable to move and there is a danger they may swallow their tongue. We were taught that in a real emergency to prevent the casualty from swallowing their tongue we would have to secure the casualties' tongue to their lip by means of a safety pin. As the dear old warrant officer lay on the stretcher I explained to the class that I was now about to place the safety pin through the casualties tongue and into his lip. This, I said, was a practice very familiar to all RAF firemen and quite painless.

The poor old warrant went a very whiter shade of pale and the training staff went much the same colour. I went on to say that, on this occasion, I would not demonstrate that practice but I did turn the stretcher upside down and leant it against a wall just to demonstrate how secure the casualty was. As the course progressed, I gained in confidence and despite those pre presentation flutters, I enjoyed public speaking. In later life as Chair of the Liverpool Duke of Edinburgh Award Scheme and the Officer Commanding Liverpool Air Cadets, I regularly made speeches at Liverpool Town Hall, the two Liverpool Cathedrals and St George's Hall not to mention many other lesser venues. Then there are my Court appearances as a Probation Officer. Many of my Probation colleagues are terrified of entering the dock and giving evidence, I meanwhile, have no hesitation in making a short or long address to the Court. I never learnt those skills during my lengthy Probation training (three years) but I learnt those presentation skills during that four-week course at Stanmore Park. As well as the public speaking aspect of the course, equally important was the ability to interview, assess and write up an account of the interview.

This is a very difficult skill to learn and we were required to master this skill very quickly. We were fortunate that the training staff knew their subject material and they would demonstrate good and bad interview technique. We would also watch some training videos and then commence our own interviews; initially we were tested amongst ourselves. We were given a script and that formed the basis of the interview. There was little room for deviation; we were required to obtain essential information and trained not to waste too much time on irrelevant information. It was relatively straightforward at first but raw recruits were brought in for us to interview. Once again all interviews were recorded and there would be a lengthy debrief highlighting any good or bad techniques. All interviews had to be completed within forty minutes and the write up was also timed another forty minutes. We were not allowed to take notes during the interview; according to the textbooks, this is not a good technique as it spoils the flow of the interview. It is very hard work not taking notes and trying to remember all that was said but as soon as we qualified we all took notes and referred to them when completing our write up. All candidates for RAF service had to meet six criteria. Those came under the following headings; socially acceptable, trainable, adaptable, reliable, trustworthy and satisfiable. Each criterion had its own key components and, all the time, you were assessing whether the candidate met the six criteria.

Some criteria were relatively straightforward. If an individual had a dislike of the Police or authority, then that was normally a reason to reject. Likewise, a loner or unhygienic individual was unlikely to be accepted. Nebulous areas included drinking habits, girl-friend/boyfriend situations and financial state. The most difficult and problematic was the satisfiable criteria. If an individual was over-qualified and applying simply on a whim, then that was a major cause for concern. Believe it or not, we had to decide whether the candidate would be happy in their chosen trade. All questions had to be open ended; who, why, what, when, and where (the five W's). Any direct questions and that constituted a failure with all that entailed. We were also expected to show no emotion, be friendly, and sympathetic but remain objective. I carried out my first professional interview twenty-five years ago and here I am now still interviewing almost every day and I'm using the same technique learnt at Stan-more Park.

These days I either write reports for the court on individual of-fenders (Pre Sentence Reports) or a variety of other criminal reports relating to risk assessments. I use the same technique and style in all my interviewing and it appears to work well. I have interviewed just about every type of offender from the murderer, the psychopath, the paedophile, the rapist etc and I always ask the five W questions and never show any emotion. I have to cringe sometimes especially when listening to a remorseless account of an awful offence. In my civilian life, I have witnessed the most appalling interview techniques. Some probation colleagues I have known always use direct questions and many ask and answer the question at the same time or offer excuses for the offender's behaviour. Without doubt, the two big stress factors in Probation and Social Services are report writing and attendance at Court. Ironically they are two aspects of my work that I still enjoy. Social work colleagues will have had minimal training on interview technique. During my two-year Diploma in Social Work course at Liverpool University I had one rather pathetic hour-long session on interviewing skills. Those course colleagues absent that day (about 50%!) all qualified without any input on that subject matter. Not only do most Probation colleagues find interviewing stressful but also the writing up of those interviews is another trauma that induces unnecessary stress and subsequent sickness.

Anyway, I was making good progress with my recruiting course. I'm reluctant to say I was enjoying it, as there was the omnipresent fear of that sudden tap on the shoulder that meant failure. Although the course only lasted four weeks our working day went from 8 am till about 10pm. We had to constantly rehearse our presentations and interview technique and then when I went to bed I would cram some theoretical information. The one break in this gruelling programme was a Wednesday night five a side football game. Staff verses the trainees. This was a staff generated activity and I remember Squadron Leader Wilson was a keen footballer. It would be fair to say that when I commenced the course I was probably the quietest member of our group perhaps somewhat in awe of my colleagues. However, as soon as I stepped on to the five a side court I was in my element and this helped to improve my confidence within the group. I remember my very first kick of our very first game I volleyed a ball at the staff goal, one nil in the first few seconds and we never lost a game during those four weeks. Those games were a wonderful respite from the gruelling training programme. Sport in any arena is a great leveller and particularly in the RAF. The course was drawing to a close and we were preparing for our final examinations. We had to complete a forty-minute presentation, an observed interview and the written examination. I chose to give a presentation on the history of association football, another chose to give a presentation on squash ball warmers, which was very funny another chose war games. All trainees, along with an invited audience, had to sit through all the presentations.

We would draw lots to see what order we would present and it was really difficult trying to remain attentive during another's presentation. All the time you were rehearsing in your head your own presentation totally oblivious to what was being said by your colleague. We did however plant questions so we had to remember when to ask the question. The final day duly arrived and those of us still standing were given our pass marks and more importantly our new posting. I received very good marks and was later interviewed by Squadron Leader Wilson who informed me that I had excelled in all aspects of the course. He went on to say that my relative shyness and lack of confidence was an initial cause for concern but they were

impressed with my resilience and "transformation". Words of encouragement and kindness go a long way and I have never forgotten
that man and in the years that followed I always sought to encourage
and praise others. I was posted to the RAF Careers office in, St
Helens. I have no idea why St Helens, but off I went back to Coningsby to inform Anne that we were on the move again, our sixth
move in the sixth-year of our married life.

Staff from the Liverpool and St Helens RAF recruiting offices.

St Helens is located about four miles from where my parents were
living and about the same distance to Anne's parents. This was a bit
of a disappointment to both sets of parents they were used to spending their holidays with us. However we were to see our parents
almost on a daily basis and this proved very important during Peter
and Christine's formative years and our parents later years. I had to
set off for St Helens on my own, leaving Anne behind once more to
sort out our married quarter. I would travel back on a Saturday
afternoon and return to St Helens very early on a Monday morning.
One of my brothers had recently bought his own property and I
moved in with him and his family. I was initially offered a married
quarter at RAF Haydock but when I visited the site I was not impressed. The RAF camp had closed but "headless families" were still
using the married quarters. This was a military term for service
families that had separated for whatever reason; death, divorce or

desertion comes to mind. The dependant relatives were effectively of no fixed abode and were accommodated at these rather sad places. I visited the quarters and was quite shocked at what I found. Houses were covered in graffiti; gangs of local youths and men preyed on these isolated, very vulnerable people.

RAF recruits from St Helens.

The residents that I spoke to all told me varying degrees of appalling stories. I refused to take over a married quarter on that site and was summoned to Warrington Army barracks to be addressed by a Major who insisted I take over a surplus quarter at Haydock. I refused and contacted my own superiors and an RAF Officer came out from MOD to hear my complaint and view the married quarters. Shortly after that visit the Haydock married quarters were condemned, the houses demolished, the land sold and the families remaining re housed. I regularly pass the site of the old married quarters and think what may have happened if we had moved in alas; we never did and justice was done. I was still separated from my family and tried to obtain a married quarter at RAF Burtonwood but that was closing down. Anne suggested we consider buying a house, just for the three years we were expecting to stay at St Helens. Within a few months of that suggestion, we moved in to our own, three bedroomed, mortgaged home in St Helens.

The enormity of moving my family from the relative security and safety of a RAF married quarter patch in rural Lincolnshire to one of the most socially deprived areas of the UK never crossed my mind. I was totally unaware of what lay ahead, especially for my family. I had a new job, once again working fairly long hours, but it was quite interesting and I was still very much in the RAF, working with RAF colleagues.

More RAF recruits from St Helens.

I noticed a big difference in the type of work I was doing but I was quite preoccupied planning for the next interview school visit and a hundred and one other things. Anne and our two children meanwhile were taken away from the RAF world, their friends, school and were effectively in a very different environment. Anne had no RAF neighbours who were generally supportive to each other no wives' club and none of the every day gossip that permeates through married quarters. Peter and Christine were moving away from their own circle of friends and, significantly, they were changing school. I encountered no personal difficulties assimilating myself into a civilian community but I had some advantages. Most people in the country had a high opinion of the RAF; consequently wherever I went I received a favourable reception. I was issued with a RAF car with the words RAF Careers emblazoned on the side. I parked the car at home (the security situation is very different now) but, having said that, late into my recruiting tour a RAF careers vehicle was booby trapped and the car exploded killing the RAF Careers Sergeant who I knew.

RAF Careers St Helens staff.

People of all ages were keen to stop and talk to me, elderly people would want to talk about their war time experiences in the RAF, others would stop and ask me about a relative in the RAF and occasionally a young person would ask me about RAF careers. I was visiting schools, colleges, and careers' conventions throughout the region, including the Isle of Man. I was participating in Town shows throughout the Northwest with the occasional overnight stay in North Wales and the Isle of Man. I was then a very busy person and there was quite a good social side of recruiting duties. My poor family meanwhile was coming to terms with their whole New World.

Author, Geoff Glover, Dave Ashcroft OC 969 (St Helens) Air Cadets, Jim Abbott.

Anne was happy to be in her own home with her own furniture and able to paint and decorate at will. We had a small garden and could lay seeds that we would see sprout and I'm pleased to say we had good neighbours and our parents were only a short bus ride away. Peter and Christine meanwhile had moved to a totally alien environment. For a start, St Helens people have an accent and dialect all of there own. My two children had an accent familiar to most service children who had moved around with their parents. In other words Peter and Christine spoke quite "posh", at least that is what people said who spoke to them. I still had a noticeable Liverpool accent, not the Cilla Black version or the Harry Enfield version but most people knew where I came from.

Some St Helens folk have a tangible dislike of Liverpool people, who get the blame for crime and disorder that took place within a hundred miles or so of our wonderful city. I was generally accepted, probably because of my job, and people would say, "you're not a proper scouser", which I am. However, Peter particularly was coming in for some ridicule and as one becomes familiar with child behaviour, children can be very cruel. Anne and I took a keen interest in all that was happening at school and the teaching staff all thought Peter a "wonderful" boy. How he coped during those first few months must have been difficult for him but he seemed to be settling down very well. On reflection, even from a very early age, Peter had been very good at sport, especially football. The infant school had a football team and Peter went more or less straight into the school team and became and remained captain of his junior school and senior school football teams. I often thought how Peter was coping at school and with his new peers and it came home to me one evening when I was just arriving home.

We had a small park just at the end of our road within sight almost of our house. As I passed the park I could see a large group of young children who were surrounding two small boys who appeared to be fighting. Being the upstanding citizen I was, I stopped the car and went over and in the middle of this melee was Peter and another young boy fighting. As I asked what was going on Peter said, "it's alright daddy I'm only play fighting." Peter, in his naivety, and innocence really thought these children were play fighting but they were in fact testing him out. Most children were unaware who I was and, being in uniform, some probably thought I was a Policeman. They stopped fighting and I let Peter remain where he was while I went home, changed and came back in my sports kit and every evening I was free I would organise football games at our local park. My mate from the RAF Careers, Jim Abbot, would also come across to the park and he and I would pick the teams and play sometimes twenty or thirty aside. Jim was a bit of a novelty to the kids, with his strong Scottish accent he generated a lot of interest amongst the children. Parents would come over to watch and then I would rope in some parents to play and this became a regular feature of our time at this address. I obtained football bibs from nearby RAF Sealand and we would play tournaments usually Scotland v England with Jim and I captaining our respective countries. I was at this time relatively fit and was still doing the odd five-mile run. All this activity helped Peter settle into his new home. Although new to the area, we became well known very quickly. Peter soon had a good circle of friends who all knew his Uncle Jim and myself from our football activities. Peter also joined the local cub pack. I became involved in this activity and enjoyed the lads and dads weekends away. Christine, on the other hand, was much quieter than Peter but she settled down quickly and became a member of a local brownie pack and joined a local dancing school, which she enjoyed. She was also very close to Peter. They were regularly seeing their grandparent's, aunt's, uncles and cousins and I think this helped them settle in to their new life.

My posting to St Helens meant this would be Peter's sixth school (including nursery) and he was only seven years of age when we moved. That is a very disturbing feature of service life and, given my preoccupation with my career, I gave little thought to the possible impact this may have upon Peter's maturation. As a matter of note, Peter did well at school, went to University and captained the English Universities' football team at Wembley Stadium in 1996. Peter is employed as an estate agent in the West Kirkby area of the Wirral. An area familiar to those who may have passed through the old RAF recruit camp at West Kirkby. Peter's actual schoolwork was at a lower standard than that which he was undertaking at his school at Lincolnshire, consequently, he stagnated for a bit. I was not aware of this but Anne was and she was always asking for homework, which was not always forthcoming. Before long, we were very settled in the community, we used the local swimming pool, parks and gardens and frequented the library quite a bit.

Work for me was very interesting and satisfying. I used to enjoy basically all aspects of the work, the general enquiries, testing, interviewing, and processing of applications. Our office consisted of two Sergeants, a Sergeant Victor Borg and I and a Corporal, the renowned Jim Abbot. We had an officer in charge who was based in the Liverpool RAF careers office and he or she came to our office about twice a week. We were a friendly little team and Jim and I became very good friends, as did Anne and Jim's wife, Sharon. Victor Borg was by trade a Steward and had spent most of his service on VIP and Air stewarding duties. Many servicemen who work closely with or work directly for senior officers tend to adopt their characteristics, either by design or default.

Vic Borg could quite easily speak like the rest of us and then if he saw fit he could speak as though he had a plum in his mouth. Jim and I often thought that Vic thought he was a class above us and the candidates applying for service but we could both deal with Vic easily enough. We would wind him up in the usual service banter style. Ironically when Vic retired from the RAF he became a financial advisor and the Tory councillor for Birkenhead. Both his job and his community activity were right up his street and well done to the man but I would never let him deal with my finances and he would never get my vote. When I arrived Vic was the SNCO in charge, which meant little really, as the main man was Jim Abbot, our administration corporal. Jim made all our appointments and allocated the work, which we all shared equitably. Our day started at 8am, we would have a batch of ten candidates to test at 9am, mark the papers and then give out the results. That alone could be a difficult start to the day telling some hopeful candidate for service that they had failed. Often parents were waiting in reception, which further compounded the bad news. Those who passed the aptitude test were sent off for a medical. On their return, we would check the scores from the doctor and that again could be a difficult and sensitive time. If a candidate failed the medical we would have to inform them.

We never knew why they failed, we simply looked at the scores on the medical envelope. Most came back from the doctor with a score of two or three but a score of four meant they had a medical problem that rendered them unfit for service. We had to advise them that they had to contact their own doctor, who would in turn have to write to our doctor. It was very sad on some occasions; often we got to know the candidates and their families quite well and it fell to us to tell them that they failed the medical. That is never an easy business but it goes on every day in most military recruiting offices. Those who had passed the test and medical were shown several RAF videos, usually of the trade they had applied for, and given a briefing of what to expect at interview. An interview date would be set and references sent for. We usually did what we called one long interview a day and wrote that up. Amidst all this routine work we had lots and lots of phone calls and general enquiries. Most days one or two of us were out of the office completing a school visit and then of an evening we visited all sorts of youth and community groups either showing a RAF recruiting film or undertaking a presentation. Tuesday was always attestation day. The successful candidates, some of whom may have been involved with us for a year, were now at the end of the process and formally joining the Royal Air Force. Parents were invited and the boss would travel over from Liverpool and conduct the small but very important ceremony. We would change into best uniform and attend to all the paperwork and attend the attestation. During my tour at St Helens, I once estimated that I must have been involved with over a thousand young people who joined the RAF from the St Helens office. Bearing in mind that it averages out that for every candidate, who actually enters the service, there are a hundred who apply and are not successful. I must have interviewed many hundreds of young people who applied for RAF service. Prior to commencing recruiting duties I had never spent any time at a desk. My RAF career had been spent jumping in and out of huge fire trucks in all sorts of weather and at all times of the day and night. I was now very much desk bound and into a reasonable daily routine. At least I could go to the toilet when I wanted and eat my meal at leisure. As an RAF fireman we were constantly interrupted, accidents and emergencies always took precedence over domestic matters. Despite my early doubts about this type of work I was enjoying the work, I was also more in contact now with others who were not firemen and not connected to the military. I toyed with the idea of night school and when I suggested it to Jim he decided to enrol as, did Vic. All three of us enrolled at St Helens technical college Jim for GCSE economics; Vic geography and I went for sociology. Jim used to say, "you cause a fight George, Vic you select the location and I will sort out the financial implications". As it was, we all passed our chosen subjects and the RAF also paid our course and exam fees.

This was my first foray into further education and I was thirty years of age when I obtained my first GCSE. The following year I enrolled for two GCSEs English and geography and the same for the next couple of years. I did Law GCSE and found this both interesting and easy to assimilate. It reminded me of my fire service examinations when we were required to cram masses of information; once the exam was over most was forgotten. The law exam is taken in two component parts, the criminal law exam and the law of torts exam. I remember sitting the criminal law exam and thinking to myself I had done very well. The following week I had to return to sit the tort exam. Well the night before the tort exam we had a leaving party for one of the recruiting Sergeants at the Liverpool careers office. Tom Dunleavy was one of the all time RAF characters of his generation an, MT driver by trade, a native of Glasgow and a loyal member of the Orange Order. He used to drink in Liverpool City centre with all sorts of characters and he looked very much at home amongst some of Liverpool's finest. His do arrived and we obtained the services of a kiss 'o' gram that came dressed as a nun. When she arrived, Tom initially thought she was a nun and I had brought her and he made a beeline for me.

"See you, you do-gooding bastard, why have you brought her". Just as he was berating me, the woman came over, and, in a flash, Tom said, "Listen Miss, I never invited you so please leave and take him (me) with you". The woman lifted her skirt and Tom disappeared underneath, we laughed as we heard his ripe language and when he re-appeared her clothes disappeared and she chased Tom around the room with whips flaying.

The next day I had to be at college at 9am for the tort exam. I duly arrived, registered and opened the exam paper. My mind went completely blank and all I could think of was last nights shenanigans. I couldn't answer one question, and by ten past nine I was ready to leave the exam room. I thought, that's it, a failure, but when my result came I had obtained a grade 'C', I must have done very well in the criminal law exam. Tom is also remembered for a passing comment he made to an enquirer. A young man called in to the Liverpool Careers office and asked about officer careers. It was Friday afternoon and Tom was eager to get away. He asked the enquirer if he had been circumcised. "Why do you ask that", to which Tom replied, "because you have to be a complete prick to be an officer in the RAF". On the Monday morning, Tom was reprimanded. The enquirer had returned home and told his parents what happened. His father just happened to be a retired senior, RAF Officer.

We used to have some great times at our Liverpool office parties. There was a local Police station just a few yards away and there were always a few Policemen drinking at our office bar and a few other invited guests. Jim Abbot was another great RAF character. A talented sports person who played cricket and football to a very high standard and he was also a member of a local bagatelle team (a St Helens form of bar billiards). Jim could also knock back a few beers and entertain all and sundry with his interesting and amusing stories. Jim and I developed a good stage double act, almost telepathic at times. We became quite good at entertaining our audience and could adapt our act to different age groups and organisations. We were often asked to talk about the RAF at Round Table dinners, civic functions and the like. There was no end of people who would ask questions or relate stories of their time spent in the RAF. I remember one time we were at a function at The British Legion in Wigan. We showed a film depicting life in the modern RAF and then gave a brief talk about RAF careers before retiring to the bar. I was engrossed in an interesting discussion when an elderly Wigan gent interrupted and in a very stern and distinctive Wigan dialect stated, "I can never forgive you Sergeant for what you done". As ever, I remained polite, and asked him in a nice way, to explain what I had done wrong. "Burma 1943, you never came back to collect us". It transpired he was in Burma and was awaiting RAF transport support, which never came. I was unable to convince him I was not even born in 1943.

We were always highly susceptible to provocation. Militancy in the Merseyside area was rampant. The miners' strike was at its height, there was civil unrest in Liverpool and other areas in the country and there was still a big CND protest. Individuals would ask the most politically loaded question and rather than enter into an argument, I would always decline to comment. Jim, however, would rise to the bait. Jim lost a brother, murdered whilst serving in Northern Island with one of the Scottish Regiments. This deeply affected Jim especially, when he had a few beers and talk turned to terrorism. Jim had very strong political views, somewhat different to mine. None the less, he was entitled to his views but, as servicemen, in the public eye, we had to keep them to ourselves. In the early part of our tour we put up a marquee at the St Helens show. The largest free show in England apparently. This was a huge event, attracting thousands of visitors during the three-day event. There was a huge military presence, bands, fly past, paratroopers, etc. The council however, was keen to disassociate themselves from the military and in the end the military withdrew and went elsewhere. In our marquee we set up a beer tent and when the show closed for the day we opened our bar. All perfectly legal and non-profit making but we had some wonderful parties involving show people, military personnel and many others.

The late Fred Dibnah, a well-known TV personality who in those days drove a steam tractor. Fred frequented our bar and I remember him saying to me, "don't you know me, I'm Fred Dibnah, I'm famous". No disrespect to Fred but I replied, "I don't know who you are and I bet your not as famous as that man other there" (Jim). With that we watched as the various visitors came into the marquee and I said, "let see who says hello to Jim and who says hello to you, Fred". Everyone who entered the tent went straight across to Jim and greeted him. Fred conceded defeat.

I organised Jim's leaving do when his tour ended. I was given free use of the St Helens cricket club and a free buffet. The guest list included two previous Mayors of St Helens, doctors, dentists, a few dozen Air Training Corps staff. All members of St Helens cricket club, his bagatelle team, football team, bin men, road sweepers and I managed to contact several airman and women who Jim had helped join the RAF. It was a memorable night. I gave the first of about ten speeches that night and each speaker had nothing but the highest praise for Jim. He could certainly walk with Kings yet still retain the common touch could Jim Abbot.

Life at the office was never the same without Jim, but life goes on. Our next office Corporal was the antithesis of Jim. Chris McCoy had no sporting interests or social life; his only interest was collecting comics. Whereas Jim and I would happily accept an invitation to talk to the community about the RAF, Chris had to be encouraged and consequently lacked the enthusiasm that makes for a good public speech. Vic Borg also moved on and in his place came an RAF Policeman also called Chris; if I gave out his surname he would probably sue me. This individual was without doubt an outstanding RAF Policeman destined to go far in his trade. He too was selected for recruiting duties, apparently RAF recruiting staff were all selected on the basis that they were the very tops in their trade. Consequently the public and candidates were speaking to NCO's who were knowledgeable, presentable, and "sensible". Royal Navy and Army recruiting staff were, at that time, all retired personnel. There is a huge difference between a top RAF Policeman and a good recruiter, for a start we had to be civil and polite to all we spoke to, we were, the public face of the RAF. Chris had come from a very sensitive RAF Police job, I never quite knew exactly what he did, he refused to speak about it and I never bothered to ask. Chris saw every non-, RAF police person as an enemy of the state and a potential insurgent. I would pass the interview room and observe Chris interrogate a terrified candidate. He would slip back to techniques used during his RAF Police training and those were certainly very different to those taught on the recruiting course. I would have to remind him we had a totally different role now. Chris tried desperately to get off recruiting duties, without success. His wife remained in a married quarter, a hundred miles or so from St Helens consequently, he completed the whole of his three-year tour residing in the St Helens YMCA. Sad to say but the YMCA is a bit of a den of iniquity, full of all sorts of delinquents, drug users and ne'er-do-wells. Despite that, none of them ever made any contact with Chris, god help them if they did.

After Jim and Vic left the office, it was my turn to start preparing for my next posting and a return to my trade. By now I had become heavily involved at night school and began to think very seriously whether I wanted to remain an RAF fireman for another twenty years with all the turmoil that entails. Anne was extremely happy in her own home; the children were settled in school and had their own little after school activities and a good circle of friends. I was at the nineteen year stage in my career and I could either apply for service till I was fifty five or come out after my twenty two year engagement. I thought long and hard and sought Anne's advice, but, as ever, she left it up to me. Throughout my RAF career Anne never once complained about my job, or the RAF way of life. I decided I was going to come out after twenty-two years and notified the RAF authorities. I was entitled to apply for a last tour of duty. This was accepted practice, subject to the exigencies of the service, of course. I applied to complete my last tour of duty at the St Helens Careers office and I am pleased to say it was approved. We did have an excellent record at our small office; we were in fact putting almost as many recruits in to the RAF as some of the big city recruiting offices, with five times as many staff. A small caveat was included in the agreement and that was that I completed a tour of duty in the South Atlantic. That seemed a reasonable offer to me, but I was worried about being separated from my family. Either way I knew separation was inevitable, but this seemed the lesser of the two options. Prior to setting off for my six months away from home, there were many domestic chores I had to sort out. Not least I was involved in a dispute with the local authority regarding the secondary school I was supposed to send Peter to. I had visited this school many times and was not at all happy with it. I obtained detailed information about school academic results, and this school came bottom of the pile in the Merseyside area and that probably meant that it came bottom of the pile nation-wide.

I made an application for Peter to attend another St Helens school, which was just out of our local area. That application was rejected. I contested the decision and appeared before a tribunal. This was no more than a formality and I knew that the decision had already been made. I was informed that it was appropriate to send my son to the local school and I could almost read the thoughts of the tribunal panel. All but one were local councillors. Who is this silly man who thinks his child should be treated differently to others but I was different, I knew how bad the school was and how good the school I preferred was. We had even put our house on the market with the intention of moving into the school catchment area. The councillors in their collective ignorance thought they could make a party political broadcast to me and tried to explain the virtues of comprehensive education. I was in no mood to listen to their drivel and explained to them my own experience of a comprehensive education. I left the tribunal having lost the first round of this my biggest ever challenge. Although wounded I would fight on and letters went off to the Prime Minister, Education Secretary and the individual councillors. I had no need to write to the one panel member who was not a councillor and that was the school Head Teacher; Brother Victor. I had during my recruiting days visited Brother Victor and his staff many times. His hands were to an extent tied but he knew how determined I was to ensure a place was obtained for my son at what I knew to be the most appropriate school for him. I wrote my final desperate letters just prior to my journey to the Falklands. When I arrived at the Falklands, amongst the pile of letters waiting for me, was a letter from the local authority, Peter had been accepted for West Park School.

9. South Atlantic Bound ~ RAF Stanley

Distance is nothing it is the first step that is the most difficult.

This was without doubt a difficult and demanding tour of duty not least because I was going away from my family for five months. I had often spent periods of time away from my family but these were short detachments and various training courses but never of this length and in these circumstances. My son, Peter was ten, and my daughter Christine, was eight years of age so they understood I was going away from home and would be absent for some time. I did discuss the situation with Peter and Christine individually and I had asked Peter in a very adult way to look after his little sister and his mum while I was away. I know Peter took his responsibilities very seriously and I think this helped him manage while I was away. I was, however, worried how Christine and Peter would manage during this relatively long period of separation from their dad. They had the wedding of their cousin (also a member of the RAF) to attend and Christmas was on the horizon. I knew there would be difficult times for them and indeed Anne.

In service married quarters it is the norm, almost, to see families without a father figure. He would be serving overseas, but it is a bit different when you live in the civilian community. As ever the time comes around when you must pack you bags and depart. Another of my favourite singers is the late, great, Ray Charles. His classic, "Oh its crying time again your going to leave me I can see that far away look in your eye," aptly sums up the moments leading up to separation. Even, the toughest of individuals, must feel a tinge of sadness when they say goodbye to their loved ones for a long period of time. I was no different, but I knew if I treated my departure with calmness and ambivalence my family would react in a similar manner. That was my plan but as soon as I lost sight of my family I was overcome with emotion, especially as Christine was clearly upset and the expression on Peters' face as he tried to act as an appropriate adult upset me more. Still to this day, I remember Peter trying to hold back the tears as he comforted his sister and his mum.

If ever I were asked by Sue Lawley, to be a guest on her Desert Island Discs show, Harry Neilson's song, "Without You" would be my number one choice. My number two would be Stevie Wonder's "I Just Called to Say I Love You", which was a Christmas hit in 1984. my number three would be John Lennon's classic, "Give Peace a Chance".

The journey to the Falklands began on 7th September 1984. Arrangements were made for our office Corporal, Chris McCoy, to collect me at 6am that morning. Knowing Chris McCoy as I did, I half expected him to arrive late so I duly telephoned him at 5.30am, sure enough, he was still in bed. However, we set off for RAF Innsworth arriving at 9.30am. One may think why I have such an accurate recollection of this journey and the subsequent tour; well I kept a diary, here before me now. One of my great regrets is that I never kept a diary previous to this episode, but so be it. On arrival at Innsworth there were literally hundreds of servicemen and women arriving at the same time, being kitted up prior to being bussed across to Brize Norton. After a few hours at Innsworth we set off for Brize Norton. There was nothing to do when we arrived at Brize other than check in and await our flight, there was nothing laid on for us either. In all my service days I had never really gone hungry but there was no meal at Innsworth and no meal laid on at Brize Norton. The drinks and sweet machines were emptied very quickly and all and sundry were complaining about the lack of food. Our flight departure time was 10pm, I left home at 6am and it was now 7pm and I had not eaten since 6pm the previous day. It was serious business, although hunger pains do, to an extent, take away the pains of family separation. I had allied myself to a group of SNCO's and officers who were equally ravenous. "My MP will hear of this", some said, however my breathing apparatus training came into play and I thought it best to conserve energy, say nothing and think only of the meal I shall devour once airborne. Fate plays many tricks and, as I sat listening to the increasing complaints, from nowhere I heard someone calling me. "Hello Sarge", said, SAC Michael Marner. Michael was a young airman well known to me, a Liverpool lad who I had processed his application for RAF service. It took him a few years to enter the RAF due to changing entry scores and his weight problem but, to his credit, he stuck at it and here he was a fully-fledged cook at Brize Norton. "Hello Michael how's your mum and dad," who I knew socially. "I'm pleased to see you fulfilled your ambition". "How are you Sarge" he said. "Well Michael excusing my language but I could eat a scabby dog". "I'm the duty cook," said Michael. "Can't you feed us." "But, Sarge, there's hundreds of you." I thought that was the end of the matter but, he gave me the nod, as they say in Liverpool and I followed his head signals. Out of earshot he told me he was under strict instructions not to feed any of the transiting personnel, "but you can have my tea if you want". "Well that would be very kind of you Michael" and off I went to make my excuses to my new acquaintances, most of who were now in a comatose state.

The Uganda – rust bucket or Queen of the South Atlantic?

I made my way to a secluded spot in the kitchen and enjoyed a wonderful steak, egg and chips. I did feel somewhat guilty but later that night, I was the senior RAF Firemen on board the departing VC10. I may well be required to assist in any emergency that was my conscious cleared.

We departed Brize at 10pm stopping at Dakar (Senegal) at 2am. After a brief refuelling stop, it was off to Wideawake airfield on Ascension Island arriving there at 7am. No time to admire the volcanic island of Ascension, we were all airlifted by Chinook helicopter to our transport to the Falklands, the SS *Uganda*. Sat out in the harbour was this rather rusty looking ship. I had my doubts whether the vessel was seaworthy but she was, and she had an air of impregnability and that calmed my fears. I was allocated to my cabin and my roommate was a Royal Engineer SNCO, a nice chap who didn't snore flatulate or talk in his sleep admirable qualities in a roommate. All SNCO's were given an hour or so to store kit and then present themselves for the inevitable briefing.

The Uganda (starboard side).

There was an air of apprehension and excitement permeating throughout the ship after all we were about to embark on a journey into the unknown. However after several briefings including one from the Ship Warrant Officer (SWO) it soon became clear that this was no jolly. Once the officer core left the briefing room we were addressed by the SWO, a wily old soldier, who made it plain he wanted no problems during our journey. As well as several hundred service men onboard there were also a hundred or so civilian trades-men and labourers who were going to build the new airfield at Mount Pleasant and a group of women cleaners. The SWO informed us that all the labourers were recruited from a job centre in Glasgow, there were no police checks carried out so it was highly likely there might be some unsavoury characters amongst them. We were told that the accommodation for the other ranks was unsuitable and unpleasant so there could be some dissent amongst the troops. As I was to find out, the other ranks, which were mainly Scots Guardsmen, were provided with a five-foot bed (a leftover from Uganda's days as an educational cruise ship for children).

We were informed there was a guardroom complete with cells; there was a weapons locker, and a makeshift morgue. It was indeed a very sombre briefing. After the SWO's stark briefing, he asked for volunteers and read out a list of duties that had to be undertaken. There was a short pause after the SWO read out the comprehensive list before asking for volunteers. RAF Senior NCO'S are not renowned for volunteering; consequently there was a gasp as I volunteered to supervise the evening bingo sessions. I had previously had some experience of organising bingo sessions at RAF Laarbruch and I thought it better to volunteer rather than be coerced into some other duty, which is exactly what happened to my colleagues. Once the briefing was completed I was asked to remain. I was informed by the SWO that as I was a RAF Fireman I would, along with the other RAF Fireman on board, have to assist the ships' crew in the event of a fire. No problems with that and off I went to sort out the first bingo session, which was to take place in a few hours. We sailed from Ascension that night at 6.30pm.

The bingo session became a main feature of our journey not least because all the women on board attended and that was sufficient motivation to encourage the few hundred men away from their respective bars. The first few days of our journey were relatively relaxed. Yes, we had a few fire drills, man overboard drills, air attack drills and we had to undertake compulsory PT; which I also volunteered to supervise; but we were in a tropical climate, wearing khaki drill and it was relatively congenial atmosphere. We would be averaging 300 miles a day, and each day, I could feel the temperature dropping, the sea swell rising and the atmosphere intensifying. The closer we came to the Falklands the closer we came to a possible air strike from a renegade Argentinean pilot. Rumour had it that there was a cadre of Argentinean pilots who had lost family members during the conflict and they were prepared to launch a kamikaze attack on the Uganda; a nice thought before retiring for the night. However, we ploughed on through the South Atlantic seas, heading for the infamous Roaring Forties. I remember one night, half way through our voyage; we were bouncing about more than normal. I was calling out the bingo numbers and there must have been a swell of thirty feet or so. The Uganda creaked and groaned and I could see apprehension on the faces of my audience but the show had to go on. The SWO was there in his usual pristine appearance and stoic demeanour and, whilst he remained there, unperturbed, all was well. That night I remember a dream and in my subconscious I thought I was on the Big Dipper at Southport fair. When I awoke I knew I was not on the fair, but in the middle of a natural Big Dipper; 'The Roaring Forties.'

The journey continued amidst heightened tension, more drills, more PT and more rumours. Despite my secondary duty I still had to take my turn as, 'Troop Deck Sergeant'. This entailed visiting the troops at meal times and listening to their complaints, which I thought were legitimate. Ironically, the Army and Navy lads made few complaints but the RAF lads were not slow in coming forward with their complaints. There really was a huge difference between the living conditions for the other ranks and the Officers/SNCOs. We travelled as first class passengers at a cost someone once told me of £2000 per first class passenger, great news for P&O shareholders. We enjoyed silver service facilities in the mess, excellent room service and bar prices that were ridiculously low.

Mind you, the other ranks never criticised our standard of living. I think that is in part, because they knew that all SNCOs in their day, had been other ranks. Although, the vast majority of passengers were Scots Guardsmen, there was quite a large contingent of RAF lads and a small contingent of RN lads. The RN lads adapted very quickly to conditions onboard the Uganda and I suppose for those lads it was a pleasant enough journey. It was the RN lads who suggested we introduce crab football into our PT activity. For those not familiar with crab football, two teams of any number play it. The players have to squat, place hands behind their back and then chase a football. It is quite arduous and physical but it is ideal in small, confined areas. The matelots were expert at it, and also very competitive. Inter service rivalry quickly developed and the SWO thought it a good idea to introduce a knockout competition organised by, yours truly. I played for the SNCO's team but cunning and tenacious as we were, we were no match, for the physical prowess of the younger teams, and were eliminated in the early stages of the competition. As ever, in service sport, of any level, there was a hotly contested final followed by an equally boisterous celebration.

Another sporting activity on board the Uganda was table tennis and I played this sport every day during the voyage. It was a bit like, the pub pool table, syndrome; the winner stayed on. In all due modesty I stayed on for long periods of time and could in the right frame of mind hold my own at table tennis in most company. Again a table tennis competition was planned which like the crab football competition attracted a large crowd. Rumour had it that bets were being placed on who would come out the winner. I had, over a few days, played just about all the military personnel and I thought I was in with a chance. I progressed through the championship and made it to the final. In the final I came up against one of the ships crew; I'd never seen him at the table prior to the competition and he came in as a wild card, so to speak. Well, he battered me five games to nil and I could see his civilian counterparts delight as they collected their bets. Nevertheless, I thoroughly enjoyed playing table tennis in the South Atlantic seas. Dealing with motions of the ship, as well as the opponents rallies, made the game a bit more exciting.

A less energetic activity, a game played regularly by RAF Firemen is a card game, called Good Morning Jack. I introduced it to my circle of friends and it became popular very quickly throughout the whole Ships Company. To play the game you deal out all the cards face down. Five or six players, is an ideal number, although you can play with a minimum of two. Players lay the cards down individually turning them over in the centre of the players. If a king is turned over players have to salute, a queen players bow, a jack players shout good morning jack and for the ace, players place their hand on the card and for the ten, one has to stand up. Sounds simple and straightforward but some players can get completely muddled, especially if played during a drinking session. Some would stand for the king, salute the jack, etc and it is quite funny to see some of the antics, especially if you have a slightly nervous player. Before long the Uganda reverberated to the words, "Good Morning Jack" and the heated disputes as teams argued who was last to act. The winner by the way, is the person who legitimately got rid of all their cards first. I was quite chuffed, in many ways, when I heard the old Navy chiefs playing the game; once again the RAF fire service made a valuable contribution to a service activity.

On a more serious note, life on board the Uganda was becoming quite tense. We had permanent lookout duties, more fire drills, abandon ship drills and you could sense the tension increase as we drew closer to the Falkland Islands. Gone went our tropical kit and we were now wrapped in foul weather gear and only the hardy went on deck. Another interesting feature of the journey was the appearance of Arctic Terns, a bird then, like most others completely alien to me. Many years later, having developed an interest in ornithology I was on holiday in Northumberland. There is up there, one of only a few breeding places for Arctic Terns. Apparently, they lay their eggs and, when hatched, set off on an epic journey south, something like 8000 miles. There are a group of volunteers who, during the nesting period remain on site, protecting the eggs and baby terns from predators. I was speaking to a few of theses dedicated individuals and one asked if I had ever seen an Arctic tern before, he was positively elated when I said I had seen then in the South Atlantic Ocean.

Our journey was nearing its end and, during my Orderly Sergeant rounds, I came across a civilian worker, unconscious on deck. I commenced basic first aid whilst summoning the medical officer who took the man to the sick bay. I was informed later through the grapevine that the man had died and his body placed in a makeshift morgue in the galley. That was never confirmed but situations like those remind you of your own mortality. We arrived at Stanley on 21 September and prepared to disembark. Rather than an airlift off, a small landing craft did the job. I was notified that I would be in the first party to disembark and off I went; another memorable journey safely completed. On arrival at Stanley Harbour there were a collection of fire vehicles on view. I made my way over and the RAF Fireman Sergeant I was relieving, he handed over the crew to my control and, departed very quickly to embark on the Uganda. I was taken to the fire section, changed into crash kit and no sooner done; we were deployed onto the runway to standby for a Phantom aircraft recovering.

Stanley airport.

RAF Stanley fire crews and RAF Regiment staff.

RAF Stanley – the road to work.

Author at the British Forces cemetery San Carlos.

Argentinean soldiers' dugout, somewhere in the Falklands.

F4 about to land RAF Stanley Mk 9 and crew waiting.

Phantom refuelling in the South Atlantic.

C130 (Airbridge) going home.

Troops accommodation, RAF Stanley -The Coastels.

Larry Teague and author Tumbledown mountain.

End of a lovely days walk somewhere in the Falklands.

Falklands scout group receiving their scout firemen's badges.

The Falkland Islands only fire truck..

Phantom engaging the RHAG – RAF Stanley.

I remember distinctly the air traffic controller calling for the crew commander over the radiotelephone and for a few seconds I unintentionally ignored the message until one of my corporals nudged me. "They're calling you, Sarge". Prior to mounting this MK 9 and taking my position in the front passenger seat, I hadn't been anywhere near a fire truck for the last four years. Yet here I was, operational on one of the busiest airfields in the RAF. The atmosphere in those first few days was quite surreal. Aircraft of all types were flying around the airfield and there seemed to be none of the usual order and circuit patterns associated with normal RAF airfields. Each aircraft type had its own coded call sign and, without disclosing any state secrets, a Phantom for instance was a Goose, a Hecules an Albert and the extended Hercules was a fat Albert, a Harrier, a jumping bean and so on. These call signs allegedly, were designed to fool the Argentinean spies, but I'm sure it didn't take long for their agents to break this code. In addition to the situation in the air there were the remains of shot up Pucara aircraft all over the place, bomb craters everywhere including the famous crater left by the bomb dropped by the Vulcan. We used that crater as an emergency water supply. There was generally a tense atmosphere about the place akin; I would say, to a battleground, a bit of a cross between Mash and Apocalypse Now.

That first shift was a very difficult experience; I had no introduction or familiarisation, it was straight to work on what is a physically and mentally demanding occupation, certainly a bit different to the time just spent on recruiting duties. I literally survived that first shift by the support provided by my crew. Having said that, you can take the man out of the fire service and give him a nice desk job but you cannot take the fire service out of the man. The core fire service tasks remained the same but this was a strange airfield, surrounded by minefields, peat bogs and other obstacles that could seriously jeopardise the task. Added to those difficulties the Phantoms carried live weapons and I mustn't forget that other Falklands factor, the f.....g weather. If the wind was coming from the south west, (South America) it could be quite pleasant, however, the prevailing wind was normally a south easterly (South Pole) and it was usually wild and raw. As the shift continued into the evening then night and early morning, I was truly knackered. Only the night before on the Uganda I had enjoyed a first class meal washed down with a nice bottle of

Chardonnay, yet, here I was with a few sandwiches, eaten between deployments. I remember being very cold, damp and mentally exhausted. It is hard, at the best of times; listening to radio messages in a moving fire vehicle, on a windswept airfield, but messages such as, "proceed to the eastern alpha two geese and a fat Albert inbound" was very confusing for this Sergeant Fireman. When we did deploy to the Phantom aircraft it was always a RHAG engagement (Rotary Hydraulic Arresting Gear). The Phantom always engaged one of the five RHAGS on the runway. If the hook missed the first, it would then engage one of the remaining RHAGs, or in a dire emergency, it would engage the barrier. RHAG deployments had to be a very slick operation by the fire crews. Phantoms always operated in pairs; consequently when one landed, the other was never far behind. There really was no margin for error. Such was the importance of this task, on each of the two fire crews were two technicians whose sole purpose was to ensure the RHAGs were serviceable 24/7. We used to call these technicians, raggies. They were very much part of the fire crew and followed the crash combine wherever we went, our own groupies. When the Phantom hook engaged the cable, the crew deployed to their pre determined positions and commenced the rewind.

My job as the crew chief was to approach the aircraft and give instructions to the pilot when to release his brakes and when to move away once he was freed from the cable. On each side of the runway were the rewinding drums. I would signal to the firemen controlling the drums when to start and stop the rewind. Signals had to be clear and succinct and responded to immediately. If one drum rewound too much it could pull the Phantom off the runway and into the peat bog; not a nice thought, especially when there are other aircraft in the circuit waiting to land and with no diversion airfield for thousands of miles. Signals were given by batons during the day and illuminated wands at night. Voice messages were out the question, given the noise of the Phantom engines and prevailing weather conditions. On some occasions when the winds were particularly strong, when I approached the Phantom I would take two firemen with me. Each would lay at my feet (not in exultation) and hold on to my legs as I passed instruction to the pilot. Another regular airfield task included disconnecting the RHAG cables from their drums and dragging them off the runway whenever the Hercs' landed or took off.

There was a risk that the cables could become entangled in the Hercs' double wheel bogie. This was a physically arduous task often carried out in appalling weather conditions and with great urgency. The cable could be covered in snow, or ice, or both, but the job had to be done and very quickly at that. Then finally, at the end of a long shift, it was the fire crew's responsibility to place the denials on the runway. This entailed collecting some dilapidated refuelling bowsers from MT and driving them onto the runway. In theory the denials, according to those much higher up the system than any fireman, would deter any Argentinean Pilot from landing at Stanley airfield and causing damage. From that first shift I was never happy with this situation; we were not checked out to drive these vehicles and they were almost obsolete and not roadworthy.

It was a task carried out at the end of a long shift and, prior to the first aircraft departure in the early hours of the morning, they had to be removed from the runway and returned to MT. My main complaints about this exercise however was the fact that it took my crew away from their fire trucks and, in the event of a Phantom scramble, we had to remove the denials asap otherwise the aircraft could not take off. As soon as I could, I made my protestations to the senior air traffic control officer (SATCO), who listened to my complaint but thought it best if we carried on with this established practice. Then, early morning one the Phantoms were called to readiness and ordered to scramble. Two Argentinean aircraft had been picked up on radar and were seen to be heading our way. As the Phantoms sat on the end of the runway desperate to get airborne, I received a message from one of my crew that one of the denials would not start. Nothing unusual about that I thought, this is not the first time this has happened but there was an incursion of the Falklands, no fly zone about to happen and the Phantoms were effectively grounded. It was with a sense of satisfaction, when I told all the crew to deploy to the troublesome denial and she was unceremoniously pushed of the runway into the bog, never to be seen again and that was the last of our denial task.

My first shift completed, I made my way to the Coastel to my allocated room, showered, had breakfast and then commenced my arrival procedure. I met my boss, a Flight Sergeant Fireman (Ron Laughton). I was surprised to find I had been put straight on shift even before I had 'arrived'. I was soon to learn that the flight sergeant had already formed an impression of me before we met. He was not pleased with the idea of a recruiting sergeant taking over one of his fire crews. He simply thought I was a shiny, with no experience of crash crews and, he more or less, abandoned me to my fate He never took the time to find out what experience I had; he had formed his own impression, before even setting eyes on me. He made no effort to welcome me and, putting me straight on shift with no familiarisation or briefings was a potentially dangerous thing to do. It didn't particularly bother me; I had confidence in my own ability as a RAF fireman and I had previous experience of managing fire crews, which I don't think he ever had. It is not unusual in the RAF fire service to come across SNCO's who had spent no time on crash crew duties; some specialised in fire prevention work, or had seen service on small domestic units. The fact that I was selected for recruiting duties and later detached to Stanley was not of my choice, but as ever, I got on with it. The flight sergeant and I did not become friendly but I saw very little of him and he was hardly likely to interfere with my role as a crew commander. The crew I assumed responsibility for consisted of three corporals, eight airmen, and the two Rhaggies. They had obviously spent some time listening to the flight sergeant and, being firemen, they sensed an opportunity to usurp my role and attempt to run the crew, as they wanted. Consequently, I had a few points to make clear. I upset straight away a couple of the louder members of the crew, one of who went to see the flight sergeant to make a complaint. It was an issue to do with operational efficiency, I was right, he was wrong and that was the end of the matter. I made my point and the rest of the crew soon realised I was no pushover; I had not travelled all this way in miles, and years, to be undermined by a few bullies. I informed the crew that I was no shiny but a fire crew chief that would not tolerate bad practice. The message got through, although I knew I had a lot of work to do to bring the crew up to the standard of previous crews I had managed.

Like it or not, once you take up your position on a fire crew, of any size, you have an awesome responsibility. You are there primarily to save lives and to deal with a multitude of incidents, some catastrophic, some more mundane. You become part of a jigsaw, a missing or broken piece and that jigsaw is useless. Those first few weeks on crew were not very pleasant. I didn't know any of the crew consequently my reputation was not known to them. They knew I had been on recruiting duties for the last four years and had no idea of my previous crash crew experience. I was effectively starting from scratch, all over again. Being a fire crew commander in the RAF is a wonderful position to hold. You have total control of the management of the crew. The everyday issues relating to training, morale, welfare, motivation, and deployment rest entirely with the crew chief.

When a fire service crew is responding to an incident there is rarely another in a position to offer advice or assume responsibility. An RAF fire service crew, in my opinion, is a direct reflection on the crew commander. Poorly turned out crews, lacking in enthusiasm and personal pride in what they do, will no doubt be managed by an ineffective leader. On the other hand, a crew of lively, enthusiastic individuals, keen to develop their skills and knowledge, is more than likely to be managed by an effective leader. One is taught the theory of management during promotion training courses but to complement that training one has to have observed the many good leaders who exist in the RAF. I had, by this stage in my career, met many bad leaders. Conversely, I had worked with some outstanding ones. They probably didn't know it themselves but they were the positive role models who I strived to be as good as: Bob Burns, Steve Davey, Paddy Fleming, Dennis McCann and many more. As a crew commander one soon learns the skills of management; how to get the best out of your crew, how to make the less able feel important and how to put down the bullies.

During my recruiting days, I completed a course of further education, which I found most enjoyable and rewarding. Sociology was one of the O levels and A levels I sat and passed. Whereas I have little time for those who use sociology degrees as a means of obtaining well-paid employment, I found the scientific study of human group dynamics extremely interesting. A fire crew is often strange set of human beings. For a start they are all relatively fit, robust, fearless and run the risk of losing their lives in the course of their duties. The vast majority of firemen are not by nature academic but they are not without intelligence. Those who aspire to promotion will need to obtain academic qualifications and maintain a high state of physical fitness. Many firemen are extremely well motivated and see their job as a vocation or the fulfilment of a long-held ambition.

Others can become disillusioned; lack of promotion opportunities and, in the RAF fire service, a lack of incidents can present problems for some. An RAF fire crew leader is in a unique position. By the very nature of the job he is required to train, motivate and then lead his crew into action. He is also responsible for their general welfare and is expected to participate in crew social activities.

In the military, social and sporting activities play a crucial role in maintaining morale. I also believe that a happy and fit crew is more likely to be an efficient crew. Managing a crew who are a long way from home has its own particular problems. I had always been keen on sport and liked nothing more than a sporting event with my crew and then a few beers afterwards. It was very different, though, at Stanley. In the first place, we never had a full day off throughout our detachment. Duty finished at 7am and we were back on duty the following morning. A drinking session followed by an early start the next morning was out of the question. Some lads were prone to the occasional binge drink, but being seen inebriated was a chargeable offence and carried a £400 fine. I did attend a 'bring your boss' function in the NAAFI one night, but it was a bit of a damp squib. I left early and reminded the lads before I left that we were on duty as normal in the morning.

One thing I did do while I was in the Falklands was organise hill-walking activities, initially just for my crew but after a while I used to organise a Sunday walk and take my mates from the sergeants' mess out for a walk. These were usually day workers and Sunday was their day off. In a way I was very fortunate. I could obtain a four ton truck, collect packed lunches and had permission to go basically anywhere on the island. As a Sergeant Fireman I needed to know the local topography – after all, an aircraft could go down anywhere on the island and we would be required to respond. I also needed to know the location of the many minefields scattered around the place; some very local to the airfield, others dotted round the island.

After only a few days on the island I briefed my crew that I was planning a day's walk to Mount Tumbledown, which is about half an hour's drive from Stanley. The climb was only 2,000 feet. I could only ask the lads to volunteer and although there were a few moans all but one of my crew agreed to participate. The normal procedure for coming off shift was to breakfast, shower and then kip until about 3 or 4pm. I couldn't adjust to this system; if I slept till 3 in the afternoon I couldn't sleep at night. I got into a routine of breakfast, shower, potter about, write my letters, went to bed about 9pm and then up at 6am. In a further effort to motivate my crew I agreed to drive to Tumbledown. I had, therefore, the extra task of collecting the vehicle from MT and then collecting the packed lunches.

We departed for Tumbledown at 9am. Weather conditions were, as ever, changeable and depending which way the wind was blowing we would either be very warm or extremely cold. The walk went well; I knew some of the history of the battle that took place there and explained what I knew. The lads bonded well and I thought it was a great opportunity to get to know my crew better and for them to get to know me. We returned to camp about 3pm, time for a shower and lunch before settling down for the night. The next day, the lads were full of our walk, telling the off-going crew of their antics, and I felt a sense of satisfaction at seeing the crew so animated. The Flight Sergeant, however, was none too pleased. He thought I should leave the crew to their own devices when off duty. He soon changed his tune when OC Regiment Flight came out with the crew on one of our walks. I was present as he told the Flight Sergeant what a wonderful day out he had had with Sergeant Edwards and his crew.

Throughout my tour, I did a walk on average, twice a week and did all the well-known battlefields – Wireless Ridge, Two Sisters, Longdon and Challenor many times. I never tired of my walks, although some of the crew did. After a few weeks I became an acknowledged hill-walking guide. All sorts of people would telephone and ask if they could come out for a day with me. I had no problem with that, but my crew always had first call for any walks. On reflection, it was quite a responsible task, taking up to twenty people on a day out into quite difficult terrain. Most were seeing a minefield, close up, for the first time.

Talking of minefields, near the end of my tour there was one walk I had been planning to undertake for some time, Mount Lowe. Sunday 6th December was the big day. My party consisted of senior NCOs from most sections and my mate, the Station Commander's personal assistant, Sergeant Chris Ellis, was also in the party. Mount Lowe is across the other side of Stanley harbour, so I needed transport to convey us across. I duly arranged for a motor launch to be at the Stanley jetty for 9am. I not only collected a four-ton truck to take us to the jetty but also a wonderful packed lunch from the mess. (one of the party was the SNCO in charge of the mess, so I'm not surprised we had an excellent lunch to look forward to.)

By now I was feeling very confident on the hills and expected no problems. We arrived at the jetty and there was a very young Army coxswain waiting to take us on the twenty-minute trip to Sparrow Cove. Off we sped, with sea spray all over us, and were taken to a beach to disembark. Within earshot of the entire group I confirmed with the coxswain where we were on the map and he agreed we were in Sparrow Cove. I gave him instructions to pick us up here at 3.30pm and off he sped. I took a compass bearing on Mount Lowe and I thought we may be a degree or so out but visibility was good, I could see the summit of Mount Lowe and off we went.

Sunday 6th December 1984 the author en route to Mt Lowe.

About twenty minutes into the walk we approached a minefield fence. I had, by now, seen many minefield fences and knew exactly what they looked like, but this fence seemed very different. Normally as you approach a minefield fence you see a clearly visible metal plate attached with the skull and crossbones symbol and the words '**beware mines**'. As I approached this fence I could see the metal plate but there were no words on it. I was slightly concerned as we approached and as I came alongside the notice I leaned over and saw the skull and crossbones and the words 'beware mines' *on the other side*. We had just walked through a minefield! Instead of being dropped off at Sparrow Cove we had been dropped off at Hell's Kitchen, which, I was subsequently to learn, was the most active minefield on the Falkland Islands. More sheep and cattle had been blown to pieces there than at any of the other minefields. Fortunately, I didn't know that then as I led the group over the fence and into relative safety.

To this day I have an abiding affection for penguins. When I left the coxswain earlier in the day I noticed a 'penguin walk' and chose that as my route away from the beachhead. I think it was that penguin walk that saved our lives. None of the group displayed any outward signs of fear, but they, like me, were no doubt feeling those same flushes of panic as were realised what had happened. As with all my hill walking activities, I carried a radio and a spare. I radioed in to the operations centre intending to explain our situation and seek an airlift back to Stanley. This was the one and only occasion that I could not make contact with the operations centre. On other occasions I would regularly call operations and some of the remote listening stations on the mainland but we were on the other side of Stanley harbour and there were no listening stations. I was in a dilemma but decided to continue with the walk and then I would have to work out some sort of plan to get back to the pick-up point.

Clearly I could not return through the minefield. We carried on, reached the summit of Mount Lowe and whilst sat up there I was struggling to work out a way of meeting with the coxswain at 3.30. We commenced our descent and the only solution I had was to follow the minefield fence round to the sea, where I would have to wade out and attract the attention of the coxswain as he made his way into Hells Kitchen.

We followed the fence and, come half past three, I could see several motor launches approaching our location. We were spotted, picked up and whisked back to Stanley. I realised that I would need to make a report and I could sense that something was already afoot by the large number of personnel and motor launches present. Nothing was said on our return to Stanley but on arrival back at Stanley Harbour I was told the harbour master wanted to see me, urgently. I dropped off my party and drove down to meet him. He came straight to the point and lambasted me. "You could have killed a lot of people today. Do you realise what you have done?" Then came the bombshell: "Why did you tell the coxswain to take you to Hell's Kitchen?"

"That's not true," said I. "I have my witnesses who can confirm that I asked the coxswain very clearly if we were in Sparrow Cove, to which he replied that we were." I then had to go to Military Headquarters and appear before the senior military personnel on the island (BIFFI), who again asked me why I gave the coxswain that order. I was informed that there would be an inquiry and off I went back to the coastel. By now it was early evening and I was physically and emotionally drained. I had completed a twenty-four hour shift, only that morning, rushed around getting transport, packed lunches, completed a mountain walk and then had the very blood drain out of me ... but there was more to come. By the time I got back to the coastel, word had spread and people were shouting, "have you heard about the RAF fireman mine detector" and mimicking a minefield clearance technique (i.e. walking backwards with the mine detector in front). The coastel tannoy system continuously called for me to telephone so-and-so. My boss came to see me. Fortunately I had a new Flight Sergeant, Chic Bebb, a much nicer guy than the other, and he thought it very funny. But I couldn't, at the time, see the funny side. "Well, George, I always said you had golden bollocks and you could walk on water. Now I'll have to call you no bollocks."

An enquiry duly took place; I was interviewed by the Military Police, as were all my party. It was proven that I never gave the instruction to the coxswain to enter Hell's Kitchen and apparently there had been a major breach in Army procedures. The coxswain was apparently newly-arrived (an FNG – Falklands New Guy), unfamiliar with area and should never have been allowed to travel on his own. There was a clear breach of procedure and I understand the

Army NCOs tried to cover up this highly dangerous cock-up. It transpired that several Army personnel were charged and fined for their behaviour. As for me, it took me a while to get over the shock but I was soon back on my walks but remained on the Stanley side of the harbour.

During those first few weeks in charge of my crew, I observed very carefully the crew dynamics. Some found this disturbing; others, no doubt, found it interesting. Even within a fire crew there's a self-created hierarchy system. Fireman drivers, for instance, consider themselves superior to non-drivers, crash one driver will consider himself to be very important, while crash five driver may feel at the bottom of the pile.

During those early days, I put into practice my interviewing skills. This caused a bit of a stir and I could hear mutterings within the crew. "Why does Sarge want to interview us?" Once those early anxieties disappeared, the crew, as most people do, responded well to being interviewed. I found out about their family situations, their anxieties, hopes and aspirations, strengths and weakness and quite often the roughest, toughest, fireman is a big softie and behaves in an inappropriate manner simply because he thinks he has to. Since promotion I have always been one to accentuate the positive in all my subordinates. Any good work, no matter how trivial, I would always either write to the individual concerned or mention during the daily crew briefing. After most incidents I would debrief the crew. I was, of course, also required to complete end of tour narratives, which I took very seriously. I would always remind the crew that I could only write about what I saw.

The shift system was very demanding; we started duty at 7am and finished the following morning at 7am. There were beds on the section and, subject to flying commitments, it was possible to snatch the odd catnap, but it wasn't unusual to complete a full 24-hour shift without sleep. Even when flying finished the fire section provided domestic fire coverage for the whole of the island. There were regular call outs to various domestic incidents. One of note comes to mind. I received, one evening, a telephone call from an Army officer informing me that patrolling soldiers had observed a peat fire and he suggested I deploy the fire service to the incident. I went down to the location, complete with the crash combine, and acknowledged that there was indeed a peat fire. I then informed the Army officer that he would have to alert Army HQ and request more Army personnel to be deployed a.s.a.p. to deal with the fire. He was none too pleased when I informed him that we were returning to the airfield to stand by for two Phantom recoverings and that was our primary task. I was not prepared to discharge any of our vehicle's water and notified him that the fire would have be extinguished by digging a trench in the peat to stop the fire spreading to, of all places, the RAF Stanley bomb dump. He did attempt to order me to dowse the fire with water, but once I put him in touch with SATCO he realised that he had no idea of our primary role.

It didn't take me long to get into some sort of routine at Stanley. I had no intention of idling away my off duty hours, so each day I undertook some sort of activity. I more-or-less coerced the crew to participate in sport in their off duty hours. I have always believed in trying to maintain a relatively healthy body, which in my opinion helps to maintain a healthy and alert mind – so important for a fireman. Not everybody shared my views but even the cynics became curious and attended, if only to see if they could get a sly kick at me or an elbow, but even in my late thirties I was able to avoid the reckless tackles. Whilst at Stanley I experienced my one and only sports injury; I was playing for the fire section in a competitive handball match and, out the blue, I felt this horrendous pain in my right leg. At first I thought I had been deliberately kicked, but as I spun round there was no one there. It was really painful and I had to limp off. As there was no obvious sign of injury I was being encouraged to play on, but I could hardly walk. I managed to get a lift to the medical centre and was informed by the Medical Officer that I had torn a calf muscle. I was given ice packs and some physio and that was it. I knew I had to be back on shift the next morning. It was an excruciating experience just getting dressed for work, never mind hobbling about all day. Once I climbed into my position on crash two, I tended to stay there as long as I could.

In addition to my sporting activities I would walk to Stanley, about six miles round trip, most off duty days, unless I was on one of my mountain walks. I would finish breakfast, do a bit of washing and then bumble off to Stanley or some other location. During the week I was mainly on my own and alone with my thoughts, which is no bad thing. I would think to myself how the previous shift went, the positive and negative aspects, and of course my thoughts would turn to home and my family. I would normally not bother with lunch and return at about 3pm, get my shower and commence my daily letter writing. Some days I would write five or six letters, usually in reply to the various people who took the trouble to write to me, but every day I wrote to Anne and my children. I wrote to my dad most days too. My dad, like me, enjoyed writing and receiving letters. It is surprising how important receiving letters can be. In my Gulf days, a 'Dear John' letter from a girlfriend who no longer wanted to wait for your return would be displayed in the NAAFI bar. Some lads used to get in all sorts of states if they didn't receive mail and you could sense the buzz going around when the Airbridge Hercules carrying the mail arrived. You could also feel the sense of despair from those who never received mail. Once all my letters were completed I would be ready for bed and for me lights out would be about 8.30pm and I would be asleep a few minutes later and that would be it until 6am the following morning.

Transport to work was by a four-ton truck. One of the off-going fire crew would drop the vehicle off at the coastel and we would travel up to the section in that vehicle. Invariably I would walk to work, about twenty minutes. I found that early morning exercise and relative freedom refreshing. I knew only too well that once I arrived at the section and took control of the fire crew everything I did for the next twenty-four hours would be out of my control. I was in charge of the crew but we were there to provide an emergency service. I would not know when I would eat, catch a nap, or get to the toilet. One shift, for instance, I had just sat on the toilet and a message came over my personal radio, "Stanley tower to crew commander deploy to number one BFI (Bulk Fuel Installation) a Wokka Wokka (Chinook) has crashed into the BFI". During the split second I was assimilating the message, the crash alarms sounded and one of my crew was shouting for me. No wonder so many firemen at some time in their career will be troubled by haemorrhoids. The worst situation was always when the crash alarm sounded without prior notification; even the fittest and most professional human beings can be thrown into a state of confusion when a crash alarm blurts out its bells or sirens. I knew of one fireman at Marham who suffered a heart attack on duty that was directly in response to a crash alarm. Messages coming over the radio en route to an incident can be extremely difficult to comprehend. The noise from the vehicle engine, road noise and aircraft noise, whilst at the same time, you are adjusting your fireman's kit all make communication difficult. I often used to say to my air traffic control mates it would be a good learning experience for them to spend a day on a crash truck and then they would have a better understanding of how we were trying our best to respond to their instructions.

However, once at the scene of an incident, decisions rested with the fire crew commander. Positioning of vehicles, deployment of the crew and the rescue rested entirely with the crew commander; an awesome responsibility at times. I remember an incident at Stanley when we were deployed to a fairly routine RHAG engagement. The Phantom engaged the cable and we were commencing the rewind. I received a radio message from crash one driver, "crash one to crew commander one of the crew has slipped injured his back and is unable to move". "Roger crash one leave the casualty and deploy to the aircraft". In those few seconds I could imagine the crew's thoughts as one of their mates lay injured and I was instructing them to move on and leave him. Nevertheless, the crew moved on for they too knew that their priority was to the aircraft and the aircraft in the circuit waiting to land. As it was I immediately radioed to red cross one (one of the ambulance crews) to deploy to the injured fireman. On another occasion near the end of my tour we deployed to what we thought was a routine RHAG engagement. The following citation dated the 22 November 1984 was given to all members of the crew.

On the afternoon of Thursday the 20th November 1984 the Crash Combine were deployed for an East Alpha RHAG engagement a regular occurrence for the fire crews at RAF Stanley. However the weather gave some cause for concern. Suddenly Mount Tumbledown disappeared in a gathering storm strong northerly crosswinds gusting at 50 knots were in evidence. The combine were deployed to rig the centre Alpha and stand by for two Geese (F4) and a Fat Albert (extended C130) recovering. The first goose landed safely and the cable was rewound. The second Goose also landed safely and the cable was rewound to allow the Fat Albert to land. The combine returned to normal readiness. Shortly after Wing Commander Manning (OC ops) called at the section and thanked the crew for their prompt and efficient actions. In the words of the Wing

Commander I have never seen a fire crew move so quickly and professionally and that includes my days at RAF Coningsby. I was urging you lads on from up in the tower and I was so relieved when you completed all your tasks in what must have been record time. I would like to show my appreciation for a job very well done by sharing a drink with you all. The Wing Commander then produced a bottle of Scotch whisky and asked us to join in a toast to the wonderful men of the RAF Fire Service. As the crew chief I would like to pass on my appreciation to all members of the crew;Cpl Bowerbanks Cpl Tortice Cpl Yapp SAC Haughton SAC Hawes SAC Hollis SAC Lenegan SAC Wade SAC Walton SAC Young and our two rhaggies Cpl Thomas and Jnr tech Palmer. I hope that you can look on this incident in years to come as a task very professionally undertaken at Royal Air Force Stanley.

GG Edwards
Sergeant SNCO i/c A Crew
Fire Section RAF Stanley

As a matter of interest, I declined the Wing Commanders offer of a toast. Its not very often you get the chance to disagree with a Wing Commander but we still had a long night ahead of us and there was no way any of my crew were consuming alcohol on duty, however small the quantity. We did however have our toast at a more appropriate time.

Fire fighting on an airfield is in many ways different to the fire fighting associated with the civilian fire service. On an airfield there is immediacy about the situation, there is usually little travelling distance to the scene of the emergency. It can be as little as few hundred metres in some cases. I remember one incident at Laarbuch when a Jaguar landed wheels up before our very eyes about two hundred metres from our position. In those situations there is little time for discussion, all decisions rest with the crew chief or his deputy. It is a fine testament to the training and professionalism that, regardless of the circumstances, RAF Firemen (and women these days) always have and always will respond with that one aim; to save life from crashed aircraft. Civilian firemen have that same objective but the emphasis with the RAF Fire Service is to save life from crashed aircraft.

During my Falklands tour I must have walked to Stanley many times and in all sorts of weather. I walked to Stanley one day, setting off in bright sunshine but on my way back the wind changed direction and the weather deteriorated. Normally I would have plodded on; there is a sense of satisfaction, I think, being in a gale. Its you versus the elements; everything else is of no importance. This day as I walked head down into the wind and rain and hail, a four-ton truck stopped just in front of me. This was an offer of a lift back to the coastel. I knew what the vehicle was; this was what was colloquially known as the shit wagon. This four-ton truck took, each day, waste from the coastel to an obscure beach and the waste was dumped in to the South Atlantic, not very environmentally friendly but so be it. Normally I would have waved the driver on but I accepted the offer of a lift and climbed into the back of this foul smelling truck. As I sat near the tailboard I noticed another body huddled against the bulkhead of the truck. I thought no more of it until a voice said; "don't you remember me Sarge". I looked up and had no idea who it was. In a distinct Wigan accent he said, "it's me Pendulbury". I thought for a moment who is Pendulbery and then he told me he joined the RAF at the St Helens careers office. I remembered him now, he enlisted as a general duties (GD) airman, the trade description states, candidates with neither the aptitude or ability for any trade could be considered suitable for the GD trade group. I remember interviewing Pendulbury and, at his attestation all his family attended the brief but important ceremony. Pendubury turned to me and said," you never told me I would end up in the Falklands Sarge" to which I replied, "when I joined the RAF nearly twenty years ago the recruiting Sergeant never told me I would end up sat in a shit wagon in the Falklands either". "I'm not complaining this is my second tour and I love it here and my job is great". As the only RAF GD wallah in the Falklands, his job was to look after the launderette and to assist in the removal of the coastel rubbish. Any official dhobi, (washing) was done free of charge and undertaken by Pendulbury however, if you wanted civilian clothes dhobied (washed), then you had to pay Pendulbury. I should imagine he earned a fortune during his tour. As with all overseas tours there is a chuff chart but some scribe had also penned an Ode to Stanley (probably plagiarised) that went:

~ *Out of the Blue* ~

This fucking town's fucking cuss,
No fucking trams no fucking bus
nobody cares for fucking us
*   In fucking Stanley.*

The fucking roads are fucking bad
Fucking folk are fucking mad
It makes the brightest fucking sad
*   In fucking Stanley.*

All fucking clouds all fucking rain
No fucking kerbs no fucking drains
The council's got no fucking brains
*   In fucking Stanley*

No fucking sport no fucking games
No fucking fun the fucking dames
Won't even give their names
*   In fucking Stanley*

Everything's so fucking dear
A fucking quid for a fucking beer
And is it good no fucking fear
*   In fucking Stanley.*

The fucking videos are fucking old
The fucking seats are always cold
You can't get in for fucking gold
*   In fucking Stanley.*

The fucking dances make you smile
The fucking band is fucking vile
It only cramps your fucking style
*   In fucking Stanley.*

Best fucking place fucking bed
With fucking ice on your fucking head
You might as well be fucking dead
*   In fucking Stanley.*

No fucking Airbridge no fucking mail
Just fucking snow and fucking rain
In anguish deep we fucking wail
*   In fucking Stanley.*

The fucking pubs are fucking dry
The fucking barmaids fucking fly
With fucking grief we fucking cry
Oh fuck you Stanley!

One of the most enjoyable aspects of my Falklands tour was my involvement with the Island scout group. I heard there was a scout group and I offered my services to train them up to the standard required to obtain the scout fireman's badge. This offer was taken up and I duly went into Stanley, met the scout leaders and commenced the training programme. Every other Wednesday evening I would drive into Stanley and carry out the training programme. I taught basic theory of fire; methods of extinguishing fire, how to set up a hydrant, basic knots hose-running etc. They were a wonderful group of young people and I used to enjoy my time with them. As well as my training programme, I would spend time answering questions about life in the UK. As the training progressed, I brought the young people and their leaders up to the fire section and gave them some more practical training with my crew. They loved this, driving round the airfield on the fire trucks and producing water from the trucks. Funny how people of any age love playing with water! Given the relative lack of activities on the island the scout programme became something of a major feature in the community.

Near the end of the programme, I arranged for the Flight Sergeant to test the practical side of the training and I prepared a written exam. My mate, the station commanders' personal assistant, produced some very nice certificates and he arranged for the station commander to present the certificates and fireman's badges. During the examination week there was a definite buzz about Stanley. All the scouts were known to be taking their test and it was mentioned several times on the local radio. All the scouts sat and passed their scout fireman's badge. One of the scout leaders was a young woman named Kate. Her father was the Stanley milkman and he was awarded the MBE for his services to the community during the conflict. Apparently he carried on delivering the milk throughout the occupation and subsequent battle. Kate was well known to all the military personnel on the island as she had a small slot on the Falkland Island Radio. This radio was nothing like we have at home; it was very much local news. One slot I remember was called, News from the potting shed, another gave information about what was available in the local shops; it was a 'very' local radio. What made it different was the fact that there were a few thousand, service personnel; who, were a captive audience. Kate's voice was different to all the others; here was a rather pleasant sounding young woman. I had heard Kate on the radio but was unaware that she was a scout leader. When I started my scout fireman's badge award training; almost all the young people in Stanley were involved, including Kate. There was very little in the way of activities available other than scouting. I was well received by the group and their adult leaders. Although the local people were surrounded by the military they had no direct contact and what contact they had was usually hostile.

Most servicemen remained on camp, frequenting their respective bars. As it was, the two pubs in Stanley were no more than small corrugated tin huts. I had been to both "pubs" just the once and never returned. The locals kept to themselves and I often thought we were intruders and their lives were certainly changed after the conflict. The locals were known colloquially as Benny's, after Benny in the TV soap, *Crossroads*. We, the British troops, were known as 'When-eyes' because of the tendency of military personnel to say: "When I was in…" (the Gulf, Singapore, Malta or wherever). I don't think it was a term of endearment.

RAF firemen were quite well known in Stanley; one of my prede-cessors had trained the local volunteer fire service in the use of their recently acquired breathing apparatus. RAF Firemen had also pro-vided assistance at the devastating Stanley hospital fire some months prior to my arrival. As it was, I got to know Kate and the other scout leaders quite well. Kate was a pleasant individual whose formative years, and young life, was so different to mine and the visitors to the Islands. She had never left the Island and consequently, had never travelled more than about thirty miles from her home. Her family and relatives all lived in Stanley and she had no concept of the outside world other than what they heard on the BBC World Service. Prior to the conflict, Falkland Islanders had no TV or video record-ers. There was a film shown every now and again in one of the small community centres and that was very much a family event. Films shown would have a U classification. Kate was educated in the small Stanley school and may well still be a Stanley resident. As well as instructing the scouts in basic fire skills, I would be asked lots of questions about life in the UK, my family, and life in the military. I thoroughly enjoyed these sessions; it was a break from the harsh environment of military life. I suggested to Kate that she may want to come with her friends to the fire section and watch, 'Top of the Pops', which was one of the many TV programmes brought in on the weekly Airbridge. I spoke with Kate's father and he agreed that would be no problem so long as I collected her and her friends and brought them home before 9pm. I don't know who was the more excited, the lads on my crew or Kate and her friends. Kate and her friends came to the fire section and watched mesmerised at Top of the Pops. My crew, who could at times, lounge around the crew room suddenly took a keen interest in smartening up the crew room and themselves. When Kate arrived, I was overcome with the smell of newly sprayed deodorant, but it was a very pleasant and enjoyable experience for all concerned.

I remember driving Kate home one evening and we were behind a four-ton truck. A couple of soldiers sat near the tailgate saw Kate and suddenly turned very abusive and started making rude gestures. I was embarrassed but Kate had no idea what it was all about. How different Kate's world, and our civilised world. On another occasion Kate was asked by one of my crew if she would like to come to one of the camp dances she asked her father and he said it would be all right. Camp dances were usually a sing along, with each section trying to out sing the other. I sought permission of those I thought I need to ask and it was agreed Kate would be coming to the dance.

By now Kate had a bit of a cult following on radio and she announced she had been asked by her friends at the RAF Fire Section to attend the dance this Saturday night. My crew was hosting her and I had warned my lads to be on their best behaviour. They certainly dressed up for the occasion; I didn't recognise them. I duly collected Kate and she was all excited and off I went as her chaperone. I remember walking into the dance and there were several hundred military personnel all spruced up. My lads behaved impeccably and, as the evening wore on, I was thinking what a great boost to morale this event was. Then, almost as if rehearsed, a group in one corner started singing, "get your tits out, get your tits out for the boys". Before I could say or do anything my lads, in true fire service fashion, waded into this group and the whole thing turned into a mass brawl.

Kate managed to escape unscathed with the help of the Military Police who had the presence of mind to be in the wings waiting for just this sort of thing to happen. I took Kate home and, far from being upset, she just didn't understand what they were singing and why they were fighting; strange people the Brits.

My tour was drawing to a close and I was eagerly looking forward to seeing my family. I was, in a strange way, sad to be leaving my crew behind. I had developed a good working relationship with most of my crew, borne out of hard work and adversity. Some of the firemen were great colleagues to work with. I can't name them all but, Bolland, Gill, Walton, Lenegan, Hollis, Tortice and Lucock come to mind, as dedicated, hard working colleagues, who made my Stanley tour a little easier. I had my leaving party and some very nice things were said, including references to my minefield experience and a few other funny comments. The day after my leaving do, I was about to have my first day off in five months. Consequently, during my do, I had a few drinks without having to worry about getting up at 6am for another eventful day at the office. I left Stanley on 26th January 1985.

The journey north to Ascension was nothing like the journey down. I sailed back on a flat-bottomed former cross channel ferry, The MV Karen. She had none of the Old World charm and character of the Uganda and there were times, when I thought we could have capsized. There was none of the daily routine associated with the Uganda. We were effectively on leave consequently it was a bit of a rest and recuperation before arriving home. We arrived at Ascension on the morning of 6th February and flew to Brize Norton that evening, arriving at 3am.the next morning. Corporal McCoy was there to meet me, along with my dear wife and we set off for St Helens. Absence definitely makes the heart grow stronger and my reunion with Anne was a magical moment.

My journey and tour in the Falklands completed, I just had one last thing to do. I had written to Peter and Christine's school and asked if I could collect them early from school. I knew the headteacher and most of the school staff very well and they were delighted at the idea. I arrived at the school and was met by a very excited head who took me to Peter and Christine's respective classrooms. I remember well the expression on their faces as they saw me walk in their classes. All the time spent apart, the privations of the last five months, the worries and anxieties about my family, the pressures of the job all paled into insignificance as I took hold of my children and walked them home.

The author – last shift at RAF Stanley.

10. Final RAF Days ~ A New Career Dawns

I returned to work at the RAF Careers office and had lost none of my enthusiasm for this type of work. If anything, I was more motivated and happy in the work especially, as I was returning home to my family each night. I was also making plans for my eventual discharge from the RAF, and with advice from the many friends I had made in the local careers service, I had worked out a career development plan. I carried on at night school, more to enable me to help Peter and Christine with their homework but also to improve my CV. I knew what type of work I was interested in and was gaining experience and qualifications to assist me achieve my aims and objectives. I had made an acquaintance with an ex Wartime RAF Rear Gunner (Ted Stanton) who was the local Soldiers Sailors and Airman's Families (SSAFA) representative for St Helens. Ted called into our office about once or twice a week. He suggested to me that I might be interested in undertaking some voluntary work for, SSAFA. I applied, was accepted and completed a short SSAFA welfare officers' course. I subsequently became the SSAFA representative for the Prescot area of St Helens and did this work for about three years.

I got to meet many ex-armed forces personnel who had fallen on hard times. I listened to some really sad tales but, depending on which branch of the services they served in, I could obtain quite substantial care packages for these most deserving causes. Ex-RN personnel had a welfare organisation that was staffed by full time staff and serving matelots. They also had substantial funds. Applications to the RN were usually successful and I remember one case that had a very happy ending. I received a request to visit an, ex wartime, RN Chief Petty Officer. His wife had written, unbeknown to him asking for assistance. I visited the couple at their home and initially the gentleman was quite angry and informed me in no uncertain terms that he didn't want any charity. I managed to convince him that he would not receive charity but explained that I would write to the RN and explain his circumstances. The man was now riddled with arthritis and had difficulty moving. His wife's main concern was the wear and tear he was inflicting upon their carpet as he dragged himself along the floor. I sent off my application and a few weeks later I visited the couple. When I arrived I was informed that they had received a visit from a RN welfare officer and he had agreed to all my requests. The couple were provided with a new carpet, a telephone and colour TV. In addition, a two-week holiday was organised for them both at a Royal Navy residential centre. The RN chief was a former RN boxing champion and former rugby player. He was a proud man and it upset me when he started crying when he thanked me for the part I played. The RAF also had a wonderful welfare organisation once again with substantial funds and I made many successful requests to the RAF Benevolent Fund. Welfare assistance for ex-Army personnel was dependent on the Regiment that the individual served with. The local Regiment for St Helens was the South Lancashire Fusilier's and I seem to remember they had little in the way of funds. Unfortunately the Army welfare organisation never seemed to respond in the same way as the RN and RAF. In my current occupation, I regularly meet ex military (mainly Army) personnel who have appeared before the Court. These generally sad, unfortunate individuals would have joined the military as young, physically and mentally fit individuals. No doubt they would have experienced alcohol misuse exactly like I did but many witness appalling violence and there is no mechanism to deal with these two problematic issues. When they do respond inappropriately they will be dishonourably discharged; abandoned to their fate to a society that cares little for the sacrifices these men and women made in the service of their country.

I remember interviewing a Royal Marine at our office; he was coming to the end of his engagement with the RM and was keen to join the RAF, in my trade in fact. As per protocol we sent off for his RM documents and they came back highly laudatory and made very interesting reading. This man had served in the Falklands during the conflict. According to his documents he was involved in the attack on Mt Longdon a place I had visited. When his platoon came under heavy fire and were suffering casualties he remained calm and continued with the attack. This attack was a close combat fight, hand to hand with bayonets, knifes and any other means of killing. This man later told me he put a bayonet in an Argentine soldiers' face. He has to live with that for the rest of his life. I am not a pacifist but war is a brutal, gruesome business and it appears to me there are no victors. Anyway, this man did join the RAF and two days after he arrived at the RAF recruit training school (RAF Swinderby) I received a telephone call from an irate Flight Lieutenant berating me for putting wimps in the RAF. "This man has done nothing but cry since he arrived". I tried to explain that this man had an exemplary Royal Marine record, "He's a wimp," was the reply, and he was dismissed from the RAF.

That same man is now a vagrant, a sad forlorn figure on the streets of St Helens and there are so many like him in Probation hostels, jails and doss houses throughout the United Kingdom; a sad indictment of the way we treat military personnel. I am a great fan of the poet Rudyard Kipling and, whilst his poem, 'IF', was voted the nations favourite poem, I am sure he would like to be remembered for his many other works including my favourite, *The Last of the Light Brigade*:

> There were thirty million English who talked of England's might
> There were twenty broken troopers who lacked a bed for the night
> They had neither food nor money; they had neither service nor trade
> They were only shiftless soldiers, the last of the Light Brigade.
> O thirty million English that babble of England's might
> Behold there are twenty heroes who lack their food tonight
> Our children's children are lisping to honour the charge they made
> And we leave to the streets and workhouse the Last of the Light Brigade
> *(Abridged version)*

In addition to my SSAFA duties, purely by chance one evening I noticed an advert in the *Liverpool Echo* for unqualified youth workers. I sent off for the application and, to cut a long story short, I was interviewed and accepted. I began work at the Speke community centre two nights a week supervising sporting activities. It was something of a revelation, the language and some of the staff's apathy, but I thoroughly enjoyed the work. When I arrived the lads played sport and the girls just watched. I was having none of that and convinced the lads that the girls should play a more active role. In fact, the lads ran the centre. When I left the confines of the staff room almost all the other youth workers could not believe that I was going to participate in the activities. There were supposed to be some real hard cases amongst the lads and there was a pecking order on the pool table, only a certain few lads played on it and the girls were not allowed. That soon changed. I also contacted other youth centres and arranged five-a-side football matches. I had access to a mini bus and I would take our team and supporters to various youth centres across the city. It is unbelievable that most young people who live in a big city never leave the confines of their own immediate area. All the 'hard cases' were the most terrified and attached themselves to me when we left our centre. Back in our centre they were loud, boisterous and strutted about as if they owned the place. It was all a big bluff, a charade; underneath they were as insecure and anxious as the next person. It didn't take me long to win over the hearts and minds of the club members and we were soon sat together discussing issues such as discrimination, crime, anti-social behaviour, etc. The girls were coming more to the fore and able to express themselves without fear of verbal abuse.

All was going well and then I received a message that a young offender was being released and was returning to the centre, bent on causing havoc. All my charges, who by now had stopped swearing, spitting and strutting around like peacocks, suddenly returned to their old ways. Staff members were terrified and showed it openly. This obviously confused the young people and sent all the wrong messages. I was warned to expect trouble; this released prisoner was not happy with what he had heard about the new regime at his centre. I thought no more of this and went about my day job and carried on coming to the centre two nights a week. As his arrival drew nearer, staff, were booking holidays, and even the young people were frightened. As previously mentioned I am a great fan of the film, High Noon and I felt a bit like Gary Cooper as I went into the club to find this anti-hero waiting for me.

I thought the young people genuinely felt sorry for me and expected me to be harmed or offended in some way but I just carried on as if he wasn't there. I had planned a visit to another centre for a friendly football match and was just about to leave with my group when he asked if he could come with us. I informed him that I had a full team but I would give him a trial next week to see if he was good enough to play in the team. This didn't go down too well but he had no choice. I soon learnt that this young lad was no different to any other child and within a few weeks he became one of my key footballers and one of the best behaved lads in the centre. Most people unfamiliar with military life assume that the military lead by shouting and bullying but the good leaders in the military do not operate that way. In my entire service career I never had to shout at anyone unless it was on a fire ground situation or during training on the drill-square. Even then I was only passing on instructions. Good leaders motivate; they listen, respect the individual and above all set an example. It's not the uniform that makes the person; it is the person, in the uniform that is in important. In the military you are recognised by visible rank markings but that really means nothing; to get the best out of your subordinates you need to understand why they are behaving as they are.

I remember completing one of my RAF leadership courses when we spent some time looking at Maslow's hierarchy of needs. Maslow is a renowned sociologist and social philanthropist. Why would the military choose Maslow's model of leadership; probably because it was the best!

I became very involved at the centre and got on well with staff and the young people in particular. The centre manger was a very pleasant woman who was keen to make changes and welcomed my ideas. She was keen to organise a residential staff training weekend but finances were tight in those days; this was the time Derek Hatton controlled Liverpool City Council. However, I was well known at RAF Burtonwood and able to obtain accommodation there, free of charge. Staff there, like any other RAF personnel were very keen to support community activities. I put it to the centre manager that I could obtain free accommodation, free food and input from the local American airmen based at Burtonwood. She was over the moon and asked me to attend a staff meeting and explain to the staff what was available. I duly did this and all present were very keen except one. This woman said it was inappropriate to be involved with the military and tried to convince others not to attend. She was overruled but still came along with her dour face and opinionated views. This was supposed to be a training weekend for staff with a bit of fun thrown in. Most extremists (and I have met a few in my Probation career) in my experience, don't know the meaning of fun and happiness. However one Friday evening we set off for RAF Burtonwood, which was about half an hours' drive away. We had an enjoyable first night with some good icebreakers and a few beers thrown in. Old sourpuss moaned about this and that and then a RAF Squadron Leader, the base commander, joined us for a drink. Suddenly she became excited and asked me who this man was. He was indeed a handsome, debo-

---

nair character, with a charming West Coast of Scotland accent. She literally drooled all over him and I, not particularly concerned for her infatuation, explained that this man was a Royal Air Force pilot and had flown aircraft, that carried nuclear weapons. It didn't make any difference; he could have been the Butcher of Belsen she would, if given the chance, succumbed to his every whim.

As it was she became over excited, consumed too much alcohol, too quickly and was taken to her bed never to be seen again till we returned home on the Sunday night, thank goodness. Meanwhile the Squadron Leader joined us for an evening of interesting discussion interspersed with a few free drinks. We also had a wonderful presentation from some American servicemen about morale and leadership in the American forces. The weekend proved to be both interesting and entertaining, the best way to learn in my opinion. Not long after commencing my work at the Speke community centre, I was asked by the manger if I would be interested in undertaking a twelve-month youth workers' course. I had to attend a college in Liverpool City centre one night week plus four residential training weekends. There was a fee involved but if I accepted the offer I knew the RAF would pay. After a little deliberation I decided to give it a go and went on to complete quite an enjoyable course. The residential weekends were like no other activity I had previously undertaken. There was a lot of alcohol consumed, a lot of shenanigans going on which I avoided at all costs and little study. As part of the course I had to undertake a placement at another youth centre. Most course members were familiar with other centres and had made prior arrangements. I, meanwhile, had no preference where I went and left it to course tutors. I was asked if I would be prepared to complete a placement at the David Lewis Centre in Stanhope Street, Liverpool 8. I knew the area very well, my parents' first home was about two hundred yards from the centre (Ashwell Street) and my job on leaving school was in Grafton Street which is also located not far from Stanhope Street. In addition, when I was sixteen years of age, I obtained part time work selling seafood's ("cockles and mussels alive a live oh") and my patch took in Stanhope Street as well as Parliament Street and Windsor Street, notorious areas of Liverpool.

That job incidentally paid very well but it was very enjoyable and I met some very odd characters on my round. Parliament Street then was a red light district and I would stop and talk to many of the girls as they waited for business and I went about my business. I would also meet many seafarers looking for girls and I would point them in the right direction. I made many friends in the various pubs I visited and got to know all the landlords and customers quite well. I would give some elderly persons free kippers and salt fish and I would also sit and chat to them, which I used to really enjoy. I had no motive for this other than I liked listening to their stories, mainly of the war and service in the Merchant Marine. However, this good will gesture paid dividends. I could walk freely and safely in probably the most notorious area of Liverpool. I remember one Saturday evening being followed and, aware that other cockle and mussel salespeople had been mugged, I was a bit anxious. I went into the Windsor Castle pub, now demolished, and mentioned it to the manager. He in turn mentioned it to a female customer whose mother I used to give kippers to. She came outside with me and watched as I was followed. She caught hold of the potential assailant and head butted him. It was the first time I had seen a woman fight and the first time I seen a nose split open. I had a few more scary episodes but I survived and, as a matter of note, when I joined the RAF I travelled back to the same pubs only this time I was in my RAF uniform.

Life in those days was a lot more straightforward and servicemen were made very welcome, especially in the south end of Liverpool. However, my placement at the David Lewis commenced and I was required to attend one night a week and complete several written assignments. The David Lewis Centre was predominately used by young black people and staffed mainly by black community and youth workers. This was a new experience for me and I was based there just after the Liverpool riots. As part of my placement I was required to interview young people and obtain their views on a variety of subjects, not least relationships and attitudes in relation to the Police. This was an enlightening experience and it saddened me to see and hear overt racism committed against young Liverpudlians for no other reason than the colour of their skin or the area in which they lived. I also experienced first hand quite overt racism on several occasions. One incident, I was invited to participate in an under tens five-a-side football competition in Queensferry, North Wales. Ours was the only club from Liverpool to accept the invite and our team worked hard in training prior to commencing the competition. I obtained a good kit for the boys and worked out some tactics, which basically meant, getting the ball to our two front players; a brilliant young black footballer, Leroy Patel, and my son Peter who played alongside Leroy. We had an outstanding goalkeeper and an excellent team spirit. I emphasised to the boys it didn't matter how well we did, what matters is we enjoyed ourselves, played as best we could and behaved as best we could. This little team of mine were trained in the Bill Shankly way, and non of my team had ever disputed a referees' decision, used bad language and always had to maintain their composure. They were expected to tuck their shirts into their shorts, socks pulled up and if I substituted a player they would have to come straight off.

Off we went to North Wales, fairly confident and determined to do well for the city. I did the necessary booking in and attending for the draw. Teams were mainly schools and youth clubs from all round the Queensferry area; there was quite a large attendance both in terms of teams and spectators. We were the only team with any black players and the only team from Liverpool, which generated considerable interest. We had no spectators other than a few substitutes. We played our first game according to plan and as soon as we went ahead and I sensed we had this game won, I made my first substitutes bringing off Leroy and Peter. No messing about they came off hugged their replacements and we went on to win the game comfortably. All my players knew, despite their young age, that they hand to shake hands with the referee and the opposition players. I did the same with the opposing managers. The next game came along and we won again and again. We reached the quarterfinal and by now there was quite a large crowd watching each game. Those teams knocked out remained to watch and there was quite a bit of noise during each game. We reached the semi-final with no incidents with any opposition players, no incidents with the referees and there were no histrionics when we scored and won our games; quite the opposite. This was the finest football team I had ever been involved with and they knew how proud I was of them. During half time of the semi-final Leroy started crying. He told me that a man had been calling him a monkey and 'the N word'. He pointed him out and I went straight over and sure enough, he was an overt racist who had probably never had any contact with black people. I asked him why he thought he could abuse a ten-year old boy. He thought it funny; I didn't. I asked for his name, which he refused to give. He was a youth leader and I advised him that I intended to take the matter up with the local authority. I went back to my team and asked them to go back on the pitch and respond to this hostility by playing our best football. The second half got under way and this man and a group near him started making further racist remarks.

I stopped the game and brought my team off. I spoke to the organisers and explained that we were returning home unless those shouting racist abuse were removed from the ground. We had done no wrong whatsoever, behaved impeccably, and men who called themselves teachers and youth leaders were abusing us. They were eventually told to leave. We made it to the final and came back to Liverpool with the winner's trophy.

That was not my first or last experience of racism. Years later when I was the officer in charge of Toxteth Air Cadets I often encountered racism directed towards the young black cadets in my charge. I briefed all my cadets and staff that I would not tolerate any form of bullying and racism is no more than bullying. Sometimes on our travels throughout the UK people would be aghast when they saw a smart young black Air Cadet and even more horrified when they found out they were from Toxteth. However, these outstanding young people were great ambassadors for their city. Racism to me is an evil, wicked disease, and I cannot understand how people can behave that way. To abuse people solely on the basis of their colour is abhorrent. People like me, who have spent a long time in the armed forces, know what an outstanding service and sacrifice black people have made in the service of their country. That's not to say racism does not exist in the Armed Forces, it does, but I do believe there is no place in the modern British military for racists and efforts are being made to root out this evil.

I duly completed and passed my youth workers course' and my placement at the David Lewis was coming to an end. I had thoroughly enjoyed my time at the David Lewis, made some wonderful friends and thought the world of the youngsters who frequented the club.

My son, Peter, and daughter Christine were now club members and enjoying their time at the centre. I had to make a decision whether to return to the Speke Centre or remain at the David Lewis. At the Speke Centre I was paid, I think it was £5 an hour. If I remained at the David Lewis I would be an unpaid voluntary worker.

After speaking to the manager at Speke and explaining to her my career plans when leaving the RAF she was of the same opinion as I that it would be better if I remained at the David Lewis. An amicable agreement and I went on to work at the David Lewis for many years. Several years after leaving the RAF I was accepted at Liverpool University for the two year Diploma in Social Work course. Consequently, I applied to the Home Office for sponsorship as a Probation student. This is a very lengthy and complicated process involving more interviews more tests and more references. I am very pleased to say I was accepted as a Home Office student and I know that the manager of the David Lewis (Winston Douglas) provided the Home Office with a character reference supporting my application.

My time in the RAF was drawing to a close and my careful resettlement plans were more or less coming to fruition. I was quite confident of securing employment either as a youth worker or my other option as a careers officer. I had attended for interview at Nottingham University and was accepted for the one year Diploma in Careers Guidance Course commencing in January 1988. I was due to leave the RAF in September 1987. I had about nine months RAF service left when one day a man came into the office making enquiries about his daughter joining the RAF as a nurse. I did the usual presentation and at the end of the presentation this gentleman (John McCabe) mentioned that he in fact was an ex-RAF Policeman. I had a chat with him about various things, not least my career options when I left the RAF. He told me that he was a Probation Officer and one thing led to another and I became a Probation volunteer working directly for John. This was another new area of work for me and one I have now been involved with for nearly twenty years. I was due for discharge from the RAF on 2nd September 1987 and in July of that year a vacancy was advertised for a Probation Service Assistant at the St Helens Probation Office. I applied, was successful, and with permission from the RAF duly commenced work for Merseyside Probation Service on 12th August 1987. I had an interesting first few weeks in my Probation career, still a Sergeant in the RAF but also a Probation Service Assistant. About this time I received a message from a RAF Officer asking me to call in at the RAF Careers office in uniform, on the 2nd of September, my last official day in the RAF. I attended and was met by my wife, (who kept that a surprise) the Inspector of Recruiting, (a Group Captain) and many of my RAF colleagues. A few pleasant and complimentary words were said and I saluted for the last time and walked back to the Probation office to carry on with my afternoon Probation duties. My RAF journey began from the centre of Liverpool and ended just a few miles down the road. I remember walking those few hundred yards back to the Probation Office and thinking to myself. That's it, the end of my RAF career. Twenty-two years, a few thousand miles, hundreds of different people thousands of incidents and experiences all gone, in the blink of an eye almost. However, I have recorded the journey as best I can and I hope it brings pleasure to some and encourages others to record their tale.

Last day in the Royal Air Force, RAF Careers office St Helens.

Postscript

Nine months after leaving the RAF I arrived home from the St Helens Probation office one evening to receive a message from my daughter that she had taken a telephone call from an RAF Officer and he wanted me to contact him urgently. I was none too pleased and a bit anxious and I racked my brain trying to think what I could possibly have done that required urgent attention. Reluctantly I telephoned the number given and was notified that I was to receive a visit this evening from my last Commanding Officer, Flight Lieutenant Hughes. He was, I remember, a decent chap and if it hadn't been for the fact that I had a lot of time for him I would have asked him to call at another time. He asked if my wife and children would be at home when he called and I said they probably would and with that he said I will be at your home in about an hour. We waited anxiously and I was mentally preparing all sorts of excuses for things I hadn't even done. He arrived came in to our home and asked me to sit down. By now I was about to tell him I was a civilian when he informed me that I had been awarded the British Empire Medal in the Queens Birthday Honours List that would be announced the next day. I was shocked, and surprised to say the least. I had no idea and felt somewhat humbled that someone, somewhere, had taken the time and trouble to nominate me for the award. The next day my name appeared in the Honours list and I featured in the Liverpool Echo. I had received my award for services to the RAF and my work in the local community. I began to receive telephone calls and letters from all sorts of people, all congratulating me. When I told my parents well, it brought much happiness into their life.

I know now something about the Honours system, the different categories of awards for different classes of people. Modest as my award is, it was a great honour for me, and my family. It reflected my rank in the RAF and my working class origins. Like most Liverpudlians, I am intensely proud of my origins: equally I am intensely proud of the fact that I served in the Royal Air Force as a Fireman. RAF Firemen are a peculiar breed. They can at times present as a dishevelled bunch of reprobates but that is not an accurate reflection of this happy breed.

Since its inception in 1943 RAF Firemen have rescued or assisted in the removal of hundreds of personnel from crashed or damaged aircraft, the primary role for all RAF Firemen. These types of incidents are the high drama of fire service work, the bulk of which is much more mundane but nevertheless vital. In addition to airfield interventions RAF Firemen have and continue to attend numerous domestic incidents. Times and situations change but still today RAF Fire fighters are waiting in the wings every minute an RAF aircraft is airborne. We all hoped we would never be called into action but when we were we strove to respond in a rapid and professional manner. RAF Firemen have over the years been killed or injured carrying out their primary role. Every response to an incident is an unknown quantity, it may appear routine but that can change at anytime. RAF Firemen were invariably the first to deploy to a conflict in some foreign land and usually amongst the last to return home. We worked long arduous hours and when other RAF sections closed we remained on duty. We were quite adaptable and equally at home climbing a thirty foot ladder, or donning breathing apparatus and entering an underground bunker; straddling an ejection seat or disarming live aircraft weapons on a windswept airfield etc.etc.

Author with Air Marshall Sir John Sutton after BEM presentation.

The RAF Fire service played such a crucial role in the National Fire Service disputes. RAF firemen also provided fire cover for the Queens Flight and in every sphere of Royal Air Force life; the sporting, the social and the voluntary activities firemen would usually be involved. When my turn comes to shuffle off this mortal coil and move to that big fire section in the sky I hope St Peter will ignore the fact that my record has some flaws; on earth I rallied for lost and hopeless causes. I smoked, I drank alcohol and coveted women (in my younger days) and I may have committed a few bad tackles. In my dreams I can hear St Peter say, "We cannot have people up here like you. Your life is full of sin" and then, before casting me off to eternal punishment in hell, he notices an entry on my record. Taking my hand he says, "Come this way" and leads me up to meet my maker. Before the man himself, St Peter says "Take him in Lord and treat him well, he used to be a Royal Air Force Fireman. He's served his time in hell."

Just one final anecdote, I attended for the presentation of the British Empire Medal at RAF Bentley Priory with Anne and my children. It was a very grand and very pleasant occasion. The RAF band played, citations were read and there were many senior RAF Officers present. I had never previously seen so much gold braid and scrambled egg. My son Peter, now aged fourteen had joined the local Air Cadet squadron and wanted to attend in his cadet uniform. I telephoned to ask if that was OK and after a few days I received a message that it was ok for Peter to attend in his cadet uniform, which was no more than a RAF blue woolly jumper. He certainly didn't feel out of place but looked slightly. When the presentations were over, the senior officer, Air Marshal Sir John Sutton, passed by everybody else and came straight over to Peter. He shook Peter's hand and said, "I am glad to see you have taken the trouble to wear your uniform and may I say, young man, you look very smart".

Well done to Sir John.

11. Venture Adventure ~ The Next Generation

Some time in 1987, Peter came home from school and told me that he had attended a presentation by the local Air Cadet Squadron Commander. As a consequence, Peter was keen to go along to the cadet open night and see what the Air Cadets was all about. Despite my time spent as an Air Cadet and my involvement with the cadets through my RAF recruiting duties, I had never suggested to Peter that he might be interested in joining. Peter duly went along and subsequently joined our local squadron, 1438 (Prescot). I would drop Peter off and collect him from the squadron each Monday and Wednesday night. I knew most of the squadron staff and kept well away, allowing Peter to do his own thing, without any interference from me. Initially I would wait outside and then, after a few months, I would call in and speak to the staff many who were well known to me, in particular the squadron Warrant Officer, Tom Fearns. As ever I volunteered to help out and before long I was helping Tom with the squadron football team and other little bits of work. I was asked if I would like to join the staff team. I agreed and become a civilian instructor. A year or so after that I was commissioned in the RAFVR(T). I really enjoyed my involvement with Prescot Air Cadets. They were a good bunch of young people some of whom came from fairly rough areas; nevertheless, they were competing on an equal basis with other cadet squadrons in more salubrious areas of Merseyside such as Formby, Ormskirk, Hoylake and Neston. There was a good staff team led by Bob Farrell who, along with the rest of his team, had set up their own residential centre at RAF Burtonwood air base. They, by their own endeavours, had fully equipped a couple of rooms into quality accommodation. Most weekends' cadets would spend time at the base and this was a very popular activity with lots of positive spin-offs for the young people. Prescot squadron was only a few miles from one of the most successful Air Cadet squadrons in the UK, 1982 (Huyton) squadron. I was very familiar with this squadron; I had attended many functions there and it was a squadron I visited regularly in my recruiting role. The squadron had won just about every cadet competition and there were many competitions in those days. However, the areas in which they did not excel were adventure training and the Duke of Edinburgh's award (DofE). Huyton Air Cadets were regularly the Merseyside Wing nomination for the best Air Cadet squadron in the country but the only thing that let them down was their lack of Duke of Edinburgh's awards.

Author, Stan Michael and Ted Prescot.

The benefits for young people involved in the award really are enormous. In an area of limited employment opportunities, the inclusion of a DofE award on a curriculum vitae was, in my opinion, proof to any employer that the holder of that award had proven that they were hardworking and had a bit of go about them. I was coerced into joining Huyton Air Cadets with the sole intention of developing the DofE award scheme within the squadron. Rather reluctantly I left Prescot and joined the staff of Huyton Air Cadets. This really was a fine squadron with first class accommodation, excellent training facilities and plenty of staff. Cadet numbers exceeded a hundred on parade most nights. I knew well the Officer Commanding Huyton

Air Cadets, Flight Lieutenant Stan Michael MBE. He was my first line manager when I left school and went to work at Holloway's timber importers. He was a good friend of my parents and he had an excellent reputation as a first class squadron commander. I had a great deal of respect for Stan; he had taken Huyton Air cadets from relative obscurity to a nationally renowned youth organisation. Stan's functions were always high calibre and I remember meeting Prime Minister Harold Wilson, Lord Derby, Robert Kilroy Silk (then MP for Huyton) and many others who attended Huyton Air Cadet functions. Stan organised an annual RAF Band concert, which was a very popular local event. Much as I had enormous respect for Stan, I knew I had a difficult task convincing the training team that more emphasis should be put on adventure training. I generated enthusiasm amongst the cadets and convinced their parents, that a Dof E award, was the best certificate of all, apart from the flying and gliding, scholarship awards. I could not however convince the staff, in particular, the indomitable Mr Ted Prescot BEM. Mr Prescot had been with the squadron over forty years, many of those as squadron commander. His sole purpose in life, it appeared, was to turn out, every year, the best drill team in the Air Cadets and he invariably did just that. Believe it or not drill, was always a very popular activity at Huyton and at many other squadrons, but drill was a very intense and demanding activity. Huyton cadets saw it as a great honour to be selected for the reserve drill team, never mind the actual team. Hours and hours would be spent practising drill movements at a local park. The fact that local youths watching thought the cadets were all stupid was of no consequence, the practices continued. Nearer the time of the drill competition nothing else mattered and the cadets would meet every night of the week to practice. When they weren't practising they were bulling their shoes and pressing their uniforms. Come the event, cadets would arrive in relatively ordinary uniforms and carried a shoebox. Ted would take his team away from all others and the final psychological briefing would commence. The draw would take place and the thirty squadrons in the Wing would each perform their drill display.

Some squadrons could hardly muster the mandatory sixteen cadets whereas Huyton had a reserve compliment as good as, if not better than, the first sixteen. When it came Huyton's turn to march on to the parade ground the cadets changed at the very last minute into their pristine uniforms and removed their gleaming shoes from their shoeboxes and off they would go. Every other squadron turned out to watch this ritual of precision movement and even I, a man who was trained in drill at the RAF Regiment depot, was amazed at the spectacle. Huyton Air Cadets, for as long as all present could re-member, always won the drill competition. RAF regular personnel gave up their time to judge the competition and they, like me, were hugely impressed. However, I saw my role with the Air Cadets as a youth worker and I saw little value in such an activity. I knew the drill practice interfered with school revision and this to me was more important. I also watched other cadets collecting their DofE award certificates, which were much more relevant to any prospective employer. I was at this period very keen on mountain walking. I had developed my interest in mountain walking during my time in the Falklands and was regularly walking in Snowdonia. My involvement with the Air Cadets gave me an opportunity to develop my mountain walking skills. Any member of the Air Cadets could, if they so wish, participate in the Mountain Leader Training Course. This was an expensive course to undertake but it came free of charge to Air Cadet staff. Very few staff took up this opportunity mainly because of the commitment involved and the high level of fitness required. Another drawback was the fact that the mountain leader-training course, undertaken with the Air Cadets, was completed at the Joint School of Military Adventure Training, located at Llanrwst. The centre was managed and operated by military, physical training instructors. I volunteered for the one-week basic course and completed the pre requisite preparation and training. Preparation included registration with the Mountain Leader Training Board, the acquisition of equip-ment and a logbook. Completion of the four day first aid course was also required. Details of previous mountain walking activities had to be sent off and, if you were considered to be up to the required standard, you were accepted for the course.

I was duly accepted and completed a most enjoyable mountain activity week in the Snowdonia mountain range. On completion of the course I was invited to return in a years time to undertake the one-week assessment to qualify as a mountain leader. Meantime, you had to complete thirty mountain walks in three different locations before returning for the assessment. I completed this requirement and recorded all details in my logbook. I applied for the assessment and was selected to attend a course beginning the end of November 1998. I had to prepare mentally for the written examinations and practical tests and would spend many hours on my own, walking in the Snowdonia mountain range. I arrived back at Llanrwst ready to commence the course and quite confident I could pass. Our course, twelve in number, included, a Royal Marine ski instructor, a RAF Tornado pilot, several army physical training instructors and me, a fifty-year granddad. We arrived on a Saturday afternoon, sorted out our bed spaces and kit and whilst some commenced their daily fitness routine I went for a walk. In the evening we all went for an enjoyable few drinks in a local hostelry in Llanrwst. Sunday morning saw the first of our briefings and training exercises. We were given a timetable for the various examinations we had to take and informed that the three day assessed expedition would start on the Wednesday. We were placed into four person syndicates and allocated our assessor for the week. Our assessor, nice man that he was, but only a few months previous had been beasting, (physically training) paratroop recruits. I think he was a little surprised when he met me and he made it plain he was going to 'burn me off' during the first of our mountain walks. We did a bit of rope work on the Sunday and then off we went to Snowdon.

We dismounted the mini bus, took a few bearings and with full kit on we set off on the three and a half thousand-foot climb. Nothing was said until we reached the summit. A brief navigation exercise took place and away we went on our descent. I could see the instructor casting glances at me half expecting me to keel over but I was enjoying this. We came into the Ogwen Valley about 2pm and then climbed Glyder Fawr; a fair part of this walk was undertaken in darkness. It was for me a long day, but I had no problems physically and all my equipment was comfortable. Our instructor did say on our return to Llanrwst that he thought I was "a fit old bugger". The next day we went back on to the mountains and practised our emergency carrying drills, two handed seat, blanket lift and improvised stretcher drills, all carried out in pretty bad weather. Nevertheless, we were working well as a group and we were well motivated. Of an evening we would take the various written examinations and prepare for the next day's navigation exercise. We had to pass all the various tests before we could commence our three-day mountain assessment test. We all passed the tests and began our detailed preparation for the big event, the three-day expedition. We had to carry our own tent, first aid kit, sleeping bag, cooking equipment and clothing. In addition, we had to carry three days supply of food and water, although we could pick up water (river water) on the journey. Our rucksacks were full, to say the least, and we carried no unnecessary items. Come the Wednesday we were taken to an unknown destination and began a three-day, thirty-mile assessed expedition.

We each took it in turn to lead, put out in front, on our own, unable to communicate with the group. It was a very difficult task trying to focus whilst the assessor would give a grid reference to walk to and throw in a few wobblies (exercises) along the way. He would suddenly say, one of the group is hypothermic, or had broken a leg; the leader had to act instantly and appropriately. The two nights spent sleeping on the mountains were both spent under fairly atrocious weather conditions. As it was, we didn't finish walking till about 9 p.m. We then had to produce a substantial meal and hot drink before retiring for a few hours sleep. I knew if I got into my sleeping bag dry then I would sleep ok but if for any reason, I went to bed damp I would not sleep. There is an art to keeping your inner clothing dry and I had mastered that over a few years practice. Up early the next morning and away we went again. Another long day under examination and another night sleeping on the mountains. Up the next day and a long hike back to Llanrwst to await the decision of the assessment team. This was an anxious time for most, they needed this qualification to further their service careers whilst I was more or less doing it for "fun".

We were allowed to shower and change before reporting for our final briefing and examination results. The centre manager explained from the outset that there was a high failure rate on every course, usually as high as fifty per cent. We knew that when we set off but you never think it will be you who fails. As it was, I was one of the failures. It was pointed out that on the final morning of the expedition I took a wrong turning and that was sufficient to fail, I remember the incident and I remember rectifying the mistake. It all happened in a matter of minutes but it was sufficient to fail. Two others failed whom, no doubt, would have been upset but rough, tough physical training instructors show no emotion. In a way I was satisfied with my performance. I had completed the expedition without any difficulty, no aches, pains, and blisters and none the worse for the experience. I enjoyed all aspects of the course and even to this day I find myself strangely at peace and content on the mountains especially my favourite, the magical and mystical Cadair Idris. I returned home safely and went about my normal everyday work and leisure activities. I was to learn later, that if I had undertaken the civilian mountain leader course, at Plas Y Brenin, there would have been less emphasis on the physical and more on the aesthetic side of mountain activities, but so be it. I could still lead groups on the mountains but not above two thousand feet.

Back at Huyton Air Cadets I was trying earnestly to encourage participation in adventure training and the DofE award, but I was definitely fighting a losing battle. I would arrange transport, kit, food etc and book a weekend away. Always at the last minute, cadets would decide they were unable to attend. I knew Mr Prescot was at the back of this but he would state categorically that it had nothing to do with him. I was becoming bored and felt my enthusiasm was being stifled. I had agreed to a four-year renewable contract with the Air Cadets and thought I would see that out and seek other pastures. One evening I received a telephone call from the officer commanding Merseyside Air Cadets, Wing Commander Ian Jones. He asked me to report to Wing headquarters at RAF Woodvale that Sunday. I agreed thinking that he may have an idea for an expedition that he wanted me to be involved with.

I arrived at Woodvale and was introduced to the chairwoman of 7F squadron civilian committee. She, along with the Wing Commander, had recently removed the Squadron Commander from his post. There was a vacancy for a Squadron Commander at 7F. I was invited to take on the role. I accepted and for the next ten years I experienced one hell of a rollercoaster ride as the Commanding Officer, 7F (1st City of Liverpool) Air Cadets.

On 11th October 1938, eleven months before the outbreak of World War Two, the Air League of the British Empire founded the Air Defence Cadet Corps. One of the first units to be formed, in fact the seventh was in Liverpool, this being 7F Squadron. There was no shortage of volunteers in the early days despite the fact that prospective cadets had to undergo a rigorous medical examination and selection interview. By the end of the War, 7F Squadron strength amounted to 207 cadets, eight uniformed staff and seventeen civilian instructors. Many cadets went on to serve in the various arms of the military and many lost their lives on active service. Cadets of the squadron in those early days include Cadet John Nicholls, who went on to become Air Marshall Sir John Nicholls KCB CBE DFC AFC. Another ex-cadet, Geoffrey Aird went on to become Flight Lieutenant Aird, a founder pilot in the Black Arrows (the forerunner to the Red Arrows). A more recent ex-cadet of 7F was the former world middleweight boxing champion, John Conteh. The end of the war saw squadron numbers decline and for the next thirty years 7F Squadron languished in the bottom half of the Merseyside Air Cadet league.

I had heard of 7F mainly because they had they had always been located in the south end of Liverpool. The squadron, for many years, was located at the old TA Centre at the top of Warwick Street, a place I passed many times on my way to and from work.

The Air Cadets is an organisation that is geared up for competition. There are all sorts of competitions that are fiercely fought over. However, the most important of all competitions is the Wing Efficiency, the Air Cadet equivalent of the premier league. Individual squadrons are assessed on a number of performance indicators, spread over a period of twelve months. There were five or six of the thirty squadrons in Merseyside who usually finished in the top three (a bit like the premier league). When I took over 7F they had, for many years, always finished thirtieth (bottom of the league). Cadet numbers were no more than twenty and the squadron very rarely competed in any sporting events and were not involved with the Dof E award. I remember my first parade night, Friday 10th May 1991. I arrived just as the squadron was forming up on parade. I had just left a squadron that formed up on parade in three or four flights with about eighty young people on parade.

At 7F there were thirteen on parade and a handful of staff. However, as soon as I saw the building I knew there was potential to develop. I did say to Wing Commander Jones, "There is only one way this squadron can go and that is up." Ian Jones, always one to have the last word, responded by saying, "That is not quite true. If things don't improve the squadron could be disbanded." Those who know anything about the Air Cadet Organisation will be aware that a squadron with the letter F means it is one of the founder squadrons. 7F was only the seventh squadron to be formed and in the cadet hierarchy it is prestigious to be a founder squadron.

I was quite excited about the prospect of getting my teeth into developing the squadron. I knew I had the enthusiasm and the wherewithal but, as ever, there were problems and challenges to be overcome. During my RAF career I had only known one way to operate and that was full steam ahead. Quite often that upsets those who don't share my enthusiasm or are reluctant to change. In the military it was quite easy to adopt this style of management, especially if it proved successful, but in a voluntary youth organisation things are a little different. The few staff at 7F had been there for many years, twenty years in some cases. The previous commanding officer was very different in style to myself and he appeared to let others manage and dictate direction. He and his staff were keen on shooting. There was an indoor range on site and staff and a few cadets would often use the outdoor ranges at RAF Sealand. I had done my compulsory shooting during my RAF days and was in fact a RAF marksman, but I was not over-enthused about shooting as a youth activity. As I set about my own recruiting campaign, the last activity I would promote, in an area well known for gangland killings would be shooting. I was going into schools encouraging young people to consider all the sporting activities you could participate in and the opportunities for adventure training. Straight away I was in conflict with my staff team. I was told, in no uncertain terms, that 7F is not interested in sport or adventure training and things would remain as they are, regardless of what I thought.

One senior cadet came to me in a rather confrontational manner and told me I was unwelcome and should leave now. He had some support amongst the staff but rather than intimidate me this was the all the incentive I needed to make changes. I had recruited quite a few new recruits and I focussed on looking after them. Also, by all sorts of ways and means, I started to bring in new staff. Stan Michael had retired from Huyton Air Cadets and was effectively pushed out, a great shame but a great bonus for me. I managed to convince Stan to come and work for me and what a great asset he proved to be. He took on the role of looking after and training all the new recruits. No one is more old school than Stan Michael, but the difference with Stan, he was receptive and willing to change. He saw the new recruits as cadets and would always call them by their surname. I, meanwhile, made it may business to know all the cadets first names and a bit about their family circumstance. All the cadets knew they could come and see me at any time during parade nights and I would certainly not shout at them or embarrass them, as others had done before me. The most important people in my squadron were the cadets and they knew that. Without cadets there would be no squadron and every cadet was made to feel important. Before long, young people were calling at the squadron asking to join. I interviewed every new recruit and kept a record of that interview. I would look for their particular interests or hobbies; some had none and came for all sorts of reasons. That was fine by me as long as they abided by my one rule, discipline. Most people will think that discipline means shouting and bawling and blind obedience but the RAF definition of discipline was quite simply, organised good manners. I would say to all recruits, "Show respect to staff and your peers regardless of colour, creed or ability and we will show you respect". I had a little logo above my desk that went; it does not matter how much money you have in the bank, what type of car you drive, or what clothes you wear, what matters is that you are important in the life of a young person. Each parade night I would take a class and start teaching map work or first aid and after a few minutes we would be involved in a discussion about my job, crime, youth culture, any topic that generated interest. I have always had strong views about racism and I have completed many anti racism courses. I have also have witnessed racism first hand and I genuinely believe racism is wicked. I would often bring racism into our discussion and the cadets soon learnt that I had strong views about this subject.

7F squadron is located in a unique area of Liverpool. Leave the squadron building and turn right, walk a few hundred yards and you were in the leafy suburbs of middle class Mossley Hill and Aigburth. Leave the building and turn left, walk a few hundred yards and you entered Toxteth with all the images that conjures up. Cadets came from the left and the right and from the different schools in the catchment areas. Some cadets came from The Blue Coat school, Liverpool College others came from less well-known schools but I welcomed all. I insisted that the cadets did not wear school uniform at the squadron. I also asked those cadets who had uniform if they wanted to travel to the squadron in civilian clothes and change in to uniform when they arrived at the squadron. No one ever did. I used to be so proud of the cadets when I saw them stood at a bus stop or walking home through Toxteth in their cadet uniform. I remember one time; I was travelling to the squadron at a time of heightened tension amongst the criminal fraternity. There had been a number of gangland murders and Police roadblocks were in abundance. I pulled up at a roadblock and as I was answering the Police Officer's questions I noticed one of my cadets stood at a bus stop. He was in uniform, beret on, standing upright, smart as a guardsman totally oblivious to all that was going on. The presence of that young Air Cadet brought some semblance of normality to a very difficult situation. I mentioned to the Police Officer that the cadet was a member of my Air Cadet squadron, even the Police Officer was impressed. That young man, David Hart, lived in Fernie Street, which is off Northumberland Street. My nan and granddad lived in Fernie Street all their lives. My dad was born and raised there and I always felt a bit nostalgic whenever I was in this wonderful part of Liverpool. Young David Hart was an unassuming individual, very polite and a bit reticent. However, over the years David spent with 7F he developed into a real character. The cadets were an ideal platform for David to develop the obvious latent talent within. He first came to prominence when we were putting on a drill display at a Toxteth, old peoples' home. The old people, as ever, were delighted to see the cadets in their uniforms and the drill display was very entertaining.

The cadets finished their display and we were enjoying tea and biscuits when David suddenly stepped forward and, without any prompting, he burst into a melody of old time songs. He captivated his audience and had obviously learnt those songs from the parties he attended within his own family. David also developed into a top class middle distance runner and was the wing 1500-metre champion for many years. David became one of our senior cadets and was extremely popular with all other cadets and very well liked by all staff. David applied for the RAF, he passed the test and interview but failed the medical. Would you believe it, he was underweight for military service. I am pleased to say David put on weight and joined the RAF as a supplier. Under the old regime at 7F, David may well have been sent away. He came from the wrong side of the local area (the left side) and he never went to one of the more favoured schools but he benefited enormously from his involvement with the Air Cadets. Many cadets, like David, lived in an area of Liverpool that was plagued by drug and alcohol abuse. Gangland warfare was an everyday fact of life but even today, in Britain's worst towns and cities, there are young people who overcome tremendous difficulties and develop into decent, law-abiding citizens. It is, in my opinion, important that the government of the day invest in organisations that provide purposeful and meaningful opportunities for young people to develop, rather simply than build more prisons.

Back to my early days in command of the squadron. Right from the start of my 7F career I was encountering problems with staff. To be fair, I was like a bull in a china shop but I was on a mission. I either made changes or let the place deteriorate. I tried to win over the staff but that failed so I set about bringing in more new staff. Stan Michael's appointment went down like a lead balloon but Stan, like me, was blessed with thick skin and did what was asked of him, with great aplomb. I gave Stan sole responsibility for recruit training. Come the formal enrolment parade Stan was given licence to plan and execute the parade. Previous to my arrival there was no enrolment parade of note. I thought it very important that cadets had the opportunity to show off their new-found skills to an invited audience of family and guests. Stan Michael was in his element in this department and there was an excellent relationship built up between him and the many recruits he trained. There was an age gap, almost sixty years, between Stan and his recruits but I used to enjoy watching him work with the cadets. Ex cadets, still to this day, speak with great affection about Mr Michael. My daughter Christine spent many happy years as a cadet at 7F and she regularly asks me, "how is Mr Michael? Another wonderful acquisition was the appointment of Terry Shaw, as a civilian instructor. I knew Terry; he was a neighbour of Stan Michael and he enjoyed photography. I contacted him and asked him to take some cadet photographs for publicity purposes. He was happy doing this but when I asked him to join as a member of staff he was a bit reluctant. He had no instructional experience, he would say, but I convinced him he had a role to play. He joined the staff team and proved to be an outstanding asset to the squadron and a great friend of mine.

Terry had recently retired early from Ford's factory at Halewood on the grounds of ill health. His hearing had deteriorated and he was troubled by arthritis. However, I convinced Terry there was a place for him at the squadron. Terry became embroiled in the million and one tasks involved in adventure training, building maintenance and the mini bus. He became an invaluable asset and the cadets thought the world of him. He would spend hours at the squadron fixing things or he would be out scrounging things, no task was ever too much trouble for him. I knew I was making great demands on his time but his wife, Irene, told me he was extremely happy being involved and that was all I needed to know. I also recruited another star in Alan Birkett. Alan's son was a cadet at the squadron and what a fine young person Neil Birkett was (now Constable Birkett, Merseyside Police). I managed to convince Alan that he would be made very welcome as a member of the staff training team. Alan joined the squadron, initially as a civilian instructor, but went on to became the Squadron Warrant Officer, a crucial role, and one undertaken extremely well. Alan became another invaluable asset and great friend. Alan had a keen interest in camping and hill walking and his knowledge and experience was put to great use over the next ten years. In addition, Alan was a qualified swimming coach; another wonderful attribute put to great use. A woman called at the squadron one evening and offered to run our canteen. June Long had heard that I was looking for staff and I welcomed her with open arms.

Every youth organisation should have a June Long. June was everyone's agony aunt. When the cadets were falling in and out of love and friendship it was June they all turned to. June was the sympathetic ear for all troubles, whether that be serious family problems or petty squabbling, June dealt with them much better than any social worker I have met and I have met many. June had many other attributes that complimented our developing squadron. She was hardworking; dedicated and always put the cadets' best interests first. June would accompany cadets to their various activities, whether that be flying, gliding, sporting or social events. June was always available and I know that the cadets always made a point of thanking Miss Long for her support. I knew I had the nucleus of a good and supportive staff team developing around me.

Another great acquisition was Steve Banks. Steve's daughter Janine was a cadet at the squadron and I had spent a week on an expedition and Janine was part of the group. So impressed was I with Janine's behaviour, attitude and enthusiasm, on my return home I made it my business to visit Janine's parents who had a butchers shop on Lark Lane. I did not know Janine's parents but arrived at their shop introduced myself and explained that I had called only to say, what a pleasure it was to have Janine as a member of our youth group. Shortly afterwards, Steve and his wife Jean were members of 7F. I now had in place a top class team of multi talented people, ironically none of whom, had any military experience, but so what. I had in the space of a few months created a lean, mean, training machine. I also recruited a young woman, Bernadette Ferguson, who I knew from my time at Huyton Squadron. Bernie was another wonderful acquisition; she had lots of enthusiasm and she enjoyed outdoor pursuits. She was also familiar with the cadet-training syllabus and had been a member of the all-conquering Huyton drill team. Bernie eventually became my nominated deputy and later joined the RAF as an administrative clerk. Bernie was by far the youngest member of staff but she was crucial to my great master plan. What we all had in common was enthusiasm, commitment and a deep respect for each other. I was technically in charge but I made sure I was seen to be no more, or no less, important than any of my team or any of the cadets in my charge. I was, however, still encountering difficulties with the staff I inherited. They appeared to be waiting for me to do something drastically wrong, and be dismissed, like my predecessor, but I was surrounded by people who shared my enthusiasm and who were becoming good friends.

I had another plan up my sleeve and rather boldly, I wrote to Lady Jean Stoddart and asked Lady Stoddart if she would take on the role of squadron President. I had met Lady Stoddart only once previously, at an Air Cadet function. Although only a very brief encounter I thought to myself afterwards, "what a lovely Lady, how pleasant and engaging". On assuming command of 7F, my letter was in the post to Lady Stoddart. I was surprised, but nonetheless delighted, when I received a reply from her agreeing to be the squadron President. Lady Stoddart is the wife of Wing Commander Sir Kenneth Stoddart KCVO AE JP former Lord Lieutenant of Merseyside and a former Battle of Britain pilot. Lady Stoddart agreed to be our principal guest at the first of our carefully choreographed enrolment parades. I also decided to take a chance and write to Sir John Smith CBE (the chairman of Liverpool football club) and asked him if he would accept the title of squadron Vice President; I'm delighted to say he accepted. I had never previously met Sir John but I was aware that he was born in Liverpool 8, left school at 15 with no qualification and went on to be a hugely successful businessman and international sports personality; he was also an ex RAF administration clerk. 7F squadron headed notepaper now had printed on it two of the most well known and well-respected Merseyside personalities. Consequently, when I was writing begging letters on behalf of the squadron, I would usually get a very favourable response.

I also changed the squadron badge from a rather dull, lacklustre logo to a rather colourful red Liver Bird with the Everton Football Club Motto underneath. *Nil Satis Nisi Optimum* (only your best is good enough).

The redesigned 7F Squadron badge.

Now that my new training team was in place, I was confidently going into local schools recruiting. I knew that if a young person made the effort to come along and see what we had to offer they would be interested in joining. It was, in my opinion, important that every visitor was greeted in a friendly manner and the building looked clean and tidy. Everything was in place to commence the development of the squadron and prepare to take on the might of Huyton, Ormskirk, Neston, Maghull and the other big players in the local air cadet world. Successful air cadet squadrons don't need to have huge numbers; what you do need is a committed staff team and cadets who are equally committed and the odd one or two who are good at sport.

By pure chance, one of the new recruits, Jane Edwards, discovered during her cadet days, that she could run. Jane lived in Eslick Street (in the Dingle) probably best known as the location for the TV series Bread. Jane was a waif of a girl who looked frail and likely to be blown away in a gust of wind. However, beneath that exterior was a very tough character. Jane came to prominence in the wing cross-country event in the autumn of 1991. We managed to enter a full team and this was the first time for many years that 7F had been seen at a cadet sports event. I was a marshal out on the course, and when the race was over I made my way back to the start point. A colleague of mine mentioned that he had heard that 7 F had done well and he thought we had the first home in one of the races. I thought it may have been my niece, Jenny Rummens, who I knew to be a good runner but I was soon to find out it was Jane Edwards and she had apparently won by a mile or thereabouts.

Once all the races are over cadets have to get changed into their uniforms and attend a presentation. This was Lady Stoddart's first attendance at an air cadet event in her capacity as President of 7F. I was talking to Lady Stoddart when up walked Jane Edwards. In her own inimitable style and manner she asked me if I knew how to get into tights. She had one leg in and the other out. I asked June Long to take her over to the cadet minibus and help her. At that time I did not know Lady Stoddart that well but she saw the funny side of it. For the next ten years, Lady Stoddart attended almost every squadron sports event, enrolment parade and visited the cadets when they were undergoing their DofE Expeditions. I have met many people on my travels but never such a kind, caring and fun-loving person as Lady Stoddart. The only time she and I disagreed was when she wanted to undertake a slip-line ride across a ravine near Fairbourne. Lady Stoddart was in the queue, waiting to go, when I reminded her "there is a minimum age for participation and I suspect there will be a maximum age." Far be it for me to disclose a Lady's age but Lady Jean had seen wartime service and I suspected she was an octogenarian.

'Lady Jean' – as we all called her, was equally at home listening to my briefing, chatting to a member of staff or more importantly, listening to a cadet's story. Most of the squadron, including myself, had never met a real Lady (in every sense of the word) but we now had our own. It used to make me very happy when I would see the cadets of their own volition, run across to Lady Jean whenever she arrived at one of our functions. There was no formality, just genuine warmth and a mutual respect. I would often tell Lady Jean of the personal circumstance of a cadet, particularly if there were hardship or family problems. Lady Jean would always, without any fuss, help out as best she could. Every annual expedition would see Lady Jean arrive with a car full of provisions for our bar-b-q. No amount of pleading could convince Lady Jean to take any money for the costs incurred; quite the opposite, I was told not to mention it again and I never did.

As for young Jane Edwards, she was our first sports star and as others followed we were gradually becoming a force to be reckoned with on the sports field. Incidentally Jane Edwards joined the Royal Navy and I understand that remains her career to this day. When I first arrived at 7F we had no sports kit of any description, no camping equipment or mini bus. Steve Banks suggested I write to Eddie Amoo, the lead singer with the Liverpool pop group The Real Thing (of 'You To Me Are Everything' fame). There followed a cheque for £400 and we now had brand new boys and girls sports kit with the words 'The Real Thing' emblazoned on the shirts. We were still in a lower league to the premier squadrons but we were competing in every event and, if nothing else, we were the best turned out, best supported and best behaved.

Known to some as Toxteth Air Cadets we were often looked down upon by other staff and cadets. Consequently I insisted we behaved impeccably and showed good sportsmanship. All our sports teams were encouraged to thank the sports referees and officials, something that became accepted practice to all squadron cadets. I also insisted we were magnanimous in victory and gracious in defeat. We were, however, not seen as a threat at this time to the big players, consequently we were always underrated and treated with a degree of indifference. As we progressed we would encounter hype and attempts to discredit us, but by now we were operating with a high degree of camaraderie and cadets would support each other.

I mentioned to Lady Jean one time about the lack of sports equipment and she suggested I write to Slazenger's head office. I wrote and shortly afterwards I received an invite to travel up to their main warehouse in Wakefield. I borrowed a mini bus and off I went. On arrival I was told take as much equipment as I needed. The managing director was a former Air Cadet was delighted to be helping a founder squadron and inner city youth organisation. The fact that Lady Jean's and Sir John's names were on our headed paper obviously had an influence.

Returning home I was able to kit out the squadron with hockey kit and donated the rest to the Wing. In addition to Lady Jean's involvement Sir John was also taking a very keen interest in our activities. I had a few meetings with Sir John both at his office in Brunswick Dock and at his office at Liverpool Football club. Sir John and I got on very well. He would regale me with his stories of the eighteen trophies won by his beloved Liverpool Football club during his reign as club chairman. He was also very proud of his Liverpool 8 roots. I always found Sir John a very down to earth, no-nonsense sort of person. He once told me a tale of a footballer arriving at Anfield to sign for the club.

"He had an agent with him," said Sir John, "so I refused to speak to the player unless his agent left the room." How different from the world of football today.

I invited Sir John to one of our enrolment parades and asked if he could bring a Liverpool player with him. He attended and brought Bruce Grobbelaar with him. Bruce was fantastic. He inspected the cadets and gave a wonderful, inspiring talk. Bruce was a former soldier in the Zimbabwe Army and signed our visitor's book, as 'Corporal Grobbelaar'.

We obtained some good publicity out of this event and consequently we were getting more and more young people joining the squadron. One other resource I tapped into was the Toxteth Community Police Liaison Officer, Constable Lol Jeffries. I had a meeting with Lol and from then on we became good friends and Lol did a great deal of work for the squadron. So impressed was Lol with the cadets that he actually joined the squadron as a member of the civilian committee. There were many mutual benefits of our involvement with Lol. For a start Lol could obtain transport for our us, including the Merseyside Police coach, but I would also take referrals from him. In the course of his Police work Lol met many young people who he thought could benefit from being involved with our organisation. I would interview those people and invariably they would join and do well.

To each enrolment parade, of which there were normally two a year, we would invite the current High Sheriff, a senior Merseyside Police Officer and other local notaries. The Lord Mayor of Liverpool came to one enrolment, as did the Lord Lieutenant of Merseyside. Quite often our guests would be surprised to see that amidst all the despair and social deprivation there was a thriving Air Cadet squadron. On one occasion, at one of the squadron organised Merseyside Police Band concerts an elderly Lady came up to me and handed over £20. She was so impressed with the cadets turnout and deportment she donated the money to the squadron; a very kind gesture. Lol, on his police beat, would meet the cadets and this in turn generated better police/community relations. Lol also had access to various schemes and opportunities and knew that if he was unable to obtain enough numbers he could always rely on 7F cadets to help out. Through Lol cadets were participating in sailing events and many cadets joined the Toxteth steel band.

One Police activity we did particularly enjoy was the River Mersey Raft Race (now defunct). Lol suggested we enter a team and we did just that. We had to build a raft, obtain oars and lifejackets. We had no training or no practice run so I was quite anxious when we turned up for our first raft race. I had warned our team to be on best behaviour. I had heard that there was a lot of flour throwing and water bombing and the like but the rules clearly said that was forbidden. We arrived, complete with untried raft, at the Albert Dock and launched our raft. It floated, I'm pleased to say, unlike the Sea Cadet raft which, when launched, carried on to the bottom of the Albert Dock. We duly set off with a crew of staff and cadets but no sooner had we taken our first stroke when we were bombarded with water bombs, flour bombs and water cannons. We were defenceless but from then on we revised our tactics and competed on an equal basis for the next ten years. The raft race was good fun, especially if the weather was decent. We also got some good publicity for the squadron and the Air Cadets in general. Cadets thought nothing of throwing themselves into the murky waters of the Mersey; I always declined but did, as a youth, swim in the same waters, which were much murkier in the 1950s.

Events on the squadron had moved so quickly that I was hardly aware of the undercurrents that still existed. I knew I was making progress in improving the efficiency and effectiveness of the squadron but at the same time I knew I had a few detractors within. I did try my best to work with all staff but there was no way things were going to stay the way they were. Things came to a head when I announced that the squadron annual awards were to take place. I made an announcement that all staff would nominate the cadets who they thought should receive an award. This did not go down well, but I was supposed to be in charge and I made that decision. Training staff were, after all, working with the cadets on a regular basis.

This caused mayhem and the Wing Commander was brought in to try and reconcile all sides. There were basically two sides; the civilian committee and old staff group and myself and my new staff group. The Wing Commander realised that the situation was irreconcilable but knew that I was acting in accordance within my terms of reference. Consequently, I went ahead. The civilian committee, few in number as they were, resigned in protest. From there on in 7F effectively became under new management and the rise from the ashes continued at a great pace.

I did have an inkling that something like this was imminent and I had in mind a few people who, if asked, would probably volunteer to help me out in my hour of need. The first person I approached was my secretary at the St Helens Probation Office, Jean McCooey. Jean very kindly offered to take on the role of secretary and she did an outstanding job. Jean had being doing some voluntary administration work for me in her lunch hour or at home of an evening. She would type up kit lists, route cards and, before I gained the skills, would type letters for me. My sister-in-law Margaret Rummens offered to act as treasurer – and what a thorough and meticulous treasurer she proved to be.

I had also met, at a cadet function, a gentleman by the name of Lieutenant Colonel Jim McGrellis MBE. I wrote to Colonel McGrellis and asked him if he would consider joining the squadron civilian committee. I am very pleased to say he accepted and shortly after joining became chairman of the committee – and what an asset he was. Colonel McGrellis had been a cadet in the squadron way back in the 1950s. He joined the Army as a boy soldier, leaving many years later in the rank of Lieutenant Colonel; not bad for a Liverpool 8 lad. Colonel McGrellis was the commandant at the Altcar Army camp, near Southport and consequently we spent many weekends at Altcar camp, a very popular activity with the cadets ... and staff for that matter.

Colonel McGrellis was the final piece in the jigsaw. He came to us with a wealth of military experience and business acumen. The cadets respected him enormously; he was, after all, a Liverpool 8 lad who had made good. He, like Lady Stoddart, was the ideal role model for the cadets. Both Colonel McGrellis and Lady Jean always made time to speak to the cadets and by virtue of the fact that they came out to see the cadets undertaking their expeditions, this further enhanced the rapport between the cadets, Lady Jean and Colonel McGrellis. The training staff was now a first class team and the three main players on the committee were highly professional and hugely talented in their own sphere of work.

Colonel McGrellis did some outstanding work raising funds for the squadron. He was regularly in dispute with the National Lottery fund. He would put forward a thorough and meticulous application for a grant and this would normally be rejected on some nebulous grounds. He would attend Lottery Fund briefings and meetings and, in the end, mastered the art of obtaining a lottery grant. Never one to embellish or overstate a case, he persevered and obtained many grants from the Lottery which were put to great use. Colonel McGrellis's finest achievement at the squadron was to obtain a brand new 16-seater mini bus from the Sports Foundation. This was a first for any Air Cadet squadron and the cadets were always delighted when they turned up for their various competitions in their own squadron mini bus and trailer.

I did inherit two very talented instructors from the old group, Tim Robinson and Clive Forder, but my new staff group was increasing in numbers all the time. I also inherited a few excellent cadets. One cadet I did inherit was a young woman named Loretta Dunne. Loretta was selected for an air experience gliding trip; nothing unusual in that, most cadets get that opportunity. However, from the outset Loretta demonstrated a natural flying ability. There followed a basic and advanced gliding course, a flying scholarship course culminating in Loretta obtaining her private Pilots licence, all before she was eighteen years of age. Loretta lived in the Walton area of Liverpool but travelled across the city to join 7F. She became an acknowledged aviator of natural ability. I remember her applying for the RAF as a Pilot. She passed all the necessary exams but was two centimetres short in her arm length; consequently she failed the medical. Loretta was an 'A' star pupil in all her school and cadet examinations; she was good at sport and had a very pleasant person- ality. Undeterred, Loretta went on to study astro-physics and may well be an astronaut now.

I also inherited two other excellent cadets, Michelle Barlow and Rebecca Robinson. They both went on to become senior cadets within the squadron. Michelle was outstanding at drill; she had previously been a majorette so had learnt co-ordination at an early age. Rebecca, like Michelle, had a very pleasant personality and manner. The cadets all thought they were wonderful and consequently we were developing a friendly, lively team spirit. We were undertaking more and more residential activities at Altcar Army Camp or Lord Derby's Estate. Both locations were only a few miles from the squadron but could have been a million miles away in contrast. An interesting aside about our camps at Lord Derby's Estate. At this time I was a student Probation Officer undertaking a placement at the Kirkby Probation Office. I had met Lord Derby several times. He had no problems with the cadets camping on his estate and would often call across to our campsite and have a few words with staff and cadets. I briefed him one day, about our plans to undertake, a DofE, bronze expedition, from his estate. We planned to set up a base camp on his estate and then move off to the scout camps at Tawd Vale and Bispham Hall. Lord Derby expressed concern about the cadets crossing the East Lanc's Road. I had assured Lord Derby that staff would cross the cadets over the road and then the cadets would set off on their expeditions. The day before we were due to arrive at his estate, Lord Derby telephoned the Probation Office at Kirby and asked to speak to me. I received a message from one of the office administration staff stating there was a man on the phone from the Derby Arms Pub wanting to speak to me. I thought to myself I have never been in the Derby Arms Pub but took the call only to hear it was Lord Derby. He just wanted to check that all possible safety checks were in place, when the cadets left his land and crossed the East Lancs Road.

Another funny Lord Derby story… When I was at Huyton squadron there was a wonderful member of staff named Kathy Murphy – 'Mrs Murphy' to hundreds of Huyton cadets. Amongst Kath's many duties was managing the tuck shop, but she went off and completed an instructional technique course. On her return, a function was taking place at Huyton squadron. I was in conversation with Lord Derby and Wing Commander Ian Jones. Kath interrupted our conversation to ask Ian Jones a question. "Excuse me sir, but I have just

returned from my instructional technique course and there is something that worries me"

"What is that, Mrs Murphy," said the Wing Commander.

"I don't understand why you have to have Aids before you can
give a good lecture." She had clearly got 'visual aids' mixed up with
'Aids,' the illness! Nevertheless, Kath was an outstanding community voluntary worker who gave considerable time and effort to the
young people of Huyton.

Lord Derby was also a great supporter of Huyton Air Cadets. We
could camp on his land as often as we liked and he regularly joined
us for our barbecues. I always found Lord Derby quite a shy, retiring
gentleman. I'm sure he wasn't; as a holder of the Military Cross and
a former Guards Officer, he would have seen some action in his time.
I also found Lord Derby a very kind man. I asked him once if we
could organise a fun run around his estate, he agreed and we did that
for a few years and, raised a lot of money for local charities. Interest-
ingly, when Lord Derby died, his coffin was brought out of the estate
on a horse-drawn trailer. No pomp, no circumstance, which is quite
unusual, for a senior member, of the British aristocracy but those
were Lord Derby's wishes.

7F Squadron expeditions to Lord Derby's estate proved extremely
popular with the cadets. It was always interesting, undertaking a
residential activity, and watching the most unassuming person
develop into a natural leader. By now cadet numbers were on the
increase. We had a wide cross-section of young people from various
backgrounds. We had cadets referred to us by Lol Jeffries. We had
fee-paying school children, the academically very bright child and
the more pragmatic individual. We also had a good ethnicity mix.
Our age ranged from thirteen to twenty. Consequently, undertaking
an activity that in some cases numbered fifty children; required a lot
of organisation and a lot of observation. Many things could go wrong
but in all my years at 7F there was never any serious incident. I was
once summoned to see the TA Centre Battery Commander (Major
Tom Richards) where we were located. I knew when I was summoned to his office it usually meant a telling-off. On this occasion
Major Tom called me into his office and looking at me rather sternly,
said, "Your cadets have been fighting with the Army Cadets and the
Army cadets have made a complaint." My heart sank. I had always
warned my cadets that fighting was totally unacceptable and I would,

without hesitation, dismiss any cadets involved in fighting. In those few brief moments I was genuinely disappointed; I really believed that none of my cadets would let the squadron down. Major Tom informed me that the culprit was Cadet Jane Edwards. I told Tom I would go and speak to Jane and report back.

I duly spoke to Jane, listened to her version of events and went with her to see Major Tom.

"Tell the Major your version of events Jane."

"Well Sir, as I came into the barracks some Army cadets started shouting and swearing at me. They called me a scruff and started throwing stones at me."

"What did you do?" asked Major Tom.

"I went over and hit them."

"How many Army cadets were there?"

"About ten," said Jane.

"Case dismissed," said I, and apart from a little advice to Jane, no more was ever said about that incident.

Each year cadets have the opportunity to participate in an annual camp. A week at a RAF station is the highlight of the cadet calendar for many, including myself. My first camp with 7F was at RAF Brawdy in West Wales. This was a long coach journey, I think it took about ten hours but I always found travelling an enjoyable activity. Not so for many of the cadets who, due to a combination of excitement and overindulging in sweets, were travel-sick. Concern had been expressed about the driver of our coach and it appeared that he had exceeded the maximum driving time, although he denied this.

On our journey home the driver pulled in to a lay by and removed his tachograph. I was sitting in a front seat alongside Steve Woods. Steve, as well as being a civilian instructor with the Air Cadets, was a department of transport vehicle inspector. He took a few notes and the following Monday he arrived at the coach depot and the drivers' log was checked. I understand the driver was heavily fined for his dangerous behaviour. A few weeks after returning from Brawdy I was asked if I would like to undertake another annual camp. I was at this time a student at Liverpool University so the opportunity of another paid annual camp was too good to miss and off I went to RAF St Athan. On this occasion my daughter Christine, who had joined the squadron, travelled with me. It was interesting showing her and her cadet friends our old married quarter. I really enjoyed annual camp. I looked upon it as a great opportunity for the cadets to see exactly what the RAF was all about. It was one such visit to RAF Coltishall in 1965 that convinced me that I wanted to be a fireman in the RAF. I am sure there are many young people who were motivated to a RAF career by their own annual camp. I always enjoyed the sporting and social side of the annual camp. There were lots of enjoyable activities laid on for the cadets and for those staff who wanted to get involved. There was also an entertaining evening's activity in the respective staff messes. I remember taking 7F squadron to RAF Machrihanish for an annual camp. The cadets and staff travelled the 350 miles by coach while I went up the day previous in the squadron mini bus (a Bedford midi). I had to travel a day early to sort out the staff and cadets accommodation and to take over from the previous cadet camp commandant, as we were called (camp comedian some said). The journey up to Machrihanish was very pleasant. Anne had prepared me a wonderful packed lunch and I had a good selection of my favourite music cassettes to keep me company. The drive down the A83 from Inveraray to Campbletown was fantastic and must be one of the most scenic routes in the UK. I arrived relaxed, having had a doze in a lay-by alongside Loch Lomond. When I had unpacked and sorted out my room, off I went for a few miles run. That evening I took over responsibility for the cadet accommodation and had a pleasant few pints in the officers' mess. The next day I had a stroll around this rather remote and barren RAF station while I waited for the coach bringing the staff and cadets. The cadets left Liverpool at 9pm on the Friday evening and arrived at camp about 10am Saturday morning. This was a big adventure travelling overnight, and I know that the cadets were excited about the prospect. I was waiting at the guardroom when the coach arrived and I watched as the cadets and staff disembarked.

First off the coach was June Long. June came straight over and informed me that the cadets had not slept a wink throughout the journey. When the cadets came off the coach they looked cheerful enough but poor June looked knackered and I'm not surprised. That particular week's camp turned out to be very eventful, in many ways. Our week at Machrihanish coincided with the start of the Royal Family's summer holiday in Scotland. In those days, the Royal party travelled to Scotland on the Royal Yacht and the first port of call was Campeltown. The Queen and Prince Philip disembark and undertake a walk about. I was asked by the station commander to take our cadets down to the harbour and join the crowds who were waving flags. As the Royal party came ashore Prince Philip made a beeline for our little group, said a few words and asked one of our cadets a question. I think it threw him a bit, expecting the child to reply in a Scottish accent she replied in a broad scouse accent. Later in the week we were undertaking a hill walking exercise and enjoying the views overlooking the Mull of Kintyre, when a land rover pulled up alongside us. A head popped out and who should it be but Paul McCartney, he was as much surprised as Prince Philip but at least Paul could understand the broad scouse accents. Paul McCartney was born and raised in the same area of Liverpool as many of our cadets. I thought we may have been invited back to his place but he never offered, although he was very nice with everyone. Another highlight of this camp was my meeting with one of my best mates from my RAF days. When on camp I would always call in at the fire section, just to see if I knew any of the firemen. I called in to the fire section at Machrihanish and there was Warrant Officer Bob Lowe BEM. Bob and I were together at RAF Lindholme and RAF Laarbruch. I never thought for one minute all those years ago that Bob would end up a Warrant Officer. Likewise, I never thought I would end up a Flight Lieutenant in the RAFVR (T). I was in uniform when I met Bob and I am sure he did not know whether to salute or shake hands, but we were always good mates and that remains the case to this day. Bob arranged for all my staff and I to attend a special function put on by him at the Sergeants mess'. On camp, Officers, SNCO's and civilian Air Cadet staff used different messes, but on this occasion we were able to enjoy a pleasant night together in the best of all the messes. Despite my long RAF service, many of those as a SNCO, now that I was an Officer I was not allowed in to the Sergeants mess unless I was invited and the person who invited me would have to obtain permission from the senior sergeants mess member. Protocol and etiquette, but such was service life. Annual camps for the cadets would entail a bit of flying, in whatever aircraft were available, sporting activities, section visits and a variety of exercises.

Station staff would devise some escape and evasion exercise or river crossing exercise. Quite often the station personnel were more excited about these exercise than the cadets. Whilst at Machrihanish we were taken over to the far side of the airfield to be given a tour of the American Seal unit, based there. I had no idea who the SEALs were or what they did but a few of the cadets had seen a film about the Navy Seals and they briefed me. On arrival at the unit, a very smart and very well decorated American Seal welcomed us. We were given a briefing outlining exactly what the SEALS do and were shown some of their sophisticated equipment, including their weapon firing range. We were all suitably impressed and as we were leaving I asked if the SEALS would like to meet us in the station gym for a game of basketball. "I shall see what I can do" replied the American serviceman. Later that day I received a telephone call, "see you at 7pm tonight, station gym". Amongst the cadets we had some very good basketball players both male and female. I selected a team and did a bit of motivational work and off we went to the gym. As I walked in, there before me were these giants, all built like proverbial brick toilets. I introduced our team, briefed the Americans that we were all Liverpudlians many from Toxteth and the game began, with me refereeing. The Americans knew, if they wanted, they could probably annihilate us but they were finding our size and turn of speed difficult to manage. They won but we did get a few baskets and when one huge SEAL picked up one of our female cadets and placed her in a basket, I called time. We spent the night in the company of the SEALS and they were, to a man, great with the cadets. I was given one of their baseball caps and the cadets were treated to free Coca-Cola and burgers. I got to know some of the SEALs quite well that week. I would regale them with stories of Liverpool and the personal circumstances of some of the cadets. I would tell the SEALS about the good and bad side of Liverpool and how the cadets overcome many obstacles and prejudices to do what they do. As a result of my tales, the SEALS arranged for one of our cadets to spend a week at their base in Italy. Young Rebecca Robinson was chosen to undertake this trip of a lifetime. Shortly after returning home she set off on her all expenses trip to the SEAL base in Italy.

I enjoyed quite a few more annual camps with 7F including, RAF Coltishall, RAF Bulmer, RAF Buchan and every one was an unforgettable experience. There was invariably the occasional problem or two but there was a whole host of support staff on hand to help out, unlike my times on cadet expeditions. One inevitable problem was cadet relationships.

The average age of the cadet on camp was about fifteen but you could have cadets as young as fourteen and as old as twenty undertaking the same activity and sharing the same accommodation. I was, in a way, better prepared than most for dealing with the problems associated with adolescence. At this time I was at Liverpool University completing my Diploma in Social Work. The syllabus included, amongst many other subjects, human growth and development, psychology and sociology. These particular subjects fascinated me. I had been brought up, one of a family of five children, but I never knew anything about adolescence, the menstrual cycle, hormones or emotions. I had always been fascinated by group dynamics and had known people who had experienced psychological problems but now I was getting paid to study these very subjects. Consequently, when I was away for a week with the cadets I could see first hand all the telltale signs of a child experiencing homesickness for the first time. Or a young person, isolated or ostracised for whatever reason, and then there were those who fell in and out of love several times a week. I would spend a lot of time in group discussions with the cadets and would encourage then to express any worries they may have. I would also go to great lengths to get the cadets to work and play together. I would encourage senior cadets to keep an eye on the quieter cadets and categorically there would be no bullying or silly rituals. When I was a cadet it was not unusual to wake up and find your eyebrows had been shaven off or, worse still, someone had blackened your testicles with shoe polish. Those two acts, in my opinion, were serious assaults upon the person. All my cadets knew I would dismiss any person who committed such acts. As the officer commanding 7F squadron I was supervising many black cadets and racism was another dismissable offence in my squadron. Other squadron staff thought I was too soft with the cadets or lacked discipline, but that was hogwash. I made it my business to know every cadet under my supervision; I called them all by their first name or nickname so long as that was acceptable. Cadets always called me sir or Mr Edwards and even now, when I meet an ex cadet of mine they still call me sir. I always say you don't have to call me sir and invariably the reply would be, "you'll always be sir, sir".

Back at the squadron we were competing to a good standard in all cadet sporting competitions and winning trophies. We were regularly appearing in the press and our cadet numbers were increasing all the time. Another little scoop that brought the squadron to prominence was our involvement with the RAF 7 squadron. I was aware of 7 squadron and knew they flew Chinook helicopters. Not long after taking over 7F, I wrote to the Officer Commanding 7 Squadron and did my normal blurb about the cadets and the wonderful work they were doing, against all the odds, in inner city Liverpool. I received a very nice reply and that was it; we became attached to 7 Squadron.

They would, whenever they could, fly up to Liverpool and take the squadron on a flight in one of their Chinooks. Even my detractors had to acknowledge that I had done something no one had done before. On one occasion a Chinook came up to Liverpool airport, collected about forty of us and flew us at low-level down to their base at RAF Odiham, near Basingstoke. We spent the day with 7 Squadron and they flew us back high-level that night. I was at the office the next day and one of my Probation colleagues mentioned that he had seen, yesterday, a huge helicopter flying out over the Mersey. He was somewhat surprised to hear that I was on that flight and had a lot to do with organising it. Also on board was my mate, Constable Lol Jeffries. Lol might be a great community bobby but he turned green, before my very eyes, as soon as we left *terra firma*.

The squadron was moving forward rapidly and we were excelling in sport, adventure training and the Duke of Edinburgh's award. Nine months after taking over command of the squadron we had an awards and enrolment ceremony. Principal guest was Lady Jean, accompanied by her husband Sir Kenneth, and our vice president, Sir John Smith. Stan Michael prepared his recruits whilst the rest of the staff nominated who they thought should receive the various awards. At this our first big parade, thirty cadets were receiving bronze DofE awards, which attracted interest from the press. Many of those thirty bronze award recipients went on to achieve their Silver awards whilst a few obtained their Gold award. To obtain a DofE award of any level takes a fair bit of effort, but to obtain a gold award is a wonderful achievement. I am pleased to say I supervised two Gold DofE award groups during my time at 7F. There is an enormous sense of achievement for staff involved in the Dof E award. It was always the highlight of my cadet year watching a DofE group return home safely from an expedition. What began as a small foray into adventure training and the DofE award developed into a hugely successful enterprise. 7F squadron became one of the largest operators of the DofE award on Merseyside, if not the UK. Bearing in mind that we were all volunteers, that is some testament to the squadron staff and the commitment from the cadets. I remember well our first expedition during the summer of 1991. Terry Shaw and I set off in a minibus borrowed from a local church, camping equipment borrowed from Merseyside Probation service and little idea how things would work out. It really was trial and error.

Awards night 1991.

Lady Jean Stoddart, the Author and new 7F recruits.

Sir John Smith talking to Rebecca Robinson.

7F cadet Jane Edwards receives sports award from Bruce Grobbelar.

Duke of Edinburgh with author and Natalie Edmunds.

The author and 7F cadet David Honeywell (now Dr Honeywell).

Author with Sir Bobby Charlton and Dave Webb.

Andrew Weightman Award.
Author, Mr & Mrs Weightman, Andrew Weightman, The Lord Lieutenant of Merseyside and his wife, Lady Stoddart, Lieutenant Colonel McGrellis.

New sports kit sponsored by The Real Thing.

My daughter Christine receiving sports award from Alan Birkett,
7F Squadron Warrant Officer and sports officer.

7F Cadets at RAF St Athan.

7F Drill Team RAF Sealand 1998.

One of 7F squadron Chinook Flights with 7 Squadron.

All-boy 7F D of E expedition group.

All-girl 7F D of E expedition group.

Steve Banks and one of his D of E groups.

7F Gold Dof E group 2002.

7F Gold Group at St James Palace.

A remote site.

A Dof E group on the move only 49 miles to go...

The Campsite at Fairbourne.

Happy birthday Paul Edwards (Fairbourne base camp).

Fairbourne Camp staff and cadets.

Canoeing on the Mawddach Estuary.

Raft race crew.

We survived that first, small expedition without incident and the six cadets participating returned home safely. The year after, fifty-five cadets, twelve staff our squadron President, our Padre, and Lol Jeffries participated in this expedition. We travelled out in the Merseyside Police coach and had TA drivers to transport all the equipment; that included a field kitchen, mess tents and a whole host of ancillary equipment. This was big business now. We had a control tent depicting the weeks activity, maps indicated where each of the six person groups would be operating at any given time. We had emergency action plans on display, with nominal roll forms, next of kin details, medication records, all available in case of emergency. Staff were allocated tasks; the less physically active ran the base camp, usually Terry Shaw and June Long. This was a vital task and never once in all our expeditions did June or Terry let any of the cadets down. Alan Birkett was responsible for the day to day management of the cadets and he also took responsibility for supervising one expedition group. Chris Legge ran a comprehensive training programme, Ian Hurley looked after the transport logistics while Steve Banks, Bernie Fergusson, Paul Edwards, Louis Adams and I went out on the mountains checking on the various expeditions. Quite often we could have six or seven different groups undertaking expeditions of various duration and mileage. We used to have what we called a baby group, usually the youngest cadets, the first timers. They would normally walk the length of the Mawdach estuary, about ten miles, and set up their camp back at base camp under the watchful eyes of June and Terry. It was always interesting and amusing watching young people trying to cook a meal for themselves or set up a tent for the first time. Some cadets took to it like ducks to water. Usually the more experienced cadets led by example; but one cold, wet and ill-prepared night under canvas was usually enough to convince a young person that they should really try harder if they were going to enjoy camping. On arrival at Fairbourne, Alan Birkett would allocate the cadets to their tents and then we would have a few ice breakers, little games and familiarisation exercises. Sunday would be a full training day and for those preparing for an expedition it would be last minute equipment checks. Come Monday, individual groups would set off on their various expeditions. We would have a bronze group undertaking a two-day expedition of fifteen miles duration. Their route took them to the lower regions of Cadair Idris.

Their night stop was at Kings Youth Hostel, a relatively safe area. The next group was the silver group, undertaking a three day expedition covering thirty miles and two nights on Cadair Idris.

This was quite arduous and required a good level of fitness, navigation and camp-craft skills. As ever, a good deal of determination was always required. By this stage, the silver group had probably been together as a baby and bronze group so they were usually good friends and knew each other's strengths and weaknesses. Then finally we had the big one, a gold expedition undertaking a four-day expedition covering a minimum of fifty miles in remote and wild country. To get to this level, all participants would have been through all previous stages of the award, although that wasn't always the case. The cadets undertaking these ventures were being assessed by a local, DofE award gold assessor, usually he or she was a Snowdonia Park Ranger. Any young person who achieves a gold DofE award has my utmost respect. It is a wonderful achievement and I am not surprised that all Gold awards are presented at either Buckingham Palace or St James Palace. I had the great pleasure of attending a gold group presentation when our first Gold group received their Gold awards at St James Palace from the Duke of Edinburgh. Those young people went through their bronze, silver and gold with the squadron and all staff were very proud of their achievements. Our fist major expedition took place in the summer of 1992.

I selected a base camp at Fairbourne near Dolgellau, an area I knew well. I was not familiar with the campsite and had never previously met the site owner, Stuart Eves. All bookings were made through the Defence Land Agent who paid the owner. I think it was two pounds, per person, per night. As we were numbering about seventy people on site, quite a large amount of money passed over to Stuart. He took to our cadets and, despite the early difficulties he had understanding their accent he soon became a good friend to all at 7F, so much so, that he would travel across to Liverpool for our annual awards ceremonies. All the local people were aware that we were from Liverpool and sometimes, Liverpool people can get an unwarranted bad press. That never ever happened on any of our adventures. The squadron made friends wherever they went and were always great ambassadors for Liverpool. Hardly surprising that the local shopkeepers made the cadets welcome; they bought their supplies from them. Staff would be out on the various routes checking all was going well. At that time mobile phones hadn't arrived on the scene but we had made an application to the Lottery for a grant to purchase hand held radios. We were successful and the radios proved invaluable to staff and entertaining for the cadets. We set up a radio station on the highest accessible point on Cadair Idris and our radioman, Clive Forder, would remain on station all the time the cadets were on the move. We always made a great play of welcoming the group's home, especially the gold group. When all the expeditions were completed we had two days general activity; horse riding, canoeing, dry slope skiing and of course our Friday bar-b-q and evening party in the Springfield Arms.

Staff would usually have a pint or two in the Springfield Arms or the Fairbourne Hotel but we always had a duty driver and support staff on site. I would normally have a pint on the Friday and that was it for me. Taking this amount of young people and staff away, under these circumstances, invariably involved a whole host of incidents, some major, some minor. Trips to Dolgellau hospital occurred a few times a week but we had an otherwise impeccable safety record. While we were undertaking an expedition in the Cadair Idris region, a scoutmaster fell and died. I was aware of a Boy Scout who got up in the middle of the night, left his tent, fell and died. These sorts of situations are always at the forefront of your mind when leading a large expedition. Much as I enjoyed the expeditions, they were becoming increasingly difficult and I was always glad to get home safely. Fairbourne was not all work and no play; we had lots of time spent with the cadets around the campfire telling stories. Cadets used to enjoy this purely voluntary activity and our scary stories got worse each year. We used to make up stories of shipwrecks off the coast of Fairbourne beach. Storytellers would say that in olden times, ships leaving Liverpool would be deliberately lured on to Fairbourne rocks and the ships ransacked.

Every July, August or whatever time we were out rumour had it, that ghosts would come ashore seeking out people with Welsh accents. This was enough to convince our group that they should speak in an even more pronounced Liverpool accent. Terry Shaw was the cadet's favourite storyteller and, out of sight of the cadets, he would place seaweed outside a couple of tents and that was sufficient to convince the cadets that the ghosts were about. Terry would also drag a chain around the perimeter of the site, further exciting or terrifying the cadets. On another occasion, one evening, Terry put a white sheet over his head and left the campsite intending to walk down the road and enter the campsite by another entrance. I caught site of Terry walking down the road at the very same time a Police car was coming his way. This was the only time I had ever seen a Police car at Fairbourne. Terry, great man that he is, was hard of hearing and sometimes it could be difficult communicating with him. I had to run over and explain to the Police Officer exactly who Terry was and what he was doing otherwise I had visions of Terry getting whisked off to the local psychiatric hospital.

Some evening's cadets would put on a sing a long act or they would come up with some story of their own. Often they would do a skit, depicting the various staff characteristics – all good fun. One unpleasant incident comes to mind. One late autumn we were undertaking a long weekend expedition. The nights were drawing in, which always increased the risk of harm. A group of local youths came onto our field intent on causing trouble. They started throwing bricks and stones at our tents and one of the younger cadets had been ridiculed as he made his way back from the shop. By this stage in our development we had one of Merseyside's finest kick boxers, Paula Edwards, and we also had a few promising amateur boxers. There were a few other cadets who could hold their own in any company. I went across to this group and told them that if they wanted to continue to incite a riot then my cadets, most of who were from Toxteth, would happily oblige. Most of them, I said, had lived through the riots in Liverpool and many of them were champion boxers and martial arts experts. I asked the group to leave us alone and we never ever heard from them again. I understand from my local Fairbourne friends that the group calmed down after that and led a more orderly lifestyle. They probably realised they weren't as tough as they thought they were.

Some of our cadets were in fact quite tough. They could no doubt mix it with the best but never once in my ten years in charge of the squadron did I ever encounter any violence, insolence or bad behaviour. Quite the opposite, these young people were always polite, well-mannered and showed great concern and compassion for each other. Another incident of note highlights the strong sense of teamwork and care for each other prevalent at this time.

We had a group of cadets undertaking a silver expedition. They had completed the first day in very hot and humid conditions and arrived safely at their first night-stop. The next morning the group set off on the second stage of their three-day expedition. This entailed a climb across one of the Cadair Idris ridges. One of the group became ill and was having breathing difficulties. The group took shelter from the sun, administered basic first aid and made a decision not to continue. They set up an emergency campsite and two of the group set off to summon help. This was our normal operating plan but no group had previously aborted their expedition. The group leader, Andrew Weightman, set off with another cadet, to find the nearest phone and make contact with me. He called at a remote farmhouse and was given permission to use the occupier's phone. Steve Banks and I set off to collect the group and return them to base camp. Prior to returning to base camp I made contact with the occupier of the remote farmhouse and thanked her for her assistance. This elderly lady was in fact a retired former Liverpool Hospital matron. She told me that when Andrew called at her home he showed great composure and was extremely polite. He briefed the lady what had happened and she in turn informed me that she was of the opinion that Andrew deserved a commendation for his actions. The lady agreed to put it in writing and, on my return home, I nominated Andrew for an Air Cadet commendation, which he duly received.

It may seem, on the face of it, that this was nothing special but here was a fifteen year old boy under pressure, in difficult and demanding terrain who had to make an important decision. Continue with the expedition and the ill child's condition may well have worsened. Andrew sacrificed his own opportunity to complete his silver expedition for the welfare of one of his group. I imagine he was under pressure to carry on, as opportunities to complete an expedition come about only once a year. This group would have spent the best part of the last six months or so planning and preparing for their expedition. As it was, we were able to arrange for Andrew and his group to complete their expedition later that year. Involvement in the squadron was, for some, the only time they met other young people who were not from their local area or school. Often it was the school truant who excelled at campcraft and led the more academic. Several of our ex-cadets are now successful business people, actors, engineers, doctors, Police Officers and many went into the armed forces, but the less successful will still remain in contact with those who went on to greater things. They have one common bond and that is the time spent together at 7F Air cadets. Shortly after retiring from the Air Cadets I received a telephone call from my friend Steve Banks. Steve informed me that his nephew, Paul Midsaeter, had collapsed and died at his home from a rare heart disease. Paul was twenty years of age. Paul was one of three Mid-saeter boys who were cadets at 7F. The family lived in Upper Warwick Street. We used to call them affectionately Baby Spud, Middle Spud and Big Spud (Paul). They were great young people and big spud, during his time with the squadron, became one of our senior cadets, well respected by his peers and staff alike. I always had a tremendous admiration for Big Spud's navigation skills, he seemed to have a natural ability to look at a map and then relate that information to the ground. He could estimate distances, bearings and the best routes with little effort and great aplomb. He was a natural leader who led by example. I was very upset when I heard the news and I was asked to speak at his funeral. I prepared my eulogy, as best I could, put on my uniform and turned up at St Malachies Church prepared to pay my respects. When I arrived there were dozens and dozens of ex-cadets in attendance.

Some had travelled great distances to be here and the sight of them upset and mourning the tragic loss of their friend upset me. As a group we had known so much happiness and laughter, this was a very sad occasion. As I stepped forward and stood alongside big spud's coffin, I had a vision of big spud calmly leading a group through a storm. This was the cue for me to speak up and celebrate Spud's achievements, during his time as a 7F cadet. I was thanked by his mother and I know words are so difficult at times like this but Mrs Midsaeter thanked all the cadets for attending and it was some comfort to her to know that her eldest son had made so many friends in his short life.

The squadron's involvement in the DofE award took a big step forward when I was elected Chair of the Liverpool DofE Advisory Committee, a body made up of youth leaders, schoolteachers, community workers etc. I never wanted, or asked for this job, but I accepted because I knew it would create opportunities for our cadets to get involved in the wider community. This it certainly did and before long 7F was playing a major role in organising the annual

Liverpool DofE awards ceremony. Staff and cadets were always in attendance either at the Town Hall; St George's Hall, or the Anglican Cathedral. Our cadets would undertake presentations outlining their involvement in the award and I would normally welcome the principal guest. On one occasion, Sir Bobby Charlton was principal guest. I doubt if Sir Bobby will be reading this, but he was a real gentleman and fantastic with all the young people present. I remember him arriving about an hour early. Strange but for a man of my generation, Sir Bobby is instantly recognisable. I had never seen him in the flesh before, other than when I was a season ticket holder at Anfield, but as soon as I saw this figure appear I knew it was Bobby Charlton. I went over, introduced myself and straight away Sir Bobby put me at ease and suggested I get on with my preparations while he went for a cup of tea. Steve Banks was stood with me so he went off with Sir Bobby to the Cathedral refectory for tea. As they made their way to the refectory they looked like a pair of old pals nattering away. Sir Bobby was great that night and gave a wonderful speech extolling the virtues of today's young people. We also got to meet John Parrot, who went to the same school as many of the cadets. One person I met a few times was Kris Akabussi. Kris is a larger than life character who gives a wonderful presentation. I had to follow him on one occasion, which was quite difficult, as his audience was cheering and clapping wildly after his wonderful tale. Kris attended one of our awards ceremonies and this event was quite unique. Kris, in his day, was one of the fastest men on the planet.

We had at the squadron two brothers Kevin, and Gary Ford. The younger boy, Gary was a comedian, always making Steve Banks and me laugh. Gary had a debilitating illness, and mobility problems. Nonetheless, he was a character. Unfortunately Gary had great difficulty walking let alone running. He would turn up for the sports events, to support his brother and his squadron mates .On one occasion we had filled every event (no mean feat) but one of our junior boys 100 metre relay team suffered an injury. We were one short for the relay and there was no one else available. We would lose points if we failed to enter a relay team. I managed to convince Gary to run.

This was without doubt the first time Gary had ever entered a race. The inter squadron athletics event was always the premier sports event in the cadet sporting calendar, well attended, well organised with lots of cheering. Lynford Christie actually began his athletic career with his local Air Cadet squadron, but Gary was no Lynford Christie. Gary ambled down to the track to great cheers from his mates. I thought it best to send him off first, he had less chance of dropping the baton or committing a lane error. To huge cheers the race began and away they went ... except Gary.

Kris Akabussi with Gary Ford and his mum.

As the cadets were chanting, "Fordie, Fordie" he was waving the baton and soaking up the applause. He walked the hundred metres, we came last but we entered every event and obtained points for that. As it was, we were the overall winners of the Merseyside Wing Athletic trophy, a wonderful achievement. Come the squadron presentation night, I introduced Kris Akabussi and explained to our guests, parents and cadets that in our midst was one of the fastest men on the planet and probably one of the slowest ever competitive 100 metre runners. Gary and his family were delighted, especially when I made great play on Gary's contribution to winning the athletics trophy. Kris Akubussi was also delighted and, as ever, made every young person feel important. My role as chair of Liverpool

DofE committee was quite demanding. I was involved in selection of staff and dealing with staff problems but it was good for the squadron. We were right at the forefront of the city's DofE events. I was invited to attend the national DofE conventions, which were always very slick events. On one occasion I went across the water to Belfast for a convention. I arranged to take some of our senior cadets, all paid for by the DofE award. I thought it would be a good experience for the cadets and if they wanted, they could make comments. On these occasions the Duke of Edinburgh chairs the event. He is always first on the platform and last to leave. He takes questions from all comers and answers them in his own inimitable style. At the Belfast event the Secretary of State for Northern Island, Mo Mowlan, the Home Secretary, Jack Straw and many more dignitaries, captains of industry, celebrities, etc were attending. Near the end of the day we were shown a video supposedly promoting the DofE award.

Next to me was one of our cadets, Natalie Edmunds. We watched the video, which was introduced by an Irish aristocrat. At the conclusion of the video, Prince Philip asked for comments. As ever, there are people on these occasions who just like to hear themselves speak and a few did just that extolling the virtues of the video. Then Natalie put her hand up. The microphone was brought over and Natalie spoke up.

"I thought that video was a load of rubbish."

I could hear a pin drop as the audience all drew breath.

"I can't go back to Liverpool and show my friends that video. It was boring and didn't show any of the good things young people get from the DofE award. There was no fun shown, no laughter and it was nothing like I have done so far on the award."

I half expected the Irish aristocrat to shout "off with her head" or some captain of industry to shout "rhubarb" but up stood Prince Philip.

"Natalie, I agree entirely with everything you have just said and well done for saying it, please see me later".

I had to take Natalie to meet Prince Philip and from that meeting Natalie was invited to the DofE head office in Windsor and was asked to review all DofE promotional material. As a further consequence of Natalie's comments, she was headhunted by the top person at BT, who had been in the audience. He invited Natalie to BT head office in London and she was asked to give a young person's view on BT to their board of directors. Not bad for a young Liverpool girl.

I have no strong views either way about the Royal family. Obviously I took the Queen's shilling, the Oath of Allegiance and remained a loyal employee of Her Majesty but I do have a great deal of admiration and respect for Prince Philip. He set up the DofE award scheme and he obviously puts a great deal of time and effort into keeping it going. On another occasion, I was undertaking a presentation at a DofE convention outlining the benefits of the award for young offenders. I outlined the work I had been doing with young offenders in Liverpool and the benefits for this type of group. An individual in the audience stood up, probably trying to ingratiate himself with Prince Philip and stated he thought I was trying to dilute the quality of the award by allowing young offenders to participate. Prince Philip was having none of it and congratulated me for my efforts and told all present that this is exactly the type of young people we should be encouraging and supporting through the award; my sentiments entirely. Some time after that incident Anne and I received, completely out of the blue, an invitation to a Garden Party at Buckingham Palace.

Then shortly afterwards, I received another invitation, to the same garden party but this one stated I was invited as the personal guest of the Duke of Edinburgh. I now had to enter Buckingham Palace via the Grand entrance not the side entrance, which is how most visitors to a Royal Garden party enter.

On the day, Anne and I travelled down by train and as we approached a Police Officer at Buckingham Palace main gate he directed us to the queue for the Royal Garden Party. Rather coyly, but none the less proudly, I showed the Police Officer my invitation card. The front gate was opened and Anne and I crunched our way across the Palace forecourt. If my family could see me now I thought and then a Guardsman came to attention and up we went into Buckingham Palace.

A charming usher took me to my position in the "garden" while Anne mingled with the other guests. There I was to remain until the band struck up and the Duke of Edinburgh joined me. In the garden was a plethora of well-known celebrities and sports stars. Here was I, the principal guest stood on my own. I was introduced to Prince Phillip and we had an interesting conversation about my work with young offenders. Amongst the many questions asked one was, did we ever get into any trouble when we were away on an expedition? I told the Prince Phillip an interesting tale of the time we spent the night in Dolgellau Police station, which he thought amusing. I also took the opportunity to congratulate him on the work he does on behalf of young people, especially the disaffected. An interesting aside about the Garden Party.

The author and wife Anne at Buckingham Palace Garden Party.

Some people think I look like the ex Everton footballer and club manger, Howard Kendall. One of my Probation colleagues, Graham Taylor, always introduced me to his mates as, Howard Kendall. I used to think there might have been a slight resemblance especially when I passed Howard in a Southport street one day. However, at the Palace several adults came over to me and asked for my autograph, "Who do you think I am," "Howard Kendall" was the reply.

7F Squadron by this time had completed its transformation. We were no longer the laughing stock of Merseyside Wing. We were competing to a very high standard in all cadet activities. We now had cadets representing Merseyside Wing in many sporting events. We

~ Out of the Blue ~

had our first ever Corps Blue, the outstandingly talented netball player, Sarah Heslop. We regularly organised fundraising events for charity and in particular, Lady Jean's main charity the Ronald McDonald House at the Royal Liverpool Children's Hospital. To this day 7F Squadron features on the house 'Tree of Life' memorial board in recognition of the £1,000 the squadron raised for this very deserving cause. We were a main player in the River Mersey Raft race and cadets were participating in a multitude of other activities.

One cadet was selected to undertake an International Air Cadet Exchange and that young man, Anthony Gallagher, travelled to America and in the process had tea at the White House with President Clinton. Other cadets went off to Cyprus and Gibraltar and Germany and of course all cadets had the opportunity to attend a Fairbourne Camp. Five years after my taking over command, 7F squadron won, for the first time in its history, the Merseyside Wing Efficiency Trophy, the premier Merseyside Air Cadet Trophy. Cadets had risen from thirtieth position to number one, a marvellous achievement. No one person could claim, or would want to claim, any credit for that achievement. The success of 7F was down to the combined efforts of so many adult staff who all had that one aim, to provide opportunities for the cadets to participate in enjoyable and purposeful activities. The cadets themselves, young people from the south end of Liverpool, proved that the youth of today, given the opportunity, will rise to the challenge. They will work together as a team, will show compassion and concern for others regardless of colour, creed, religion, age, disability or status. I am sure that young people today will still respond to a challenge and I would recommend the Air Cadets to any young person, or adult, who wants a bit of adventure and fun in their lives.

As for me, I completed a twelve-year engagement with the Air Cadet Organisation. That engagement plus my twenty-two year engagement in the Royal Air Force and my four years as an air cadet with 2359 (Woolton) Squadron brought my association with the Royal Air Force to nearly forty years. Although I had a few difficulties managing an Air Cadet squadron, I thoroughly enjoyed every minute of it. I hold no malice against any of the Air Cadet staff who disagreed with my actions, quite the opposite, every adult Air Cadet instructor or committee member, in their own way, played their part in bringing some happiness into many young people's lives (including those of my own two children) and that is something to be very proud of.

Although my association with the Royal Air Force has formally come to an end I still have a tenuous link with the RAF, in my role as secretary of the Royal Air Force & Defence Fire Service Association. This is a wonderful group of mainly retired RAF and Defence fire fighters but we do have some serving personnel amongst our membership. Our reunions take place twice a year and it is an occasion for reminiscing, mainly about times spent in RAF fire sections throughout the world. Any ex-RAF or Defence Fire Service firemen out there are more than welcome to join our thriving association.

I look forward to seeing you at one of our reunions.

~ E N D ~

Author and wife Anne at their last RAF function.